The

EMPOWERMENT MANUAL

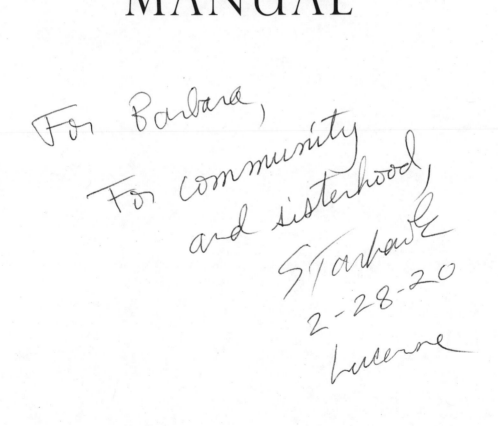

For Barbara,

For community
and sisterhood,

Starhawk
2-28-20

Lucerne

The

EMPOWERMENT
MANUAL

A GUIDE *for* COLLABORATIVE GROUPS

STARHAWK

NEW SOCIETY PUBLISHERS

Cover design by Diane McIntosh.
© iStock (Spectral-Design); Table illustration, © iStock (Vizualbyte)

Printed in Canada. Third printing January 2019.

Paperback ISBN: 978-0-86571-697-1
eISBN: 978-1-55092-484-8

Inquiries regarding requests to reprint all or part of *The Empowerment Manual*
should be addressed to New Society Publishers at the address below.

To order directly from the publishers, please call toll-free (North America)
1-800-567-6772, or order online at www.newsociety.com

Any other inquiries can be directed by mail to:

New Society Publishers
P.O. Box 189, Gabriola Island, BC V0R 1X0, Canada
(250) 247-9737

Library and Archives Canada Cataloguing in Publication

Starhawk
   The empowerment manual : a guide for collaborative groups / Starhawk.

Includes bibliographical references and index.
ISBN 978-0-86571-697-1

   1. Social groups. 2. Leadership. 3. Community power. I. Title.

HM716.S73 2011   302.3   C2011-905863-4

New Society Publishers' mission is to publish books that contribute in funda-
mental ways to building an ecologically sustainable and just society, and to do
so with the least possible impact on the environment, in a manner that models
this vision. We are committed to doing this not just through education, but
through action. Our printed, bound books are printed on Forest Stewardship
Council-certified acid-free paper that is **100% post-consumer recycled** (100%
old growth forest-free), processed chlorine free, and printed with vegetable-
based, low-VOC inks, with covers produced using FSC-certified stock. New
Society also works to reduce its carbon footprint, and purchases carbon off-
sets based on an annual audit to ensure a carbon neutral footprint. For further
information, or to browse our full list of books and purchase securely, visit our
website at: www.newsociety.com

NEW SOCIETY PUBLISHERS

MIX
Paper from
responsible sources
FSC
www.fsc.org   FSC® C016245

This book is dedicated
to Margo Adair, who devoted her life
to bringing together spirit and action
in the pursuit of social justice.

Join the Conversation

Visit our online book club at NewSociety.com to share your thoughts about *The Empowerment Manual*. Exchange ideas with other readers, post questions for the author, respond to one of the sample questions or start your own discussion topics. See you there!

Contents

Table of Questions and Exercises

Chapter 4: The Axis of Action

Chapter 5: The Axis of Learning

Chapter 6: Leadership Roles for Leaderless Groups

Acknowledgments

This book draws on many decades of working, creating, organizing and living in collectives and collaborative groups. I've learned something from everybody I've encountered along the way, and it would not be possible to name them all. But I especially want to thank all the people who have been in Reclaiming throughout the years, in my circles and covens, and who have lived in my collective household, Black Cat. I'm most deeply appreciative of all of you with whom I've had conflicts — you know who you are! — and whom I love nonetheless.

In this book, I've used real examples of conflict but with names and details changed to protect peoples' privacy. I've also created a fictional community that exemplifies many of the difficult issues groups face. The characters are invented — they are not based directly on any real people nor are they meant to stand for any person or organization.

Special thanks to Lisa Fithian and Lauren Ross, members of my training and organizing collective Alliance of Community Trainers; to Penny Livingston-Stark, Erik Ohlsen and Charles Williams, co-teachers of Earth Activist Trainings, and to Bill Aal and the late Margo Adair, co-conspirators in developing approaches to social permaculture. Donna Read has been my collaborator on many documentaries. Delight Stone and Louisa Silva have offered many sorts of support over the years and much encouragement for this book. Rose May Dance, Bill, Kore, Sabine, Mark and Leonie Lotus, my current housemates, and my partner David give me a strong and loving base of support.

Lisa Fithian, Hilary McQuie and David Solnit gave helpful comments on the manuscript. Adam Wolpert and Brock Dolman of Occidental Arts and Ecology Center let me interview them and offered many helpful resources, as did Carolyne Stayton of Transition USA. Laura Kemp offered many insights and contacts. My agent Ken Sherman has advocated for my interests for longer than either of us care to admit.

Special thanks to Betsy Nuse who wrestled the manuscript down to a reasonable size, and to all the folks at New Society.

And gratitude to all who are working to create more cooperation, co-creation and true democracy in this world. You are my constant inspiration.

CHAPTER 1

A New Era of Empowerment

Cairo, Egypt, January 25, 2011. A chanting crowd marches into Tahrir Square in the center of Cairo to challenge the power of the dictator Mubarak, who has held power for decades. A few days before, a similar groundswell of popular outrage toppled the autocratic regime that ruled Tunisia. Inspired by that success, the Egyptian activists determine to stay in the square, violating long-standing prohibitions against protest. Days go by, and in spite of intimidation, arrests and attacks, they remain until finally Mubarak is forced to step down. Their success inspires similar uprisings in Bahrain, Yemen, Morocco and Libya, transforming in a few weeks the power structure of the Middle East.

At the same time, in the US, protestors flood the state Capitol of Wisconsin where governor Scott Walker is attempting to push through a law that would gut the power of unions. From the Mideast to the Midwest, ordinary people are taking action to challenge coercive power.

These uprisings are different in structure than revolutions of the past. No charismatic leaders take control. Organization exists within the mass, and groups at the center provide inspiration, direction and momentum, but there is no command structure to issue orders to the protestors, no head for the opposition to cut off, no leader to assassinate. As one commentator put it, "The swarm defeats the hierarchy."

This way of organizing may seem to be very new, facilitated by all the tools of the Internet, from Facebook to Twitter. The Internet itself is a distributed network with no central control or center of command, and it favors similar structures.

But decentralized collaboration is actually very old, perhaps the oldest way that human beings have come together to pursue common goals. It harkens back to the clan, the council around the fire, the village elders meeting underneath the sacred tree. Long before kings, generals, armies that marched in formation and codified classes of nobles and peons, people came together more or less as equals to make the decisions that affected their lives.

Collaborative groups are everywhere. They might be a group of neighbors coming together to plan how their town can make a transition to a more energy efficient economy or a church group planning a bake sale. They could be a group of anarchist forest defenders organizing a tree sit or a group of friends planning a surprise birthday party for a workmate. Pagans planning a May Eve ritual, perma-culture students starting a community garden, a cohousing community deciding on its ground rules or a group of preschoolers playing Monster all operate without centralized structures of command and control.

When we set out to change the world, when we organize to bring about greater freedom, justice, peace and equality, we most often create such groups. Collaborative groups embody some of our most cherished values: equality, free-dom and the value of each individual.

And they can be enormously effective. In the 1970s, the Second Wave of the feminist movement was carried forward by consciousness-raising groups, small circles that met each week to share stories and experiences. Out of those discus-sions arose the issues, actions and campaigns that drove the movement. Alcoholics Anonymous and all its offshoots provide the most effective treatment for alcohol-ism and other addictions. They are structured around groups of peers who offer each other support with no experts or authorities taking control.

And there are thousands of other examples, from grassroots relief efforts after Hurricane Katrina to the collaborative art event/festival of Burning Man that draws tens of thousands to the Nevada desert every September.

Today, networks, collaboration, decentralization and the wisdom of crowds are hot buzzwords. Co-created projects like open source software and Wikipedia have not only been enormously succcessful; they are being touted as the business models of the future. Many corporations are opening up to forms of co-creation — from the Learning Organization discussed by Margaret Wheatley to Japanese-influenced consensus models to the hundreds of thousands of volunteer organizations work-ing for social change and environmental balance.

COLLABORATIVE GROUPS AND HIERARCHIES

As different as these groups and activities might seem, they have something in common. If you were to diagram their structure, your picture would look more like a circle than a pyramid or a traditional chain of command. These groups may include individuals who exhibit leadership, but they are not dependent on leaders. They may include bossy people, but they have no bosses, no one in control, no one who holds authority over the others. They are groups of peers, working together for common goals, collaborating and co-creating. Such groups are at the root of democracy, and participating in them can be a liberating, empowering, life-changing experience.

My first immersion in a culture of egalitarian collaboration came at an extended blockade of a nuclear power plant at Diablo Canyon in central California in 1981. For nearly a month, we organized blockades of the power plant, did our share of the work to keep our encampment clean, fed and safe, got arrested, made decisions together in jail about how to respond to threats and hold solidarity and changed the course of energy policy in California for decades to come. When the blockade ended, I went back to graduate school in a feminist program in an alternative university. But I felt deeply uncomfortable. Sitting at a desk, listening to lectures and complying with assignments I'd had no hand in designing seemed constricting and irksome after three weeks of sitting in circles, participating in every decision that the group made, living immersed in a structure that affirmed my core worth and the value of my voice.

Hierarchies are appropriate and necessary for some endeavors. When the house is burning, we don't want the fire department to sit down and decide in a long-drawn-out meeting who will go in and who will hold the hose. In families, adults must exercise control over children if they want their offspring to survive. In emergencies, and where true differences of skill, training and knowledge exist, command and control structures may be needed.

But hierarchies also have their drawbacks. In a hierarchy, power differentials expand, so that those who issue orders also receive the greatest status and rewards, and the bottom rungs are not pleasant places to be. The workers who do the nastiest jobs receive the lowest pay and wield the least power.

No one enjoys being a peon or a slave. Many of us submit to hierarchies for work, school or other ends because we often don't have other options. To make a living, we need to work in situations where others have control over us. But when we do have a choice — in our leisure time, our volunteer efforts, our work to better the world — we gravitate to groups of peers. In a group where we have an equal voice, we feel a sense of ownership, pride and investment. We feel empowered: affirmed and supported in developing our own abilities, skills and talents, in pursuing our own goals and standing up for our own values.

Empowered people stand for something in their lives. They take action, sometimes even facing great danger, because they know that they have the right and the responsibility to act in service of what they believe and care for. A young woman faces the cameras in Tahrir Square, smiles and says, "Today we Egyptians have lost our fear."

Empowerment comes from within — but the structures around us can evoke that inner strength and support it or deny and suppress it. Collaborative groups, when they are working well, create fertile ground where empowerment can flourish.

THE CHALLENGES OF COLLABORATION

Collaborative groups, however, face their own challenges, especially when they exist over time and strive for permanence and sustainability. It is a joy to be part of a team that works well together. But a team that spins its wheels in fruitless discussions or becomes a vicious battleground can be frustrating, enraging and deeply wounding.

Diana Leafe Christian, who studied successful ecovillages and intentional communities, found that "No matter how visionary and inspired the founders, only about one out of ten new communities actually get built. The other 90 per cent seemed to go nowhere, occasionally because of lack of money or not finding the right land, but mostly because of conflict. And usually, conflict accompanied by heartbreak. And sometimes, conflict, heartbreak and lawsuits."[1]

Diana describes a common pattern. A group of kind, compassionate idealistic people set out to form a community or change the world. For the first few months, everyone loves one another, high on that heady drug of working together toward important goals. And then a year later it has all dissolved into bitter fights and recriminations.

For there is one overriding problem with collaborative groups — they are groups of people, and people are damn difficult to get along with. Were it not for that fact, we would have already saved the world many times over. Instead, we're left down here in the muck, struggling with the irritating, irresponsible, pig-headed, stubborn, annoying, judgmental, egotistical and petty people who are supposed to be our allies.

I'm writing this book to offer what I've learned in over four decades of organizing and working collaboratively. I believe that we can become far more skillful at co-creation. When we do, our inner empowerment will flourish, our relationships will thrive and we will become far more effective at all the important work our groups undertake.

HOW COLLABORATIVE GROUPS ARE DIFFERENT

Collaborative is the term I've chosen to describe groups that are based on shared power and the inherent worth and value of each member. Brafman and Beckstrom, in *The Starfish and the Spider*, characterize what they call starfish groups as very amorphous and fluid. Because power and knowledge are distributed, individual units quickly respond to a multitude of internal and external forces — they are constantly spreading, growing, shrinking, mutating, dying off and reemerging. This quality makes them very flexible.[2] How do I define a *collaborative group*? It's a group that has most if not all of the following characteristics:

- Structured as circles, webs or networks, not pyramids or trees
- Groups of peers, with a horizontal structure, working together to create something and to make decisions
- Groups without formal authority, no bosses that can hire or fire you. (In some hybrid groups, that authority might exist but be rarely and reluctantly imposed.)
- Businesses that run collectively or cooperatively
- Groups where the major reward may not be money, but something else — creative fulfillment, impact on the world, spiritual development, personal growth, or friendship
- Often formed around strong, altruistic values — from saving the world to sharing knowledge to religious observation or community celebration
- Groups of humans — which means that motives of gain, status and power do come into play, if not overtly, then covertly
- Groups that often have few or no overt rules, but many norms
- Often ephemeral, for better or worse

When we understand these differences, we can use them to our advantage. We can structure our groups to encourage the behaviors that foster cooperation, efficacy and friendship — and discourage those annoying traits that undermine our aims. There are thousands of books, courses and leadership seminars that will teach you how to manage a hierarchy. There's much less support for co-creative groups. Throughout this book I have drawn on all the literature and research I can find, but the primary source is ultimately my own experience.

My academic background is modest — an MA from Antioch University West in psychology in 1982. But my experience of co-creative groups is broad and deep. For more than 40 years, I've been working and living in collaborative groups. In the early 1980s, I cofounded Reclaiming, a spiritual network of Goddess-centered Pagans who practice a co-creative tradition that values personal healing, deep spiritual practice and political action. I've lived collectively both in the 1960s and continuously since the early 1980s and worked collectively on hundreds of projects, including books and films. I've helped to organize political groups that work collaboratively, from small collectives to major mobilizations involving thousands of people. I've trained thousands of people in consensus decision-making and facilitated countless meetings. I've mediated conflicts for social change groups and presided over strategy meetings of protestors in jail. As a writer, organizer, activist and spiritual teacher, I've struggled many times with the contradictions of being a leader in groups that define themselves as leaderless.

I've had many wonderful, empowering and healing experiences in groups — and my fair share of painful disasters. Those disasters, my own mistakes and hard lessons are probably the most valuable experience I have to offer. Very few people have experience of how co-creative groups change over time. Many of the new experiments are still in their honeymoon phase. When an emergent group needs to undergo a phase shift, to dissolve and re-form, who can recognize the need and help to orchestrate the change? When conflicts erupt, when unexpected pitfalls open up beneath our feet, where is the experience to guide us?

It comes from the edges and the margins, where these experiments have been going on for decades. We can learn a lot from those who have pushed the boundaries, from both the successes and the failures, from the long-lived and the short-lived.

Most hippie communes of the 1960s failed — but a few survived to thrive and grow. The Quakers have survived for three and a half centuries. Reclaiming, my own network, is entering its third decade. There are other intentional communities that have also endured for decades.

In a redwood forest, there are lichens that only begin to grow on a tree when it is over 150 years old. In collaborative groups, there are patterns and structures that also only emerge over time. If we identify and learn from them, we can help groups sustain themselves for the long haul when that is appropriate or recognize when there is strength in flexibility and power in the ephemeral.

HOW THIS BOOK IS STRUCTURED

In *The Empowerment Manual,* we'll look at the factors that enable collaborative groups to thrive, and we'll also examine failures and bad examples. Successful groups form, articulate and maintain a common vision. Power and authority are balanced with responsibility. Trust is balanced with accountability. Group norms are made visible and conscious, and beneficial norms are fostered.

"Equal" does not mean "identical," and egalitarian groups contain many distinct roles, both formal and informal. Finally, we'll look at how to lead a leaderless group, how to embrace conflict and deal with difficult people.

Throughout the book, I'll bring in real examples and case studies. Most will have names and details changed to protect the privacy of all involved — and to keep me from spending my golden years dealing with hurt feelings and bitter attacks from those I might offend. And I have synthesized many of those examples into an ongoing story about a fictional community that will weave through the book.

I've also provided many experiential exercises, sets of questions and ways of working the material that go deeper than the intellectual. I encourage people to use this material in working with your own groups and with others. The more effective our groups become, the more valuable work they will achieve in the world.

EXERCISES AND MEDITATIONS

I come to this work from many decades of teaching and practicing earth-based spirituality, and many of my previous books, audio tapes and other resources are heavily weighted to the spiritual. I've also suggested rituals, meditations, experiential exercises and guided imagery in this book. Ritual and meditation may or may not be appropriate for your group — that's up to you to decide. If a group is deeply uncomfortable with anything they consider too woo-woo, it's better not to force a process on them. You can easily take the same material and present it in a different form, for example:

I'm going to ask us each to take ten minutes and write out something of your vision of an ideal world. Or — you could draw it if you prefer that mode of expression — on the table are colored pens and paper. I'm going to read a list of questions — you don't have to answer them all but let them jog your imagination.

I've often presented exercises and guided meditations in the form of scripts. They can be read aloud, but this is probably the least effective way to lead them. A far better practice is to learn the structure of the exercise or meditation, commit the bones to memory and then speak it in your own words. A guided meditation is an inner journey, so learn the landmarks and then feel free to improvise. Remember, though, that there is an art to creating a meditation that leads people into their own imagination. It needs to be just specific enough — but not too detailed. You aren't trying to get them to experience your own inner landscape, but rather to travel on their own imaginary journey. Use sensory imagery — but keep it generalized. For example, "You are walking down a path, and you smell the air around you and feel the ground under your feet and how the weight of your body shifts from foot to foot ..." NOT "You are walking on a hot desert, and you feel sharp stones under your feet and hot sun on your skin." You may be in a desert; someone else may be in a forest or on a seashore and too-specific imagery will throw them out of their journey. Keep it open, so that peoples' imagination becomes engaged.

E
X
E
R
C
I
S
E

Beginning a Session

Find a place for the meeting where people can sit in a rough circle and feel comfortable. Welcome people as they arrive, and introduce everyone. An introduction might simply involve asking people to say their name and where they are from. It could include a short statement about what drew them to the group — but beware, as you continue around the circle, those statements will get longer and longer until people are telling their entire life stories. Here are some suggestions for quick rounds of introductions.

Quick Intro

Tell us your name and something that's happened this week that gives you hope.

Weather Report

Tell us your name, and if your mood right now were a state of the weather, what would it be? Sunny? Cloudy? Stormy?

Partner Intro

Find a person in this circle you don't know, and introduce yourself and what drew you to this group. Then the other person takes a turn. You will each have five minutes to talk without being interrupted or questioned. After you've both spoken, you'll have a few minutes to talk freely about what might be common or different in your experience.

Leader: Keep time and announce each five minutes with a bell, chime, drum or your voice. After the exercise is done, call the group back together and say:

> Now I'm going to ask each of you to introduce your partner, and tell us in just a sentence or two what drew your partner to the group.

Pride Intro

(For an ongoing group) Say your name and tell us what you've done since we last met that you're proud of toward furthering the work of this group.

After introductions, review the plan for the meeting and its purpose and intentions. Ask the group, "Can we agree to this plan?" DON'T say "Are there any objections, concerns or suggestions about the agenda?" unless you want

to spend a long time hearing them and revising the plan on the spot.

If it is appropriate in your group, you might also begin with a short grounding or meditation to bring the group together. There are hundreds of suggestions in my other books that I won't repeat now.[3]

Group Grounding

This is a very simple and general grounding.

Let's all stand in a circle. Take a moment and stretch, and feel your body. Where are you holding tension? What needs to be released? Take a deep breath, let it go and bring yourself to a nice, easy, balanced stance, with your knees slightly bent. Take some deep breaths, down into your belly.

Close your eyes. Feel your feet on the ground. Allow yourself to feel the weight of gravity and how your feet push down against the earth. Let yourself think for just a moment about what you stand for. What drew you to this group? To its work and values?

Imagine you have roots, like a tree, extending down from your feet into the earth. As you breathe, let them push down through the soil and rock and water under the earth, thinking about what feeds and supports the work of this group and your own work within it.

As you reach the mantle of living fire beneath the earth, take a breath and release anything you don't want to bring into this meeting. Just let it go, on your breath, and feel the fire transform it.

CONTINUED

Now take a breath and draw up a spark of that fire — a spark of the inspiration and passion you feel for the work at hand. Draw it up through your roots, through the rocks and the water and the soil, up into your feet and legs, up through the base of your spine, and feel your spine expand and grow like the flexible trunk of a living tree. Draw some of that warm fire into your heart, and feel the heart connections you are making. Draw it up into your shoulders and down into your hands, and honor the work of your hands. Draw it up into your head and out the top of your head like branches that reach up to the sky and then sweep back down to touch the earth. Feel the circuit of energy that this creates.

Now feel the sunlight (or moonlight, or starlight) on your leaves and branches. Take a deep breath, and draw some of that down, into your leaves and down through the top of your head, through your heart and hands and belly, down through your feet into the earth. Draw in some of the energy you need to realize the vision and do the work.

And just stand for a moment, breathing, feeling yourself as a conduit between earth and sky. Now become aware that under the earth, all of our roots are intertwined. And above our heads, our branches are intertwined. We stand together, a sacred grove, sharing our vision and our work to make it real.

Let's take some deep breaths together, in and out ... our breath becoming one breath, in and out ... letting your breath become a sound, a tone that you give to the circle.

(When the tone dies away) And now let's just take in some of that energy, the energy we each need for the work tonight. And look around, and acknowledge everyone in the circle. Thank you! And now let's begin.

Anchor to Core Self

This exercise is probably the most basic and useful spiritual practice I know. I learned a version of it originally from bodywork teacher Suzette Rochat, and another version can be found in *The Twelve Wild Swans*.[4] I use it every day, as a basic wake-up meditation, under stress, when I need to make an important decision. I've taught it to activists preparing to go into dangerous situations, to permaculturalists wanting to learn how to better observe what's going on in the garden and to spiritual circles wanting to meditate in the woods.

Begin with the grounding above. Now, as you stand grounded and centered, notice how your body feels. Think of a time, place or situation in which you feel at home and comfortable, when you can just be yourself, without any masks or pretense or face to keep up. A grounded but neutral state, when you can be in touch with your deepest, creative power, without having to use it. Say your own name to yourself, and notice where in your body you feel it reverberate.

Can you find a place on your body that resonates with this state? Take a deep breath, and

CONTINUED

touch that place. Or perhaps it's a stance or a gesture, but find something physical you can create as an anchor to this core, grounded, neutral state.

Now, can you think of an image or a symbol for this state? Perhaps it's something from this scene you are remembering or imagining. It could be a color or a shape. Find something visual, and as you touch your physical place, hold it in your mind and tell yourself that by visualizing this image you can bring yourself into this core, grounded, neutral state.

Now, can you think of a word or phrase you can say, your magic word or affirmation that you can associate with this core, grounded, neutral state? Take a breath, and say the word or phrase to yourself, as you visualize your image and touch your physical place. Tell yourself that by using these three things together — your physical touch, your image and your word or phrase — you can quickly and instantly bring yourself into this core, grounded, neutral state.

Take a breath, and open your eyes. Look around you, and notice how the world looks when you are in this core, grounded and neutral state. How do other people look, when they are anchored to their core self?

Now, you can let go of the physical gesture, the image and the phrase, and still stay grounded and centered. We will practice with this anchor, and I encourage you to practice also at home. The more you use it, the more it will become ingrained, until it becomes your natural, default state in response to stress.

Really Simple Grounding

For groups with less tolerance for ritual, here's a really simple, secular grounding ….

Let's stand together in a circle, just for a moment. Take a moment to stretch and release any knots and kinks.

Now, let's all take a deep breath, and let go of any tension or distress you might be carrying with you from the day. Take a deep breath in, and out, and release anything you don't want to bring into this meeting.

Now, feel your feet on the ground. Feel the pull of gravity, and the solid contact you make with the earth. Think about what you stand for, and what we stand for together — those things we care about, the reasons why we do this work. Feel the solidity and the strength we have when we stand together. Know that any time you feel off-balance, physically or emotionally, you can bring yourself back to this solid, grounded stance simply by feeling your feet on the ground and taking a breath.

Look around now, and see your allies. Acknowledge them with your eyes, and let's begin.

Thanksgiving

The Iroquois nations begin every meeting with a Thanksgiving Address — a prayer of thanks to honor all of the cosmos. You might begin with a simplified version — asking people to share something they are thankful for and giving gratitude to all who have contributed to the work of the group that week.

Cultural Sharing

Groups that might feel uncomfortable with meditation or imposed prayer might still be open to starting with some form of cultural sharing. Musicians or poets can share their work, or any member can read a favorite poem or lead a group song. Artists get a chance to perform to a supportive audience and the group has an enriching experience that adds another dimension to the work.

Clap In/Clap Out

A leader holds her hands apart, and everyone follows suit. She counts one … two … three … and claps, and everyone attempts to clap together as one. This is a very simple way to build unity, either to begin a meeting, to end one, or both. An alternate version is a group "Yes!," either accompanying the clap or with a fist-punch up to the air.

Ending a Session

Leave some time at the end of every session for evaluation and closing.

Short Evaluation

Allow time either for free discussion or go around the circle asking:

What worked for you in this session? What could have worked better? What would you like to see in the next one?

Make sure someone takes notes that can be given to the facilitator for the next session.

Thank You Circle

Go quickly around the circle and thank each person for their contribution and for the work they've done for the group. Beware: when you thank people individually, you always run the risk of missing someone or slighting some accomplishment they feel is important. So don't be sloppy.

Or: keep the gratitude general: "Thanks to those who organized the meeting, to everyone who brought food, to those who sent out the announcement and called people to remind them, to all of you who have done so much in this last period to further the work of this group."

Cultural Closing

A poem, song or short dance jam can also close a meeting. Be aware, however, that when timing gets tight sometimes the closing gets postponed or foreclosed. It's disrespectful to singers or poets to shove them off the agenda at the last meeting. So if that's likely to happen, have the cultural offering first, rather than last.

Closing Meditation

For groups who are open to it, closing with a meditation, a grounding or a short empowerment ritual can be a lovely send-off.

Clap Out

A group clap can be used to end the meeting.

When to Have the Potluck

Before

"We gather at six for the potluck and start the

CONTINUED

meeting at seven." This allows people with tight schedules to come just for the meeting, and others who have the time and inclination to socialize.

After

A daytime meeting can end with a potluck. This allows people in the group to release the tension of formal work and relax, and also to informally carry on the discussion started earlier.

During

A meeting can be held over brunch, lunch or dinner. This works well for building trust and connection when no decisions need to be made. It's a great setting for deeper and more philosophical discussions, for tackling the big questions that tend to get shoved out of agendas. But if conflict resolution is the purpose of the meeting, hold the food or risk indigestion.

WE NEED COLLABORATIVE GROUPS

Today we face overwhelming social, economic and ecological crises, from wars to natural disasters to nuclear meltdowns. Climate change is progressing even faster than predicted. We are challenged to recreate our technologies, our energy systems, our economies, our food systems and our way of life — and to do it not over the next century but within the next few decades. We have a short window of time to either make the transformation to a world where we all can thrive or devolve into a grim future of ecological catastrophe and all the social breakdowns, war, destruction and suffering that go with it.

To choose the positive future, we need the imagination, the commitment and passion that can never be commanded but can only be unleashed in groups of equals. Those groups need to work. They need to function well, as smoothly and efficiently as the most well-oiled hierarchical machine. And some of them, at least, need to last. That's why I'm writing this book.

Let me begin by telling you a story. It's about a fictional group, and I've designed it to highlight some common patterns of conflict and confusion that plague us. So … come with me on a visit to RootBound Ecovillage.

CHAPTER 2

RootBound Ecovillage and
the Talisman of Healthy Community

RootBound Ecovillage is an imaginary cohousing community located in the Oakland hills overlooking the San Francisco Bay. RootBound was started by charismatic, visionary psychologist Eli Stern and his wife Ella. Dynamic, outgoing Eli has an international consulting practice bringing the human potential movement into corporations. Ella, warm, thoughtful, practical and more self-contained than Eli, teaches in the Graduate School of Education at UC Berkeley.

RootBound was an answer to problems the Sterns faced as a couple. As Eli grew more successful, his work began to keep him on the road much of the year. Their two children were entering their teens and becoming more interested in their peers than their parents. Ella had grown up in a close-knit, extended family. While she had a circle of colleagues and friends, she found herself longing for the kind of neighborhood she'd known in her childhood, when she was in and out of the houses of cousins, with many aunties and uncles she could go to for comfort if she skinned a knee or needed a sympathetic shoulder to cry on. In her research on education, she'd come to believe that children needed a range of adults in their lives, as role models, as caregivers and as friends. She found herself longing for more connection and community.

On one of Eli's trips to Denmark, he was taken on a tour of a cohousing community. Cohousing is a movement that seeks to lower environmental impact and create more sense of community by balancing public and private space. Member families have their own modest dwellings, while the community as a whole owns a common dining room, meeting rooms, guest rooms and gardens. Dwellings face pedestrian streets, where children can safely play, with parking consolidated on the edge of the site. Opportunities for community abound.

Fired with enthusiasm, Eli saw cohousing as the answer to their problems. Ella saw it as an opportunity to create the kind of community her theories said would help children to thrive, and her intuition said would be more fun and supportive for adults. With all the passion, drive and charm that propelled Eli's career, he began organizing such a community in the Bay Area.

All went well. Eli and Ella quickly collected a group of interested people around them. Most were also idealistic professionals: teachers, nurses, academics, therapists and lawyers. While RootBound's Vision Statement called it a "multi-racial, multi-generational community, welcoming to all genders and sexual persuasions," most potential members were white, heterosexual and in their late 30s or early 40s. Still, they included a sprinkling of other races, and RootBound consciously set aside a percentage of their space for "starter homes" — flexible, less-finished spaces that could be rented-to-buy by younger people with lower incomes. They even included a graduated-care suite of rooms fitted with grab bars, call buttons and accessible showers and toilets, where aged and infirm relations could be accommodated.

Eli persuaded a Danish architect who specialized in cohousing to design the complex, and in short order they broke ground. The buildings incorporated all the latest energy-efficiency measures: solar tiles on the roofs, water-saving features and the latest in energy-saving appliances. Potential members helped design their own units and helped keep costs low by volunteering to recycle all the construction waste. Unlike most construction efforts, the complex was completed on time and within budget, and the celebration party on move-in day became a legendary event.

At first, all was blissful. Members showed up on time for their cooking shifts, and communal meals were delicious, healthful and convivial. An Events Committee planned fun outings to the beach, to the ski slopes in winter and an annual river rafting trip in summer.

Common spaces proved not only to be useful for parties but became a resource for the larger community. A local Alcoholics Anonymous group used the space daily. Sustainable Oakland Hills met there weekly. A women's circle offered full moon rituals, and a drumming group met on Friday nights. RootBound had an Olympic-size chlorine-free swimming pool, kept clean by natural methods, with an attached hot tub. It was a great center of activity in the summer, and RootBound opened its use to people with chemical sensitivities who could not tolerate ordinary pools.

Everyone loved the name — combining as it did the sense of rooting in a home, while still travelling toward a destination. Perhaps because none of the original members were gardeners, it was only later that they realized its secondary meaning — a plant stuck too long in too small a pot that ceases to grow.

Six months after move-in day, the Membership Committee received an unusual application. TreePeople was a collective of 15 young people, all under the age of 25. For three months out of the year, they travelled in a caravan of buses converted to run on vegetable oil, planting trees in schoolyards up and down California. For the rest of the year, they did odd jobs and travelled to antiwar protests around the country, cooking for the demonstrators out of their kitchen bus. The TreePeople were looking for a home. They wanted to take over two of the low-income units and convert them into one large, communal space. They committed to make the monthly payments and contribute to the common work and activities.

TreePeople's application revealed some underlying differences of opinion within the community. Many were in favor of it. It would bring new, youthful energy into the community and would support activities in line with the vision statement.

But other folks were wary. Fifteen new people would be a big impact on the community — and the TreePeople were not only younger but marginal than most of RootBound. They wore dreadlocks, patches and lots of black.

TreePeople's living density in two units would be much higher than elsewhere in the complex. Not all members of RootBound were motivated solely by ideals. Some had joined simply because it was the only way they could afford to own their own home in the high-priced Bay Area. They were worried about their property losing value.

Nonetheless, TreePeople were accepted. They moved in and set to work with youthful energy and strength. They transformed their units into multiple small suites, with lofts above sitting and working spaces. They installed state-of-the-art Internet access. An unused plot of land had long been designated for a community garden. The TreePeople soon had it thriving, producing food for their own consumption and extra to give away.

TreePeople loved to cook, and with so many of them willing to do their shifts, it eased the burden on others. They volunteered to take extra shifts in exchange for using the kitchen between meals to prepare the food for the homeless. But they were accustomed to cooking for large groups with few resources, and their meals leaned heavily on pasta, day-old bread and bean soup. Doctor Rick Ragle was horrified to learn that many of their vegetables were "dumpstered" — collected from the produce thrown out at the end of the day by supermarkets. And TreePeople refused on principle to cook anything but vegan food. When they signed up to cook, many members began staying away.

Other RootBound members were having difficulty filling their own shifts. Eli was now not only travelling to consult, but often speaking about RootBound and advising other start-up cohousing communities. He had less and less time at home. A once a month commitment to cook didn't sound burdensome in theory — but in practice, trying to make up his shifts when he was home seemed to fill all of his spare time. He had even less time to spend with Ella and the kids. One day he came up with a brilliant idea — he would hire some of the TreePeople to take his shifts. They needed the money, he needed the time. A perfect solution! But soon people began to whisper behind his back: "Eli thinks he is above the rest of us, too good to waste his precious time cooking meals. Eli is throwing his weight around, wielding too much power."

Other busy members liked the idea of hiring someone to do their shifts. Many members had heavy demands on their time. It was easier to pay someone to cook a meal than to do it themselves, when they barely had time to eat. Still others, pushing middle age and struggling to keep their waistlines in check, were eating some variation of a low-carb diet. Meals of pasta, bread and brown rice just didn't work for them. They began to stay away from common meals. Better to microwave an Atkins Special Meal at home or go to the salad bar at Whole Foods.

The whispering increased. RootBound now had a class structure — where some people worked and others threw money around. TreePeople came to "own" the kitchen, except when they were away on tour. Fewer and fewer members came to meals. Other members had simply opted out. They didn't cook, they didn't join the communal meals or activities, they didn't come to meetings or sign up for work shifts. They paid their dues and monthly fees, but otherwise were absent.

People were also missing meetings and other work shifts. RootBound held a monthly Members' Meeting, a brunch on the fourth Sunday of every month.

Once they were highly anticipated social occasions. Eli would schedule his work commitments around them. But over time, these meetings had grown longer and longer, more consumed with minutia and more and more contentious. As Eli's schedule grew more demanding, he found it easier to stay away. And when he began to stay away, the whispering increased: "Eli no longer cares about this community. He is too self-important to come to meetings. If he doesn't bother to show up, why should anyone else?"

The sense of community, the very reason for RootBound's existence, was slipping away. Finally, at one of the monthly meetings, the issue of slipping community involvement was raised. RootBound did what groups do when faced with an uncomfortable challenge: they formed a committee.

The Community Building Committee consisted of Ella, bright and cheery Donna Darling, a kindergarten teacher at a Waldorf school, and Edward Appleby, an engineer working on electric cars. The CBC, as it rapidly became called, decided to host a program of fun events, to try and spark more community spirit. Their first event was a picnic by the pool on the first day of summer.

Donna and Ella volunteered to cook. They hoped by offering free-range, organic fried chicken and turkey hot dogs as well as vegan couscous, they could attract members from the whole range of culinary preferences. Edward was in charge of setup and publicity.

The day dawned hopeful. Overall, the members of RootBound missed their community and wanted to support the efforts of the CBC to renew it. So they turned out in large numbers. The weather was perfect — not too hot, not too cold. The children started a lively game of Marco Polo in the pool.

The trouble started when the meal was served. Edward and a couple of teen helpers set out colorful plastic tablecloths and matching paper plates. Ella and Donna set out platters of fried chicken, and Eli fired up the barbecue.

Suddenly Ella noticed Pyracantha, one of the TreePeople, sobbing in a corner. She went over to her. "What's wrong?" she asked.

"I'm crying for the birds!" Pyracantha sobbed. "I'm crying for the animals, and the insensitivity that lets us eat other living beings."

"We have a vegan soy-dog option on the barbecue," Ella offered, but Pyracantha only cried harder.

Meanwhile, Rick Ragle had stopped short at the pile of plates. "Paper plates!" he thundered. "What idiot came up with that idea?"

"That would be me," Edward said. "I thought they'd be festive."

"Festive?" Rick roared. "When the planet is frying, you cut down more trees to feel *festive*? How many forests died so you could have your little party?"

"Plates of death!" Pyracantha sobbed. "Plates of death!"

"They're 50% post-consumer recycled," Donna chirped.

"What about the other 50%? How the hell can we save the planet if we can't even practice sustainability in our own community?"

By now most of the adults and all of the children had crowded around to watch the show. "Please, Rick," Ella intervened. "Don't spoil the party."

"Oh, that's right. Don't spoil the party! Let's just drink and waste and consume and use it all up, cuz hey, anything else might spoil the goddamn party!" By now Rick was frothing at the mouth.

Eli put a fatherly hand on his shoulder. "Hey, Rickster, let it go."

"Don't push me," Rick said.

"He wasn't pushing you," Edward said. "He was trying to get you to calm down."

"You shut up."

"Screw you!"

And suddenly Edward found himself flying through the air, landing in the pool with a huge splash.

That was the end of the picnic. But the trouble didn't stop there.

Rick stomped off home and immediately posted a scathing indictment of RootBound's hypocrisy on his blog, which he also sent out to the global Friends of RootBound e-mail list.

Edward wrote up a formal letter of complaint, which he also sent out to the e-mail list, the Board of Directors and for good measure, the head of Rick's department at Alta Bates hospital and the officers of Doctors Without Borders, with whom Rick, a plastic surgeon, volunteered each summer to repair cleft palates in Africa. Edward accused Rick of being a violent man with an anger management problem.

A group of women members sent out an Open Letter stating that they no longer felt safe at RootBound when physical violence was treated with impunity.

Horrific pictures of caged, tormented chickens, pigs and calves were left in everyone's mailbox. Little Jennie Springer, age seven, found the picture and sobbed for three hours. Her irate mothers, Joan Springer and Marion Herman, accosted two of the TreePeople, Acacia and Ailanthus, and screamed at them even though they claimed to know nothing about the flyers and to eat meat themselves whenever they could get it.

The Women's Committee demanded that Rick be thrown out of RootBound. Rick threatened to sue if his contract was abrogated. Joan and Marion spearheaded a group of mothers demanding that the TreePeople go. Other members threatened to leave themselves if anyone was thrown out.

Within days, the community was splintering.

✳ ✳ ✳ ✳

Eli and Ella were near despair. For Eli, the situation was especially grueling as he was booked for a full season of talks and slide shows extolling the joys of community.

The couple were debating alternatives (the cost of real estate in Tasmania, joining a monastery in the Pyrenees, begging admission to the witness protection program and changing their names) when they received a new application for membership.

Dr. Marta Alvarez had been one of Ella's teachers and mentors in education. For 40 years, she had taught in and eventually chaired the sociology department at Berkeley. Her specialty was in organizational development and group dynamics. Now she was retiring, and she wished to move into RootBound Ecovillage.

Had the application come at any other time, Ella and Eli would have been thrilled. They both admired Dr. Alvarez. For she was not only an academic, but brought a rich and courageous personal history to her work. She was the child of a Jewish mother who had fled Nazi Germany in the 1930s. The only visa Marta's mother could get was to Nicaragua, where she had met and married Marta's father, Wilson Alvarez, a Meskito Indian from the East Coast, whose ancestors were escaped African slaves. Wilson Alvarez was the first person from his community to go to the university, where he became a doctor. Marta was raised in a small, remote village where her father had his clinic, and she always credited her upbringing in an indigenous community as the source of her insights into groups.

Marta Alvarez had been educated at Wellesley and Columbia University, where she took part in the antiwar demonstrations and the occupation of the university in the late 1960s. She returned to Nicaragua and joined the Sandinista movement shortly before the uprising in 1979. While she herself was not a guerilla fighter, she organized outreach and educational programs, drawing heavily on the philosophy of Paolo Freire and his Popular Education for the poor. In the 1980s, Marta was offered a teaching post at Berkeley, where she had influenced a generation of educators and organizers.

Ella was deeply ashamed to admit to her mentor how badly her own community was failing. But she knew that she had to be truthful. She asked for a meeting to discuss RootBound, and Dr. Alvarez invited Eli and Ella to dinner.

"Call me Marta," said Dr. Alvarez as they sat down to enjoy bowls full of her delicious black bean soup.

"Marta," said Eli, sipping appreciatively, "we would be so thrilled and honored to have you at RootBound. But here's the truth about what's been happening …" Together, he and Ella laid out the situation for her. Marta looked thoughtful.

"So that's the situation," Eli said. "I don't know if I can honestly encourage you to move in, or even if we'll be staying. I don't know if RootBound will survive."

"Your problems do sound grave and worrisome," Marta said. "But they are neither unusual nor surprising. All groups go through similar trials. Especially groups that try to organize cooperatively, without top-down leadership."

"Why?" Ella asked. "I would think that would be easier, not harder."

"It is probably the most common way that people have organized ourselves throughout our evolution," Marta said. "But for thousands of years, now, hierarchy has been the prevailing pattern. It's the model we hold in our minds. When we try to organize in a different way, without realizing it we often still apply the old model. It takes great effort to change. Sometimes a crisis like you are facing can be a blessing in disguise — as people are more motivated to make deep changes when the old ways no longer work."

Eli shook his head. "If we get through this period, then maybe I'll call it a blessing. At the moment, it feels more like a curse."

"Maybe I can help," Marta said. "After all, this is the area I've specialized in all my life."

"Would you?" Ella asked.

Marta smiled. "Well, perhaps this is a challenge for me. It will test my theories. If they work, I will have a flourishing community to move into. That will be good for me, as I wish to give this house to my daughter and her family, but not to become dependent on them. I would rather have my own friends and support around me. So I have a strong interest in making RootBound successful."

"We'd be eternally grateful!" Ella said.

"I don't know that we could afford to pay you," Eli said, 'but we'd offer you anything … the best unit available. The TreePeople would plant you a garden. …"

"We'd cover your meal shifts for a year!" Ella offered.

"I don't know about that," Eli said. "This soup alone might draw people back to the common dining room."

Marta smiled. "I will show your TreePeople how to make it. And now, as we have our coffee, I will share with you my secrets."

They followed Marta into the living room, where she served strong, hot coffee. Marta brought out a pen and a notepad.

"I am going to draw you a talisman," she said. "A powerful symbol to remove the curse on RootBound: The Talisman of Healthy Community. Watch!"

Marta drew a circle on the paper.

"We begin with a circle — the circle of community, which is also the circle of vision. Your vision — your core values, how you imagine the world you want to create, your goals for getting to it — that's the container that holds all the rest in place."

Then she drew a vertical line inside the circle.

"Here is the north/south axis, the Axis of Action. North is earth, solidity, manifestation. In this talisman, it represents responsibility. And south is fire, energy, passion. Here it represents power.

"In a healthy group, power and responsibility are balanced. Power is earned by taking on responsibilities, making commitments and keeping them — sometimes by making mistakes and taking responsibility for them. And those who take on tasks must be given the authority — the license to use power — that will make it possible to carry out their responsibilities. Together, power and responsibility make effective action possible."

She drew a horizontal line that crossed the first line.

"Now we come to the second axis, the east/west line. I call this the Axis of Learning. East is air — clear sight, the mind, oversight. Here it represents communication and accountability. To connect with people, we must communicate. And west is water — emotion, feelings. Here it is trust. In a thriving group, people invest trust in one another. But to do so, there must also be systems of accountability in place. To create trust, to communicate in ways that transcend our normal win/lose dichotomy, we must shift our focus from advocacy to inquiry, from asserting our point of view to listening and opening to others. We become a learning organization, enabling each of us to grow and develop.

"Put them all together in balance, and in the center you will generate connection, love and community that continue to grow over time. Let them fall out of balance, and like an unbalanced spinning top, the group will wobble and crash."

She smiled at them both.

"Don't be afraid," she said. "We will apply this magic talisman to RootBound, and together we will heal your community."

The Talisman of Healthy Community

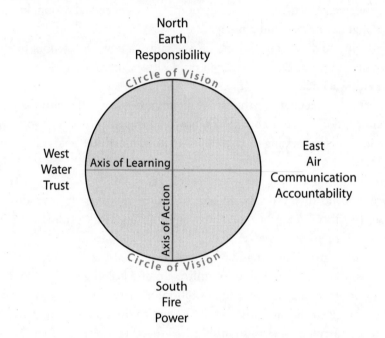

North
Earth
Responsibility

Circle of Vision

West
Water
Trust

Axis of Learning

East
Air
Communication
Accountability

Axis of Action

Circle of Vision

South
Fire
Power

CHAPTER 3

The Circle of Vision

Collaborative groups are generally started by people with a vision. Sometimes that vision is articulated and clear, expressed in a document or a set of writings. Sometimes it's embodied in the way a group organizes or the work that it does. Often it's assumed, and not made explicit. People may never have had the time to sit down and articulate what their vision is. Or they might be afraid that making it explicit will set it in stone and make it rigid and unchangeable.

But a clear vision is actually a gift to a group. An articulated vision lets prospective members know what they might be choosing to join, and it creates a standard against which your decisions can be judged.

A PICTURE OF AN IDEAL WORLD

A group vision contains many parts. First of all, it's a picture of the world you want to create, the ideal that you hold. What does that world look like? How does it feel and smell? Who lives in it and how do they interact?

Your picture of the world will influence the choices that you make and the priorities you choose. RootBound exists because someone had a picture of a world that was more communal and less isolated than the general culture. An antiwar group may form because people envision a world at peace.

Groups sometimes form around a negative vision — a shared fear or a need to stop some wrong from happening. We want to prevent a nuclear power plant from being built on an earthquake fault outside our town, because we hold a nightmarish vision of what will happen if it melts down. We might want to end policies that allow the torture of prisoners, to prevent the spread of AIDS or to end racism.

In new-age circles, I often hear people say "I don't want to go protest because it's so negative." "I don't want to give that thing energy by opposing it." "What you resist, persists." But those slogans reflect only partial truths. What you don't resist does not cease to persist. On the contrary, it generally gains momentum from its lack of opposition.

Images in our minds create frames through which we experience reality. As linguist George Lakoff says, when you say "elephant," the beast appears in your mind's eye.[1] So, yes, when you chant "no war!," war persists in your mind. But if you don't chant "no war!," if you remain silent and don't voice your opposition, war will not disappear. It will rage on, and the warmongers will not even have to go to the trouble of silencing you. You will have done it to yourself.

Protesting injustice is an important and valuable activity — but it is even more effective when we protest with a picture in our minds of justice. We are most empowered when we know what we do want, not just what we don't want.

Groups that form with fear or anger as their motivating force also tend to be short-lived. Once the threat passes, the group dissolves. That may be appropriate for some issues — once the permit for the nuclear plant is pulled, everyone may be relieved and happy to go back to watching *American Idol*.

But groups that want to create something lasting need to have a positive vision. Only a positive vision that mobilizes our love and passion can draw us away from the thousand other demands on our time, money and energy and generate excitement and long-term commitment.

One of the most powerful systems I know for generating a positive and encompassing vision is Alan Savory's Holistic Management. Savory comes from a background in land management, where he struggled for many years to understand why land was degrading in his homeland of southern Africa. Eventually, he realized that people were asking the wrong questions. They were looking at the number of cows on the land — not the overall relationship between their activities — grazing, trampling, defecating — and the health of the grass. Grasslands, he discovered, needed grazers — but managed so as to mimic the way wild herds behave in the presence of predators, bunching together and moving on quickly. It was not the number of animals but the time they spent in each area that was key.

Savory now works globally helping range managers reverse desertification, restore their land and sequester carbon in healthy soil.

What does this all have to do with vision? Savory recognized that solving the huge problems of environmental degradation required a shift in thinking — from looking at isolated parts to looking at wholes. So the key to his system is formulating a holistic goal — and that process applies not just to rangelands, but to any human endeavor.

Savory's holistic goal includes three parts: the quality of life you want, the future resource base which includes both the land and the human community, and what you need to produce.

> One of the most common mistakes is to describe a future landscape that is not much different from what you have today, when it needs to be. The mistake is understandable in many cases, because people have trouble visioning something they've only heard about but have never seen …. Young people in an African village surrounded by bare ground and starving goats and cattle found it hard to picture grassland with their livestock herded among zebra, sable, impala and other game. Having hunted big game over the same land ... this seemed simple enough to me ... until they pointed out that they could not picture something that had disappeared before they were born.[2]

A vision can and should be big. A big vision raises the stakes of our work and inspires a deeper level of passion, commitment and creativity. Each year, I work on co-creating a big ritual in San Francisco for Halloween, called the Spiral Dance Ritual. For me, the ritual is part of the larger vision of Reclaiming, our network of Pagan ritual-makers, organizers and teachers and our own particular Goddess tradition. Our mission statement says, modestly, that we are engaged in "creating a new culture." If I see our purpose as "creating a really cool event," then I might enjoy working on the ritual but it wouldn't seem that important to me. But if I envision it as part of creating a new culture, I feel a deepened level of responsibility and commitment.

And we need big visions. The realities of climate change and the dire need to reduce our carbon load — by 90% or more in developed countries — call on us to reinvent our civilization: our energy systems, our food production systems, our economy, our whole way of life. Without some big visions, we lose hope and spiral down into apathy and despair. Like the African villagers, it's hard for us to picture a world we've never seen, but unless we do so, we won't be able to create it.

There's one caveat here: a big vision raises the stakes, which means it also raises the level of risk. The risks have to be worth taking. So, for example, if your vision for a family reunion is everyone getting together in a warm, nurturing environment and having fun, you will create a set of expectations in line with the scope of the event. If your vision is to end racism in the world and you imagine your prejudiced Aunt Betty finally embracing your mixed-race child with true warmth — be aware that's a dangerous expectation, and you will be putting a load of emotion on the event that it may or may not be able to hold.

Sometimes the work of identifying a vision might bring a group closer together. At other times, it may clarify for some people that they need to look elsewhere to find others who share key aspects of their vision. Many times, some people may choose to leave the group. That's not a sign of failure, but a natural part of refining the group's identity. Beware, however, of crafting a vision so detailed and exacting that it excludes forms of diversity you might value: "We envision a multiracial, multicultural world in which everyone is a vegan who meditates twice daily." When aspects of your vision contradict one another, clarity may come from addressing the group's values.

Guided Imagery for Clarifying Your Group Vision

EXERCISE

Allow about one hour including sharing afterward.

Materials needed: Big sheets of paper and markers or a whiteboard and a Scribe or notetaker.

Find a place where you can sit comfortably. Now, take some long, deep breaths. Close your eyes. I'd like you to think about the place where this group does its work. Let yourself picture this place, with all its wonderful aspects, and all its challenges. Notice how you feel in this place, how your body feels, how you are breathing.

Now take a moment and think about those things you care about most deeply. What are the qualities and values that are most important to you? What are the things you don't want to see harmed or lessened in any way? What would you take a stand for?

Now come back to the place where the group does its work. Are those things you most deeply care about present? Are they cherished in the world this group exists in?

Now imagine that you hold in your hand a magic wand. Take a deep breath, and feel the wand in your hand. What is it made out of? How does it feel to hold it? What weight does it have?

When you wave this wand, you can change the world. This wand has the magic quality that will transform society into one that cherishes what you most deeply value. Are you ready? Let's count to three together. Take a deep breath … one, two, three … Wave the wand, and feel your hand moving through the air, the world starting to shimmer and dissolve around you. And now it solidifies again, in a new way, into that world that cherishes what you care about most deeply.

Take a deep breath … sniff in through your nose. What does the air smell like?

Open your ears, now. What do you hear? What are the sounds of this world?

How does your body feel in this world? How are you standing, breathing?

Now open your inner eyes. What do you see? Take a moment to look around you and explore this world.

Where is your home in this world? Take a moment and explore your home. Who do you live with? What is your home built of? Who built it? What are the surroundings like?

You're in your home, and you're about to share a meal with people you love. Who is there with you? Where do they live? Who cares for the elders and the children? Who cares for the sick in this world?

Now you eat together. What do you eat? Where does your food come from? Where does it grow? How do you get it? What kind of land does it grow on? How do you replenish the soil and maintain the land?

What does the land look like and feel around you? What trees grow in the forests, and how big? What animals and birds live around you?

Where does your water come from?

What is your work in this world? Where do you do it? Who do you do it with? How are you rewarded?

What do you do for fun and celebration? What are your rituals and ceremonies?

How do you resolve conflicts in this world? How do you meet threats and dangers? What are your challenges?

What happens, in this world, to those who disagree? Who hold a different vision? Who violate the group's trust?

How do you honor people in this world? How do you reward those who make great contributions?

Now take a deep breath, and take a last, long look at your home and at this world. If there's something you particularly want to remember and take back with you, hold it in your mind.

For now you are going to wave your magic wand and return to our ordinary world. But this world will remain, in your dreams and visions and imagination. You can visit it any time you want to, and it can inform your work in this world.

So take a deep breath, and thank anyone you've met in this world. Say goodbye.

And we're going to count to three again … take a deep breath, and one, two, three …

And as you come back to this world, notice the wand in your hand. As you feel it and look at it, it begins to change. You realize it's not a wand after all — it's part of you. It's something you can do, something that will bring us closer to that world that cherishes what you most deeply care about.

What is it that you can do?

Now breathe deep, and open your eyes and we take three deep breaths together. One … breathing in and out and remembering your vision … two … breathing in and out and bringing back a clear memory of your world … three … coming back now, fully awake and present in this world. Take a moment, feel your own body's edges, open your eyes and say your own name out loud. Now clap your hands three times … and that's the end of the story.

Now take a moment to share some of your vision with one other person. You'll have about ten minutes altogether.

Were there common elements in your visions? Surprises? Things you disagree about? What aspects of your visions do you strongly want as part of the group vision?

Now focus back on the big group. We're going to ask each pair to share the common elements of your visions, and/or the things you strongly want in the group vision. And the Scribe is going to write them down.

I want to be clear that there are no right or wrong visions. Everyone's vision is right for them. But we want to find out how to meld our individual visions into a common vision for this group.

(The Scribe writes short summaries on the big sheets of paper or whiteboard.)

Now we've heard the parts of our vision that people strongly want … I'm curious whether there were elements of any of your visions that your partners disagreed with or had concerns about? Let's go around and hear them, and the Scribe will write them down.

Now we've got two lists: one of common and strongly felt aspects of the vision, and one of areas of more contention. I'd like to start with the first list, and ask you all to look at it and think about it. We're going to come back to the other list later.

Now, is there anything on the list of common vision that somebody disagrees with or has concerns about? It's OK if there is, and it's very important that you voice that disagreement now. Because if you hold silent or try to make nice at this point, it's likely that it will come out later anyway.

So, we'll star the one or two things people have concerns about, and let's look at the list of what we all agree on. What an amazing vision we hold in common!

CONTINUED

But let's look at it once again — is there anything missing? Anyone missing? Anything that hasn't come up yet that should be there?

OK, that was great work! What an amazing vision we've come up with. And now I have some homework for you. Before we meet again, I'd like to ask each of you to do some creative expression of this vision. You could write about it, draw it, paint it, collect some images and make a collage, write a poem or song — whatever you like to do. Don't worry about being a great artist — the point is to express ourselves and to enjoy doing it. (In a longer retreat, take an hour and let people do the creative expression immediately.)

We will come back to the things we disagree on. But now we're going to take a break.

(10 minute break)

Welcome back. Now — take a deep breath, and let's look at the aspects of our vision that generated strong concerns. Here are some questions we can ask:

- Is this a part of the vision that people are strongly attached to?
- Is this something that we all need to hold in common, or can it be an area of individual autonomy?
- Ask yourself: Can I honestly commit to the group if people don't share this aspect of my personal vision?
- Ask yourself: Can I honestly commit to the group knowing that some people might hold this piece of the vision which I don't share?
- If not, might I be more effective in another group?
- Would there be ways to work together in alliance or coalition?

FINDING OUR CORE VALUES

Visions embody our values, and articulating those values makes them visible and allows people to accept or challenge them. Shared identified values become a common bond that draws people together and helps hold the container of the group. They can also be a standard by which to weigh decisions or set priorities.

But values can also be a point of conflict. They can divide instead of connecting us. Most people who join collaborative groups are idealistic — but they come not just with one ideal but with a whole constellation of values. My constellation might overlap with yours, but not be identical. We both might value democracy and equality, but perhaps you value promptness, while I value an organic flow of time. We both might value the environment, but you might refuse on moral grounds to eat meat and I might be a committed hunter who believes in culling the herds.

A discussion of values can be contentious if we insist that everyone involved in a group share the whole values constellation. It can be destructive if we demonize those who don't share our own values. So one question to ask is: "Is this value core to our work together?" If we're organizing a peace rally together, I don't care whether you clean your bathroom or do your dishes after every meal. But if we're planning to live together, your level of tolerance for clutter becomes much important than your position on the proposed timetable for withdrawal from Iraq.

Collaborative groups remain dynamic and alive when they respect diversity of beliefs and opinions as well as other forms of diversity. Yet we must also set the core values that define the group. Some kinds of diversity are not meant to work together: if our goal is to ban the growing of genetically engineered crops in our county, we're not going to work well with Monsanto. Yet we should also beware of drawing to tight a circle. If everyone in our group has to be a vegan, polyamorous, non-gender-specific advocate for peace, we're going to lose. To win, we need a coalition of conventional farmers, organic growers, ranchers, vineyard owners and environmentalists who might hold widely divergent views on gender bending, gay marriage and foreign policy but agree on the food system they want to see.

We come from a culture that loves dramas of good vs. evil. But in collaborative groups, we often find ourselves in contention not with evildoers, but with someone who holds a different vision of "good." For that matter, we ourselves often hold sets of good values that conflict. We might believe in accessibility and free access to information, and also believe that people deserve to be paid for their work. Reconciling these two positive values can be difficult. Do we charge money for teaching — or offer it for free? If it's free, how do we compensate teachers and organizers for their time, energy and expenses? If we don't compensate them, will the work be sustainable?

Many conflicts that arise around values are conflicts of good vs. good. Understanding that, we can stop trying to win and start looking for ways to achieve a dynamic balance — which may be exactly what the situation most truly needs. We do indeed want our projects to be both accessible and sustainable, and if we don't squander our energy bashing each other, we can unleash our creativity to find solutions together.

E X E R C I S E

Values Council

This is a heart-centered way of looking at the group's core values. Allow one to three hours or more, depending on the size of the group.

Materials needed: A Talking Stick (a specially decorated stick or something as simple as a pen or even a microphone) or other sacred object that can be easily passed, a notebook and Scribe or notetaker.

Everyone sits in a circle. The leader might begin with a short meditation — for example, the grounding earlier in Chapter 1. She briefly explains the process and core agreements:

- Listen with full attention and respect.
- Speak only when you are holding the Talking Stick.
- Be aware of how much time you are taking up, and pass the stick on.
- No one speaks twice until everyone has had a chance to speak once.

She then poses this question: "What core values do you hold that you want this group to share?"

This question will lead to open-ended discussion that may take time, but can create an opportunity for deep sharing. If time is at a premium, the question could be framed: "Name one of your core values that you want this group to share. If someone has already named a value you would have said, you can name another or pass."

The Stick can pass clockwise around the circle — or be left in the center for people to take as they are inspired to come forward. When everyone has spoken or been given a chance to speak, the group may do a second round or allow open discussion about what is common and what is different.

End with a song, a chant, a short meditation or something to bring the group together and affirm the sharing.

Values Brainstorm and Priority Setting

This is a more heady way to approach the question of values. Allow one hour.

Materials needed: Large sheets of paper or lots of whiteboard space, markers, red and green sticky stars or extra red and green markers, a Scribe or notetaker.

Welcome. I'm going to ask you to sit in silence for a moment, and think about those things that you care most deeply about. Those things you cherish and want to protect — the things you stand for.

(after a pause)

Now we're going to brainstorm our values — that means that you can just call out what they were and the Scribe and I will write them down, big, on these big sheets of paper. In a brainstorm, we don't criticize each other's contributions or comment on them ... later we'll

CONTINUED

have time for that. We just get them all out. So we'll do this for just five minutes — ready? Go!

(The Scribe and facilitator write down the values very large on multiple sheets of paper. When the five minutes are up, continue:)

OK, that's five minutes. Anything we missed, anything that you're going to go home and lose sleep over if we don't put it up?

All right. Now, I'm going to ask you all to look at this list. We're going to take ten minutes, in silence (or while musicians play — this is another opportunity to let creative people contribute to the group) and ask you to put a green star next to the seven values that are most important to you. (This number is somewhat arbitrary — it could be five, ten or three ... the smaller the number, the more complaints you'll get from the group. Larger numbers will generate more unwieldy but more inclusive lists.)

And I'm going to ask you to put a red star next to any values you disagree with or have strong concerns about.

OK — go!

All right, now we can look at the list and get a picture of which values are most important to us — which have some support and which are contentious. And I'd like to ask a couple of volunteers to write them up again in three lists:

- Values everyone supports
- Values some people support
- Values that have strong concerns

And while they do that, let's look at some of the values that have both strong support and strong concerns — lots of green stars and some red stars. And I'd like to ask the people who placed the red stars to voice their concerns.

Take time to hear the concerns and see if they can be resolved. If not, ask if this is a value the entire group needs to hold or one that can be left to each person's private conscience.

If it does need to be addressed by the group and can't easily be resolved, the facilitator should ask for volunteers — one from the objectors and one from the strong supporters, with perhaps one other who does not feel strongly about the issue, to meet before the next session and come up with a compromise. Once the group accepts that people hold differing values, there are many possible practical solutions to accommodating the diversity of views. For example, RootBound's meat-eaters vs. vegan controversy could be resolved in a number of ways: the group could decide that all common meals would be vegan or that meals would always include both a vegan and a meat option. Or that meals on odd-numbered days would be vegan and on even-numbered days a meat option would be on the table.

When the new lists are made and the group is ready to address them, move on.

Now we're going to look back at our list of common values. Remember our sheet of common vision? Let's see if our vision reflects all of our common values. Is anything missing?

CONT.
• •
•

Now let's look at the values that had some, but not unanimous, support and no opposition. Let's take them one by one and decide if we want to add them to the list.

Now let's look at the aspects of our vision that had opposition. Has any of that been dealt with in our conversation around values? If not, let's hear from those who had concerns or objections.

Great work, group. We've got a sense of our vision, and we know what our values are! Let's congratulate ourselves.

CLARIFYING INTENTION

In ritual and ceremony, everything begins with intention: a clear, concise statement of what we are trying to accomplish. An intention is narrower than a broad vision, but wider than a goal. Our vision might be of a world that embodies our values of freedom, justice and communities living in harmony with nature. Our intention might be to create an inspiring public ritual that embodies our vision and raises energy to help it manifest.

An intention is an action statement — what are we going to do? It's also a brief statement — one or two sentences, at most, with minimal extra clauses. Consider loglines — those one or two sentences in the newspaper that describe a film or a TV show. A good logline will grab your attention and, in that brief moment, tell you enough about a show for you to form an opinion on whether or not it interests you. Screenwriters learn that refining the logline helps them become more clear about the spine and momentum of the work.

A powerful intention often involves a change — either one you intend to make or one you intend to cause. Change gives an intention dynamism. It implies an arc, a rising and falling of energies directed for some purpose. Without that dynamism, our actions may lack passion or focus. I once attended a spring ritual put on by an enthusiastic group of people who had never created one before. It had many fun and beautiful moments, but with no sense of connection between them. We formed a circle and learned a dance. We blew bubbles. A fairy came out of the woods and handed out gifts to the children. But we never really knew why anything was happening, so people were amused but not emotionally engaged. Later, one of the planners asked me for feedback. "What was your intention?" I asked her. "To have a Spring Equinox ritual," she said. I suggested that next time they look for a more powerful intention, one that included some aspect of change, some form of need. Without that, there was nothing to connect the pieces.

Each year when we plan the Spiral Dance, we conduct a visioning session to find our intention for that specific year. In 2008, right before the US election, our intention was to raise the energy to help set our feet firmly on the good road, the road of life, the road that leads to a viable future.

EXERCISE

Setting Intention

Begin by reviewing the vision and values from the last session. Read the vision, look at the pictures or objects people have brought in, create the collage.

Now that we know our vision and our core values, let's think about our intention. I'd like all of us to take ten minutes, in silence, and think about the question, "What is the work of this group? What do we intend to do?" Then in one sentence, write your answer down.

If you have trouble coming up with an answer, try this: Imagine that you were making a Hollywood feature film about our group. What goal would the lead characters be trying to pursue? What difficulties would they face? What are the stakes — what will happen if they don't succeed? Now write the logline for the movie — the one or two sentence description that tells us who, what, why and what if. Then see how that works as a group intention.

A logline for an activist group might read: "Committed activists risk arrest by blocking shipments of arms to Iraq, in order to express opposition to the war." A 12-step group's logline might read: "Recovering alcoholics band together to support one another as they struggle to overcome their addiction."

(When the ten minutes are up)

Now find a partner. Take a few moments to read your intentions to each other. Now you have ten minutes to combine your intentions and come up with one common intention.

(When ten minutes are up)

Now you and your partner join up with two other pairs, to make a group of six. Read your common intentions to each other, and you have ten minutes to combine all three into one intention.

(When ten minutes are up)

Now let's come together and hear each group's intentions.

(Each group reads its intention aloud.)

Now, let's look at what was common in all the intentions. Who noticed places of common ground? Where were there differences? Let's take some time now and weave these into one common intention.

In organizing for the protests against the G8 meeting in Scotland in 2005, our intention was to create an ecovillage encampment that would model the kind of alternative society we want, one that runs by direct democracy and lives in balance with the earth.

IDENTIFYING GOALS

Goals are statements of desire — of what we want, what we hope to achieve by realizing our intention. Goals should be doable and reachable — or at least some should be if a group wants to survive and thrive. So goals are often more specific and timebound than visions or even intentions.

Our intention for the 30th anniversary Spiral Dance might be to create a ritual that honors the past and launches our community into a thriving future. Our goals might be:

- To create a ritual that is inspiring, emotionally moving and aesthetically thrilling
- To increase attendance by 30% over last year's ritual
- To raise money to support the work of Reclaiming
- To introduce new people to our tradition and community
- To assure that more experienced people mentor younger people
- To not have aging members of the group stuck with cleanup at 3 AM

Groups may rarely if ever achieve all their goals. But it is vital to have some goals that are reachable. People do not become empowered by strings of failure. We like to win sometimes. We like to cross things off the to-do list. So groups need small and large goals, short-term and long-term goals.

Our short-term goals might look very different from our big vision. Our big vision might be the free gift economy — but our short-term goal might be to pay the rent. Or as my housemate Bill often says, "We dream of the anarchist ideal of small, self-organizing communities in a world with no coercion or force. In the meantime, we'll settle for Scandinavian socialism."

Conflicts often arise when people in a group have different intentions or goals that have never been voiced. You might want to build a broad coalition by inviting speakers to the conference from 20 different organizations. I might want to limit the number of speakers so that each can have more impact. When we step back and articulate our visions, values, intentions and goals, we can find common ground.

GOVERNANCE ALIGNED WITH VALUES

Our circle of vision also includes how we function as a group. The ways we communicate and govern ourselves should reflect our visions, values, intentions and goals. Governance includes many aspects: how we treat each other, how we meet and how we schedule meetings, how we communicate, how we resolve disputes and make decisions.

E
X
E
R
C
I
S
E

Setting Goals

Begin by reviewing the work already done on vision, values and intention.

Now that we have our intention, let's think about our goals — those milestones we will pass, the markers of progress. So I'd like to go around the circle and give us each a chance to speak to this question: "What are some of your personal goals that you hope to realize through the work of this group?"

(In a very large group, you might divide the group into smaller groups or threes.)

Now let's brainstorm some of our common goals. Let's take ten minutes and we'll write them up.

Now, we can look at this list and identify whether there are goals we all hold in common, goals we disagree about, goals that are more important to some people than to others.

(You can go through a priority-setting exercise as you did for values or simply have open discussion.)

Are any of these goals in conflict with one another? Will we need to find some kind of dynamic balance between them?

Do we have the resources, skills, allies and knowledge we need to achieve these goals? If not, do we need further training? More resources? What else?

Which of these goals are completely within our power to achieve? Which depend partly on outside circumstances or luck?

Do these goals fall into an order? Are there goals we need to achieve first so that later we can work toward other goals? If we were building a house, we'd need to lay the foundation before we could build the walls. What order do these goals fall into?

Is there a time frame for these goals? Are there deadlines? Can we create a timeline for them?

In groups, disagreements often emerge between the get-it-done people and the process lovers. Some people want to devote time to building interpersonal connections, telling stories and discussing the nuances of miscommunications. Others want to get on with the work, and soon grow impatient.

A group that pays no attention to process becomes a harsh and sometimes brutal place to be. In the business world, where people are paid to do a job, we expect a no-nonsense focus on the task at hand. In groups of volunteers, people simply won't stay in a situation that becomes uncomfortable and unpleasant. When we join a group, we are hoping to find friends, to connect with others as people, not just envelope stuffers. If, instead of connection, we find ourselves on yet another grueling work schedule, we will tend to look elsewhere. So relationship-building in a group is vital.

But in a world where all of us face enormous demands on our time, people also grow impatient with too much process and no product to show for it. We come to groups because we believe in their mission and want to contribute to it. In support groups, of course, process is the mission. But if a group with a work mission abandons its focus — if it decides, for example, not to put on the ritual this year but instead just to spend time getting to know one another — it loses the forward drive that can pull people away from Facebook and into a face-to-face meeting.

Some years ago, I gave a weekend workshop in northern Ontario. As the organizers were driving me to the airport, they remarked on how well the weekend had gone. "And we're very relieved," Violet said. "We were worried that nothing you could possibly do would be as wonderful as the experience we had organizing the workshop."

"What's your secret?" I demanded. "If you could bottle what you've got and pass it on, we could save the world!"

But all she said was, "Potlucks."

I've pondered that one enigmatic word for years, and here's how I think they created such a wonderful group experience — they hit the sweet spot, the perfect balance between connection and achievement, work and play. They were a group of friends who liked one another and looked forward to getting together, sharing food and updates on their lives. As friends, there was nothing to prevent them from doing so at any time — but organizing for my workshop gave the potlucks a focus and a sense of purpose, and added the satisfaction of achievement that comes from envisioning something and making it happen.

GOVERNANCE AGREEMENTS

Having a set of agreements can be helpful for a group. When agreements are explicit and clearly communicated to new members, people know what is expected of them, what the group norms are or aspire to be and what they can ask of others. Discussing process and reaching agreements early on can also forestall future conflicts. If I'm told from the beginning that personal complaints do not belong on the group's listserv, I have something in the back of my mind that may stop me pressing the Send button at 3 AM.

Here's an example of one group's agreements:

Suggested Agreements for the Spiral Dance Cell:

1. We agree to treat each other with respect, compassion, love and humor as we do the sacred work of the Goddess.
2. Our intention is that working in this group will be nurturing, fun, creative and will help each person further their own development, while accomplishing the goals of the group.
3. We embrace passion and commitment in our work. We know this sometimes leads to lively arguments, and we support each other in putting forth our ideas freely and defending them strongly, while refraining from personal attacks.
4. Power, influence and perks in this cell are earned by commitment, by undertaking responsibilities and fulfilling them and, on occasion, by owning up to mistakes, learning from them and making amends.
5. Members join this cell by taking on organizing or coordinating responsibilities in putting on each year's Spiral Dance.
6. Members who take on a task or role commit to mentoring others and sharing the skills, knowledge and information necessary to fulfill that role, and to training successors.
7. Conflict is a part of life and of all group endeavors. If we have a personal conflict with someone in the group, we agree to deal with it openly, honestly and with underlying respect for each other and the work. We commit to face-to-face engagement whenever possible — with phone calls as a less desirable alternate. We will engage each other privately before we make an issue public. We will not try to resolve a conflict on the group listserv, other community listservs or over e-mail.

8. If we are unable to resolve or transform a conflict with someone, we agree to ask for help, support and mediation.

9. We agree to support one another by offering our help and support and, when appropriate, our services as mediators or in other roles of conflict transformation or by helping to find the right people, resources and processes to resolve an issue.

10. If a group member violates the group's agreements repeatedly and, after warnings and at least two chances to change their behavior, continues to violate those agreements, the group can, by consensus minus one, ask them to leave.

EXERCISE

Governance Session

Begin with a round or with people in pairs or threes to answer these questions:

- When have you had a really wonderful group experience? How did you feel? What made it empowering and exciting? How did people treat each other?

- What practices or agreements might you want to bring to this group from that positive experience? Generate a list.

- How has it been working together so far in this group? What has worked well? Are there practices we already have that we want to formalize into agreements? Add them to the list.

- What has not worked so well for you or felt frustrating or disempowering? Are there patterns we want to change? What agreements might we make about them? Generate another list — patterns we want to change or avoid.

- Now, have you ever had an awful group experience? What made it awful? Can we learn from that experience about patterns or behaviors we want to change or avoid? Add them to the second list.

Let's look back at our vision, our values, intention and goals. Are these agreements in alignment with our larger vision? Are we missing anything?

Ask for volunteers to take the lists and compile a set of agreements.

How will we communicate these agreements to all group members? New group members?

How will we hold each other accountable for keeping these agreements? What happens if someone violates the agreements of the group? Whose responsibility will it be to hold that person to account, and how will they do it?

THE GROUP'S JOURNEY

Imagine that your group is on a journey together. Your destination is that picture you hold in your mind of the world you want to create. Your values are the vehicle you travel in, and your intention is the road you set out upon. Your goals are the milestones you pass along the way, and your process is how you decide how fast to go, how often to stop and rest, what to eat along the way and what songs to sing.

A picture of an ideal world, a set of values, a clear intention, goals that can be realized and a group process that embodies its values — together they make up the circle of vision that holds a group in its embrace. That circle is a container — something that both strengthens and constrains. When the group needs to make a decision, to set priorities or choose new work, it can ask, "Is this in line with our vision? Will it help realize our intention? Will it help us meet our goals?"

The circle also functions like a membrane, the boundary of a cell. It connects the group to the rest of the world — by making its vision and intention clear, it can draw people in or filter out those who don't share the same drive, passion or values.

When the circle is drawn, we can begin to call in the other elements of healthy group functioning that make up our talisman: power, responsibility, accountability and trust.

CHAPTER 4

The Axis of Action — Power and Responsibility

MEETING WITH MARTA

Eli and Ella went home from their first meeting with Marta with a bound copy of her course outlines and manuscript notes. Eli read the section on Vision with mounting excitement.

"That's it!" he said to Ella. "We'll hold a vision session. Maybe we can get Marta herself to facilitate — we'll make it a retreat. Maybe a whole weekend. People will get refocused on our values and our ideals — fired up again! When can we schedule it?"

"I think that's jumping the gun," Ella said. "Let's see what Marta says."

They had arranged to meet Marta for coffee after an interview on KPFA, the progressive radio station in downtown Berkeley. They settled themselves into a table in a dim back corner of Au Coquelet, Marta's favorite café, and over steaming cups of cappuccino, Eli laid out his plan.

But Marta shook her head. "A visioning session would be premature," she cautioned. "You have too much conflict to deal with. If you were just starting out, I would recommend you begin by articulating your vision, your values, your goals and your governance early on. But now that you are embroiled in conflict, you must face and embrace it before you can get back to your vision."

Eli sighed. "I was afraid you'd say that."

"And are you going to say, 'You were right, Ella?'" Ella asked sweetly.

"Only if you bend my arm up at the elbow and threaten to break it," Eli replied. "OK, Marta, what do we do?"

"Conflict is often about power," Marta said. "Power is like fire — that's why I placed it in the south in my talisman, in the direction that corresponds to the element of fire."

She drew the quartered circle on a napkin. "Groups need fire — they need the driving energy of passion to move forward. But the group structure must contain and direct that fire — otherwise it will burn out of control. When power and authority — the license to use power — are in balance with responsibility, the group can take action. But to find that balance, we first must understand what power is. Or more accurately — that power is not one single thing. There are many types of power. When we understand them, when we create a structure that can effectively channel them, we can begin to untangle the conflicts that plague RootBound."

DEFINITIONS OF POWER

In collaborative groups, we often encounter a variety of forms of power. To work effectively, we must understand their differences.

Power-over, or coercive power, is a form of power we are all familiar with from hierarchies. It's the power one person or a group has over another, to control resources, to impose sanctions or punishments, to hire or fire. Ultimately, it is backed by the power of the state, the law and the underlying threat of force.

Collaborative groups generally try to eliminate or minimize power-over. They have no bosses who hire and fire, and often no threatened punishments. Decisions are made collectively. Many idealistic groups are open to anyone who wants to join, and have no mechanisms for kicking anyone out.

Collaborative groups foster a different type of power: *power-from-within,* or empowerment. Power-from-within is creative power, the power we feel singing, writing, making art or dancing. Empowerment can be moral courage — the power we feel speaking an uncomfortable truth or standing up for a value we believe in — or spiritual power, the force we feel flowing through us in moments of deep connection with the great creative, compassionate energies of the universe.

When empowered people band together, they can develop *collective power,* the power we have as a group when we act in concert. Another term for this is that good old trade union value of *solidarity.* To get through difficult times, we need each other. We need to know we're not alone, that we're part of a strong community that we can trust. Solidarity means that I've got your back, whether

I like you or dislike you, because we are acting in the service of common goals. It means that I don't betray you, denounce you or reveal your secrets to those who might use them against you. Solidarity means that I am willing to set aside my own individual interests in favor of our collective interests.

While RootBound has been powerfully effective in using its collective power in many ways, it is suffering from a lack of solidarity in the personal relationships that are its foundation. Solidarity has a bearing on how we look at issues of accountability, gossip and communications, and it can be a guideline for how to resolve conflicts.

There's also a fourth kind of power — it's around this power that groups often get confused and come to grief. I call this *power-with* or social power, but other words for it might be influence, rank, status or authority. It's the power that determines how much you are listened to in a group, how much weight your opinion carries and how much respect you receive. Co-creative groups, striving to eliminate power-over and hierarchy, often have difficulty recognizing and dealing with social power. Yet all human groups contain variations in status and rank, however nuanced.

In RootBound, founder Eli Stern holds no more coercive power than any other member. He cannot decide who gets to join or kick someone out who displeases him. He can't change the fee structure or the work schedule. But he does have enormous social power, of two kinds: *earned* and *unearned.*

Unearned social power is *privilege,* the power you get not from anything you've done or created, but from who you happen to be — your gender, your race, your social class, the wealth you've inherited, the opportunities handed to you. Privilege encompasses some things which should be universal human rights — access to good food, healthcare, education, a decent place to live. But it can also include unfair advantages and license to be insensitive or oblivious.

Eli's privilege comes from being white, being male, being born to an upper-middle-class family. He also holds social power that may be partly privilege and partly earned: for example, his high level of education and success. He was fortunate enough to come from a family that could send him to good schools as a child, pay for extracurricular activities, buy him cool clothes and sports equipment that helped his popularity. But he also worked and studied hard, and put forth the effort that was needed for his success. Many people with all of his privileges fail to do so.

Eli has other sorts of social power in RootBound, much of which was earned. He is the founder: he had the original idea and did the research, the organizing and the work to make it happen. He inspired others with a vision and took on many responsibilities to make it a reality. He did grunt work, meeting with attorneys and architects for endless revisions of contracts and blueprints. And he's somebody that people respect. He's idealistic, kind, charming and funny. He genuinely cares about people and goes out of his way to help others.

So at RootBound, Eli's word carries weight. People listen to him with more intensity than they do to others. If he stops attending meetings, they are seen as

E X E R C I S E

Discovering the Positive Face of Power

This is an exercise developed by Margo Adair and Bill Aal of Tools for Change.[1]

In pairs, interview one another, giving each partner a protected time to talk without being interrupted, and practicing active listening for both content and emotion.

- We have all experienced the transformation that comes out of sharing power.
- Tell me a story of a moment when you experienced a true sharing of power or maybe of a time when unequal power relationships were shifted into balance.
- What was happening? How did it feel?
- How did people relate to each other?
- What qualities were in the air?
- What values were present?
- When geese fly in a V, the flap of their wings creates an uplift for the one behind.
- How did people create uplift for one another?

After both partners have had a chance to speak, take time to discuss what was common and what was different. What have you learned that you might be able to bring back and share with the larger group?

Variation: These questions could also be addressed in rounds in small groups.

Rhythms of Power Exercise

The facilitator tells the group, "I'm going to start a rhythm. You can follow it, but I want everyone to find your own rhythm, put it out as strongly as you can to the group and try to get everyone to follow it."

Begin clapping a simple rhythm. As others join in, note the energy level and the level of cacophony which generally arises from this instruction.

Stop the rhythm, and ask people how it felt. How much did each person feel they could influence the group?

CONTINUED

Now tell the group we're going to try something different. "I'm going to start a rhythm, and I want everyone to listen hard to one another and try to find another person's rhythm to amplify and support." Begin clapping, and note what happens as people join in. Often this second round is much more harmonious but sometimes dull and static.

Stop the rhythm and again ask people how it felt. Did they like it? How much did they hear other peoples' rhythms? How much did they feel heard? How easy or hard was it to influence the group?

Now tell people you're going to do a third round. "I'm going to start a rhythm, and you can join in. I want you to listen to one another, and listen for creative impulses to support. I also want you to listen to yourselves. If you get a creative idea, go for it — put it out strongly and see if others support it. If not, look for other people's ideas to support." Let this round go on a bit longer — often it becomes highly creative and may expand into other kinds of sound and movement.

Stop the rhythm and again ask people how it felt. Did they like it? How much did they hear other peoples' rhythms? How much did they feel heard? How easy or hard was it to influence the group?

Discuss the exercise as a metaphor for how groups interact. Identify the third rhythm as our goal for the group — a place where people listen and support one another's creative impulses and ideas, and where we're free to have our own — where the spark of inspiration moves from person to person, and everyone has the opportunity to lead and understands the value of support.

of lesser value. Sometimes social power works to his advantage: people are more likely to adopt his ideas. Sometimes it backfires: they resent his ideas and go into reaction against him, perceiving him as too powerful.

Eli also has another source of power — *celebrity*, the prestige accorded to him by others outside the group. Celebrity, too, can be both earned and unearned. Prince Charles was born into his celebrity. Michael Jordan earned his. People who have read Eli's work or heard him speak know what he stands for and trust his assessments and judgments. When he is involved with a project, people transfer to it some of that trust. His name can draw people to events and into involvement and bring resources to the group.

But a celebrity in a group can also be a detriment. Celebrity is like a spotlight focused on one person — it makes that one person highly visible while others are lost in the shadows. Outsiders may attribute all of the creativity in the group to the celebrity, while the contributions of others are unseen. RootBound is seen as "Eli's community" rather than a community of strong people of whom Eli is a member.

RULES AND NORMS

Our society is full of *explicit rules* — stop on the red light, go on the green. We are taught those rules, law books codify them and they are backed by the authority of law. We may obey them or disobey them, but generally we know what they are.

Society is also full of *implicit norms,* that we are expected to obey without being taught. Backed by no laws and unenforced by police or armies, nonetheless they are strictly followed. We get into an elevator and we turn and face the door. No law tells us to, no rules are posted saying, "Face the door and don't talk to strangers." We generally don't make a conscious decision about which way to face. We just follow the norm because, well, that's the way we do things.

Norms differ in different cultures and subcultures. In African American culture, looking people in the eye is a sign of respect, a way of saying, "I see you and acknowledge you." In some indigenous cultures, looking people in the eye is an implicit threat and a powerful insult.

The norms of our own groups are often unconscious. They are so deeply ingrained that we don't recognize them as specific cultural norms — they are just how things are, how decent people behave. Norms become visible when they are violated or rub up against different norms. A warm and fuzzy Californian rushes toward a New Yorker with arms open for a hug, only to be stopped by a stiffly extended hand to shake. The Californian feels rejected, the New Yorker feels like she's just defended her personal boundaries against an unwanted assault. And norms are strong enough to cause us extreme discomfort when we disobey. Try the elevator experiment — walk into a crowded elevator and face the other people instead of the door. How do you feel? How long do you last?

As humans, as primates, we have a hard-wired ability to pick up on unspoken norms and expectations, and an instinctive urge to follow them. When someone lacks that ability, we consider it a symptom of disease, as in autism, Asperger's or Tourette Syndrome. Someone who violates the norms, unspoken though they might be, is often feared and shunned. If they don't get it, if they don't know something as basic as how to behave on an elevator, what else might they do? Think of our term of insult: "clueless."

Norms can strengthen group identity. Groups that may consciously identify as rebels and rule-breakers can still be powerfully ruled by unspoken norms. I once made the mistake of attending the Anarchist Book Fair dressed in the bright green I'd worn to a Spring Equinox ritual the same day. Of the close to 400 hundred other people there, I was the only one not wearing black. I stood out like an emerald in a coal mine, and I felt excruciatingly uncomfortable. If someone had tried to impose a dress code, if a sign at the door read "Must wear black to enter!" there would have been mass rebellion. Yet the norm was so strong that it resulted in an absolutely unified color theme.

Norms can also maintain and reinforce social hierarchies. A person from a poor or working-class background who rises to wealth and prominence has to learn many new norms — from which fork to use at a formal dinner to what length of dress to wear.

Collaborative groups may explicitly welcome people of different classes and races, yet create subtle and unconscious barriers to their full participation. Unexamined assumptions about what people know, how they should dress, how much time or money they might have available, how they should communicate can all create an atmosphere in which some people feel that they belong and others don't.

All groups have norms. How, then, can we make our groups truly welcoming across barriers of race, gender and class? How do we share power fairly in an unfair world?

EARNED AND UNEARNED SOCIAL POWER

Understanding power-with and the variations of social power is key to making collaborative groups welcoming and effective. Conflicts around social power are also one of the key reasons groups break down. Collaborative groups often try to eliminate power-over and privilege. But when they mistake social power for coercive power, or fail to distinguish earned from unearned social power, they may actually undermine their members'

EXERCISE

Questions About Norms

- What norms do we have in our group? Do they serve us, or not?
- What would we have to wear in order to be inappropriately dressed in this group?
- What might we say or do that would violate a group norm? Would that be a positive or negative contribution?

empowerment. For if a group does not consciously acknowledge earned social power and decide how people should earn it and wield it, they may end up penalizing and driving away their strongest and most committed members. Such groups may be equal — but extremely unfair. If I were to write my own list of Proverbs of Power, here's one that would be at the very top: Groups that refuse to let people earn social power inevitably favor those with unearned social power. The loudest, strongest, most educated or most charismatic get heard; those who do the actual work may be ignored.

Groups that refuse to let people earn social power may create invisible barriers to membership for those who have historically been most oppressed. In communities that have suffered from prejudice and racism, tokens of respect may be far more important than they are in more privileged groups. If you've grown up in a hostile world that denigrates your skin color or your religion, your sense of self-respect might rest on the social power you have within your group. If the larger society calls you "girl," it is all the more important to be accorded the respect of a title in your own group, to be called "Miss Jane," "Mama Sylvia" or "Brother Mo." If Miss Jane comes to a community day and people jump right in and call her "Jane," she may feel deeply disrespected. She may leave, shaking her head and never come back, convinced that the group is a bunch of rude louts or racists.

In many groups with strong egalitarian ideals, the norm is that leaders don't get perks. If someone facilitates a meeting, that does not entitle them to cut in front of the food line. Old, young, important and less important all wait together — a visual statement of the value the group places on all being equal. But in many indigenous groups, elders are served first. They are conducted to the front of the line or food is brought to them. They have earned that token of respect by surviving in a hostile world, and they are valued as carriers of culture and tradition. If they were expected to join the back of the line with everyone else, they would likely feel insulted.

To avoid these pitfalls, we must be clear about the difference between unearned and earned power. We must find ways to identify and limit privilege, while encouraging positive ways for people to earn power and respect and receive appropriate rewards.

PRIVILEGE AND ENTITLEMENT

Recognizing our own privilege can be painful. We all struggle in different ways to reach our goals, and what looks like a blissful float down a lazy river to someone else might actually feel like a long, hard pull to us. We all like to feel that we deserve what we've gotten, that we've earned whatever measure of success or comfort we've achieved. Most of us are struggling day to day to get by. As wealth has been systematically siphoned away from the poor and the middle class, even white college-educated folks are pinching pennies and working to the max just to stay afloat. We don't feel privileged — we feel stressed, strained and sometimes panicked. Yes, we know there are people much worse off, but hey, we didn't ask to be born who we are!

Acknowledging that we might have gotten a boost along the way from some form of privilege can make us feel guilty or inadequate. It's a threat to our self-esteem. So we may deny our privilege or deny that privilege exists. We may try to run away from it, joining what Native Americans call the Wannabee Tribe — Wannabee Indian, Wannabee black, wannabee anything but what you are. Or we may let in the information only to become paralyzed with guilt. But neither guilt nor denial are helpful. Instead, we need to take responsibility, to use our privilege to create greater opportunities and empowerment for all.

Privilege is easiest to see from below. When you have it, it's often invisible. When others have it and you don't — it's in your face. Privilege means greater access to resources, opportunities and information. An affluent child will have access to better food, from gestation to graduation, than a poor child. She will have better schools, better healthcare, after-school enrichment activities, more parental support through college and early adulthood — a jump-start on life.

Privilege can mean physical and emotional safety. A rich child lives in a safe neighborhood. A poor child lives in the projects where murders and drive-by shootings happen on a daily basis. Privilege can mean lack of harassment — the ability to drive home from the grocery store and not get stopped by the police, to be presumed honest and trustworthy.

Privilege can be overt. Marta tells the story of her Anglo friend Joan, whose passport was stolen when they were both in Mexico. She went with Joan to the US Consulate, who quickly, with minimal fuss, gave her a temporary passport so she could travel back home.

"Don't you have questions for me?" Joan asked. "Don't I need to prove to you somehow that I'm an American? Recite the Pledge of Allegiance, give you some baseball statistics, something?"

"Oh no," replied the smiling agent. "It's clear — from your name, your accent, your language. Now, if your name was Gonzalez or something, it might be harder. But you — you're fine."

With privilege goes a sense of *entitlement*. Entitlement, of course, is a feature of hierarchy. A boss is entitled to yell at an underling — a line worker who yells back may get fired. High-level management is entitled to eat in the private dining room; the secretaries eat in the cafeteria. Yet entitlement also has a positive aspect. We want people to feel entitled to speak up, to question, to make suggestions and changes, to put forth ideas and to initiate projects. We want social power to be fairly earned and fairly distributed.

Entitlement, too, can be both earned and unearned. At the scene of an accident, a paramedic is entitled to move a victim. I'm not. The paramedic earned that entitlement through training and experience. If an untrained person were to step in, they could do great harm. Few of us would assume that we're entitled to give medical care without training. But in other areas, we may often assume unearned entitlement.

Some years ago, I attended a gathering to bring together women of European heritage and First Nations women (as indigenous women are called in Canada). Cultural and personal clashes plagued us from the start. They came to a head when a young white woman leading a moon lodge for menstruating women decided to have her group decorate the sweat lodge poles as a gift to the gathering. She didn't know that in Lakota tradition, menstruating women aren't allowed anywhere near the sweat lodge. By touching the poles or even walking over them, she rendered them unfit for use. The moon lodge leader felt entitled to add something to another group's tradition without first learning the rules and norms. Although her intention was to show honor, her actions conveyed disrespect.

In standard American culture, we're expected to be active, self-promoting, competitive, to strut our stuff. The way to show respect, involvement and interest is by doing something. "I don't understand you people," a Lakota woman once said to me. "You're so damn arrogant! You just waltz in and start doing things and changing things. If I go into another nation, I just sit and watch. I shut up and listen, and I don't say anything until I figure out what's going on." In many indigenous cultures, respect is shown not by offering and doing, but by listening and observing.

In the dominant culture, we assume that anything not labeled "Do not touch!" is up for grabs — a sweat lodge pole, a song, a story, a tradition. In many indigenous cultures, you must ask permission to touch a sacred object, to sing someone else's song or tell a story you've heard. European colonizers felt entitled to the lands, the resources, even the lives and personal services of indigenous peoples from Africa to the Americas. We inherit that history, and while we might deplore it, we can't entirely escape it. If we want to work cross-culturally between the descendents of the colonizers and the colonized, we must be sensitive to that legacy. Taking without asking is cultural appropriation. If we come from the colonizer people, we must be especially careful to ask permission and to question our own unconscious sense of entitlement.

Back at RootBound, Carrie Cherkowsky is complaining about Eli to Gerda Griswell. "He's so damn arrogant! He came to our directors' meeting 20 minutes late, and then he just announces some brilliant new idea — he thinks it is — that completely trashes the agenda! I can't work with him!"

Eli may feel entitled to be late — or he may have rushed off a plane that was delayed for three hours by air traffic control, pushed the speed limit and sprinted across the RootBound grounds in order to make the meeting at all. But he certainly feels entitled to shift the agenda, to bring in his own new enthusiasm and try to rally the group around it. After all, he founded RootBound. If he were challenged, he might say something like, "Hey, I founded this place. I worked my ass off for years to make it happen. I'm on the board of directors, and I give a lot of time to making it work, to promoting the idea in the world. Surely I'm entitled to bring up a new idea in a meeting?"

At the other end of the spectrum, Sally Sanford is chopping vegetables for her cooking shift when three 14-year-olds burst into the dining room and skateboard around the tables. Sally, who is a bit timid and insecure, doesn't know what to do. Should she stop them? Will they hurt the floor? What if she confronts them and they won't go outside?

"Hey, kids," she says weakly. "Maybe you shouldn't be doing that indoors."

"We do this all the time!" Tommie assures her. Which is true — but not because they are allowed to, simply because no one has caught them at it yet.

Just then, Myra slips and crashes into a table, gashing her head, which bleeds profusely all over the natural bamboo floor. While the paramedics are checking her out, her mother yells at Sally, "Why the hell didn't you stop them?"

"I didn't know — they said they do it all the time. I thought they were allowed to." Sally didn't feel entitled to intervene. She suffered from too little entitlement.

RECOGNIZING AND EARNING SOCIAL POWER

How does a group get it right with all the complications of privilege and social power? How can we undo privilege and help each person contribute to the best of their potential? How do we recognize and reward those who give to the group?

In Eli's case, rather than denouncing him as an arrogant elitist and kicking him out of the community he founded, the group might simply recognize his sense of power and entitlement. Yes, he has earned a certain amount of social power. Sally's voice is simply not going to carry as much weight as his, at least, not for a long time to come. And yes, he often does have ideas that truly are brilliant. Nonetheless, the group also needs to be able to set an agenda and keep to it. So, they might say, "OK, Eli, we're going to give you ten minutes on every agenda — we'll call it 'Eli's Brilliant Idea.' If you don't have one, that's fine. If you do, there's

**E
X
E
R
C
I
S
E**

Power and Diversity Exercise

This exercise is derived from one I learned from George Lakey, combined with input from Katrina Hopkins and Lisa Fithian.

Ask people to think for a moment about who has more social power than they do, and to call out examples. Most often you'll hear things like, "white male executives," "corporate CEOs," "rich people."

On a big sheet of paper, have someone write down the group's responses.

Ask, "When you think of those groups who have more privilege than you do, what are some of their identifying characteristics?" (Usually the group comes up with a list that includes things like arrogance, denial, confidence, entitlement.)

Flip the paper over so that it covers the list and ask: "Now think of some groups that have less social power than you do. Name them ...."

Write them on the board. Then ask, "Think back to that list of qualities you associate with people of higher social power. Do you imagine that people who have less privilege than you see any of them in you?"

Flip the paper back to reveal the former page. "Are there any that you identify with?" Often the group will laugh, at this point, in self-recognition. Allow time for discussion.

"Now, close your eyes for a moment. Take a few deep breaths and relax. Imagine walking into a meeting of that group that has more social power than you do, a meeting in which you have some vital things to say. What would they have to do to make you feel comfortable? To make you feel that your presence was welcome, that your voice would be heard and that your opinions would be valued?"

C O N T I N U E D

Give the group time to experience their inner imagery. Then ask them to open their eyes and name out loud some of the things that would help them feel welcome and valued.

Ask people to stand, walk around the room, greet each other, and do those things they have mentioned.

Heritage Circle

Thanks to Margo Adair, Shay Howell and Bill Aal of Tools for Change for this exercise.

The group sits in circles of four to five people. Begin with a grounding and, if appropriate, a thank you to the ancestors for the gifts they have given us. Thank the future generations, those who will carry on after we're gone.

Now each person is given a protected time to speak. A talking stick or other object can be passed around. Those who are not speaking should listen for both content and emotion.

The questions can be addressed together, or separate rounds can be done for each. They are:

1. How did the people who raised you and their people get to the place where you were raised? Or if your people have always been there, how did the US reach your community?
2. What did those who raised you do for a living?
3. What's one strength and one thing that holds you back from your heritage, however you define it.

The group may add a fourth question that is particularly relevant to its own work or situation.

After the rounds, take some time for open discussion, in small groups or the whole group, on what is common and what is different in our heritages.

where it goes. That will give you enough time to present it and introduce it, and if there's interest from the group, we'll give it a chunk of time for discussion at a later meeting."

Eli's earned social power can be acknowledged, but also limited and constrained. He can relax, knowing that he'll have his time if he needs it. And others can relax, knowing that he won't take over every meeting and that they can get other work done. If someone else has a brilliant idea, the group has channels for them to express it. But Eli, being the smart man that he is and truly committed to egalitarianism, might also say, "Hey, don't make it 'Eli's Brilliant Idea.' Suppose we make it the 'New Brilliant Ideas' spot. I might jump in, when I have one — but if someone else has one that's not already on the agenda, they can also bring it up at that time."

Now the group has made a structural change that not only recognizes Eli's needs but opens up new room for spontaneity and creativity across the board. Sally might never feel entitled enough to insert a brilliant inspiration into a set agenda — it's simply not her style. But that open ten minutes creates a framework in which she becomes explicitly entitled to do so.

UNDOING PRIVILEGE

We all hold some level of privilege. Somewhere on Earth is the least privileged person — lowest on every possible ladder of race, class, education, health or freedom. But if you are reading this book, you have some measure of education, leisure and awareness that others do not. What do we do with our unwanted privilege? How do we relinquish this burdensome gift that we never asked for? Below are ten key steps we can take to move away from our unearned social power and step up to greater responsibility and empowerment.

EXERCISE

The Landscape of Power Exercise

Everyone stands in a circle. The facilitator asks people to step in or step back according to how central they feel to the group.

When people have had time to position themselves, ask the group if they feel this self-assessment is accurate. Is there anyone whose position they would change?

Ask the people on the outer rim to speak about their experience of the group. Do they like being in the position they are in? Do they feel they could move more into the center if they want to? Why or why not?

Ask the people who are midway to the center to speak about their experience. Do they like being in the position they are in? Do they feel they could move more into the center or step out further toward the rim if they want to? Why or why not?

Ask the people in the center to speak about their experience. Do they like being in the position they are in? Do they feel they could move more into the center or step out further toward the rim if they want to? Why or why not?

Ask the whole group: What have we learned from this? Are there changes we need to make in our structure? If so, what might they be?

Make the Invisible Visible

Take some time in the group to acknowledge who holds authority and who does not. Discuss how people feel about their role and position.

1. Recognize Privilege

Learn to recognize some of the ways in which you might hold privilege — not to feel guilty, but to be aware of the unfairness that still characterizes our society so that we can work more intelligently to change it. Release guilt, and accept responsibility for being an agent of that change.

2. Distinguish Between Privilege and Identity

You are not your privilege — or lack of it. Your race, your class background, your access to opportunity, the circumstances of your life are not the essence of your being. Rather, you are what you've done with your circumstances and opportunities, the choices you've made, the stands you've taken.

3. Know Your Heritage

Learn something about your own history, the people you come from, their traditions and stories and culture. Even among "white" people great diversity exists. Italian culture is different from Dutch. Black people are not all the same; Chinese, Japanese and Koreans all have different cultures. When you know who your ancestors were and where they came from, you may discover a rich and wonderful heritage.

4. Learn About Others

The dominant culture does not need to know much about the cultures of the oppressed — but people from oppressed cultures do need to learn the dominant culture in order to survive. As a result, many of us know little about groups that have historically been disadvantaged. Read books about other cultures, learn history from a multiplicity of perspectives, study other languages and, above all, learn about the real, current, present-day struggles of people around the world.

5. Ask "Who Is the Protagonist of the Story?"

Privilege leads us to unconsciously expect to be the star of every movie. Popular culture still reinforces this idea. Hogwarts may have a multicultural student body, but Harry Potter is still a white boy. *Avatar* may plead brilliantly for nature and indigenous cultures, but it's still told through the eyes of a white man.

If we're trying to build a broad, multicultural movement, if we're organizing across the barriers of race and class, we have to stop casting ourselves as Jake saving Pandora. Instead, we might think of playing the role of Sam or one of the others who support Frodo in *Lord of the Rings*. Support roles can also be roles of power: not only Sam, the gardener, but Gandalf, the magical wizard, Aragorn, the rightful heir to the kingdom, dwarves, elves and warriors who are strong and powerful in their own right all aid Frodo in his task. We don't have to give up our power to support another in their goals and challenges. Instead, we can put our power and privilege to use, in service of goals we identify with.

6. Be of Service

Watch, look and listen — find out what the community's aims and challenges and struggles are, and look for ways you can be of service. If you have something to offer — make it known, but wait to be invited in. If you are invited, show up and keep showing up. Share skills, resources, information and opportunities. Do some of the grunt work, not just the brain work or creative work. Do the dishes. Share the risks.

7. Earn Trust, Patiently

Trust must be earned, and that may take time. Be patient. Sure, it's painful if people don't instantly like and trust you, but when people have had a history of being exploited by those who look like you, they may not take to you instantly. Don't take it personally. Be comfortable with who you are, be of service and over time you will win that trust. And it will mean a lot more when you do.

8. Listen

When you're in a different culture, expect that norms and values may be different. You might not even realize what your own assumptions are until someone steps all over them. I remember feeling excruciatingly uncomfortable visiting a Sami friend in the north of Norway. I kept trying to make dinner conversation, and everything I said dropped into a void of silence. I had just about decided they all hated me, when it occurred to me to ask my friend, "Ellen-Marit, is it a Sami thing that you don't talk during meals?" "Why would we talk?" she asked. "We're eating!" Watch, look and listen. Expect to learn a lot!

9. Examine the Norms and Values of Your Own Group

Whom do they include, and whom do they exclude? Are there signs or symbols of belonging? The right haircut? Dreadlocks? Eating — or not eating — the right foods? Believing in the right conspiracy theories or prophecies of the End Times? Which norms reflect your core values, and which may simply be marks of belonging, subtle ways of saying, "We're in and you're out."

10. Commit to the Children

Years ago when I was perplexed about issues of cultural appropriation, I meditated and asked for guidance from the ancestors. They said, "We don't really give a damn who your ancestors were. We care about what you're doing for the children." I would define cultural appropriation as "Taking the gifts of the ancestors without a commitment to their descendents." So, don't lay claim to knowledge or spiritual teachings or entitlements you haven't earned, and then relax, enjoy and get on with the work that will benefit the generations to come.

DEVELOPING ELDERS

In many indigenous cultures, elders are accorded great respect. To be an elder is more than being old; it means being a person who has learned some wisdom from their life experiences, including their mistakes. An elder may be someone who has lived a blameless life of complete integrity, or a recovering alcoholic who knows from personal experience how hard it is to struggle with an addiction, and so can guide others.

Not everyone old is wise. For some people, aging can simply rigidify longstanding patterns of dysfunction. And some "elders" may be young, blessed with good judgment, compassion and sound sense from an early age.

Groups need elders: people who put the needs of the group first and help keep its balance. We may become elders and gain social power in many constructive ways.

By Taking on Responsibility and Fulfilling It

In a healthy, functioning group, the key way that people earn social power is by taking on responsibility. Our Spiral Dance organizing group, which puts on a major ritual each year, says clearly to people in our outreach material, "The way to have a say in how the ritual is planned is to take on a coordinating role. That could be coordinating the dancers for the invocations or coordinating the cleanup — but it means making the time commitment to organize others. Do that, and you get the inestimable benefit of coming to meetings and helping to shape the ritual."

By Helping the Group Function Smoothly

People who pay attention to social relations, who help resolve conflicts and mediate problems tend to gain social power in a healthy group. We respect those who can raise issues effectively, who identify conflicts and bring them forth so they can be addressed, who help resolve intransigent disputes and who look for ways to create good feelings in the group.

By Good Judgment

Elders get to be elders by exhibiting good judgment, being able to put the good of the group before their own personal benefit or profit, being able to look ahead, anticipate problems and deflect disasters.

By Making Mistakes and Acknowledging Them so They Become Part of Group Learning

People often fear to admit mistakes because to do so seems like losing face. But in a healthy group, a person who admits a mistake and shares the learning actually gains trust and influence. They become a good model for others.

By Showing Compassion and Forgiveness

Elders are not saints: they may get embroiled in conflicts just like anybody else. But they don't wage vendettas or hold grudges. Instead, they've learned to confront conflict, forgive those who commit to changing hurtful patterns and move on.

By Integrity and Upholding Values

If you stand for something, if you walk your talk, you build trust and social power. In a healthy group, those who speak for and uphold the group's core values gain influence — provided they act on those values themselves.

By Bringing Experience, Skills and Training to the Service of the Group

If someone is a trained bookkeeper and volunteers to be on the fundraising committee, their voice will carry more weight than someone who is inept with numbers — at least around financial issues. People who have special training, expertise or talent and bring those gifts to the group do a great service — especially if they are also committed to train others and pass the skills on.

By Mentoring and Being Mentored

When we mentor and train others, we pass on some of our skills and knowledge. When we ask for mentoring, we admit that our mentor has some quality we want to develop, experiences we can benefit from or knowledge we would like to gain — that we don't start out as equals in every arena. We invest our teacher with the authority to advise and guide us, to offer constructive critiques and to make suggestions that might further our growth.

Groups that refuse to recognize differences in social power cannot encourage mentoring. Egalitarian groups sometimes resist any structure that involves teaching or training in favor of skill shares and peer groups. A good skillshare can introduce people to a new subject or teach a specific technique — but it does not replace long-term training and development. We might learn emergency first aid at a skillshare, but when we need brain surgery, we go to someone who has gone through years of training and apprenticeship.

When we invest power in a mentor, we remain the active agent. That power, in a sense, is lent, not given away. When we mentor someone else, we hold their power in trust. Our commitment is to help further their development and the good of the group. Our overriding reward comes from knowing that our skills and knowledge will go on whatever happens to us. In a group that encourages its members to develop, grow and learn new skills, many people can eventually take on crucial roles and no one is trapped. We can be free to move on to our own new challenges, knowing that the work we've done will continue.

By Commitment and Time

People gain social power in groups through committing time, energy and creativity to the group. Someone who has a long-standing commitment to the group's goals and values should have a larger voice in decisions than someone who just showed up for the night. If not, why should they stick around?

However, there's another side to this story. If a group is composed only of long-termers, they may accrue so much social power that others feel shut out and have no motivation to join. Founders and original members can stand so tall that, like ancient redwoods, they shut out the light below them. In old-growth forests, new saplings only get a chance to shoot up tall when older trees fall and open up the canopy. Unlimited social power can turn into founder's syndrome, when the founder or originator of a group can't let go. If a group wants to sustain itself over the long term, it must put some limits on the social power even of elders to make space and light for others to take root and grow.

Time and commitment may also reflect privilege. Someone who has a heavy work schedule and family obligations may simply not have time to devote to the group, however much they care about its projects and values. While they may not be able to make day-to-day decisions or sit in every meeting, a group that serves a wider community must make room for the voices of those on the edge, as well as in the center.

By Modeling Good Self-Care

Elders take care of themselves. They commit to the group; they may devote immense amounts of time and energy to the mission, but they also take breaks, take naps and take vacations. Elders know that eating, sleeping, exercising, taking time for relationships, pleasure and beauty are important aspects of life that ultimately feed the work. They are models for others, helping to create a group culture that can be truly sustainable.

EXERCISE

Stepping into Eldership Ritual

The group may prefer a different word than "elder" to represent stepping into one's personal power and a role of respect in the group.

The group stands in a circle. Begin with grounding and anchoring to the core self.

Take a moment, and ask each person to reflect on the ways they hold power in the group and exercise some form of eldership. Also consider where their growing edges are.

One by one, each person steps into the center, states their name and a way they exercise eldership, followed by "and I do it well." "I am Eli, I founded this community and have guided its beginning, and I do it well."

The group affirms the person, by repeating their name, or with a resounding "Yes!"

Then the person goes on to state some way in which she is growing into deeper eldership. "Now I'm deepening my eldership by learning how to gracefully let go and share the limelight with others."

The group responds again, "Yes!"

The first person steps back, and another steps forward. Continue until everyone has had a chance to be affirmed.

EARNING REWARDS

In hierarchical structures, gains in power are often accompanied by gains in money and marks of status: the corner window, the best table in the restaurant. Those who receive the rewards may not be those who do the most work or contribute the best ideas. Professors may take credit for research done by their graduate students. Top-level managers are rewarded for innovations thought up by their direct reports.

Even in groups that value equality, residues of privilege may determine who receives the highest rewards of status and social power. The volunteer coordinator who devotes hours and hours to a benefit receives less acclaim than the lead singer. The organizer who spends months making a workshop happen gets far less praise than the workshop leader who flies in for two days.

Some groups define equality very strictly and attempt to do away with all perks or rewards, earned or unearned. "Equality does not recognize merit or status: all members are truly equal." Delfina Vannucci and Richard Singer state in their handbook on collective process, *Come Hell or High Water.*[2] Yet such absolute equality may be inherently inequitable and unfair. The worker who has devoted years to the collective is paid the same as the new person who has just joined.

If we don't find clear and conscious ways to reward real contributions to the group, we may burn out our best people. Over time, long-term members who have given much to the organization may leave feeling frustrated and unappreciated. Worse, we may end up awarding perks unconsciously through unexamined norms or residues of privilege. The loudest voices may get the attention of the group, or those who cry "victim" most persuasively may gather the most social power. The charismatic male who tells a compelling tale of his exploits may gather everyone's respect — while the woman who quietly does the work and keeps the group functioning may be dismissed.

What rewards can a group offer those who take on responsibilities and fulfill them?

Thanks and Appreciation

Healthy groups develop a culture of appreciation. They make a point of thanking people after the completion of a project, both privately and publicly. Moreover, they make appreciation part of the group culture and norms.

A Hearing for Ideas

Of course, in collaborative groups we want to hear everyone's ideas. But we should be especially careful to listen to those who have made big contributions to the group. We might make sure that they have an opportunity to speak at meetings or be willing to hold a special meeting to entertain a new idea. When we're holding creative sessions or visioning meetings, we make sure they are included.

Care and Tending

In Reclaiming, when people take on ritual roles that require great concentration and altered states of awareness, we assign them tenders or wranglers — someone to watch over them, make sure they don't come to harm in a trance state, make sure they are warmed and fed and helped to ground after the ritual and escorted back through the dark woods to their bunk or driven home. Tending is a vitally necessary role that can make a great difference to a priestess's state of health and physical safety.

People who take on heavy responsibilities outside ritual may also need some tending from time to time. The spokesperson who represents your group on Fox News may need someone to hold her hand afterwards and get her a hot meal. The person who is preparing for that crucial meeting with the city council might appreciate someone who will set up the projector and bring the flyers.

Sometimes, out of misguided ideals of egalitarianism, we avoid doing anything for one another that might smack of personal service. But developing a group culture that encourages tending and caring for one another can help sustain our efforts over the long haul, rewarding and safeguarding those who may take on big or dangerous tasks.

Marks of Respect

In some communities, as we've noted, marks of respect are important. Using a person's title instead of their first name, conducting the elders and the honored guests to the head of the line, reserving a parking place for a speaker — even small things can be important tokens of esteem and acknowledgment of earned social power.

A Voice in Decisions

Making formal, conscious agreements about how people gain decision-making power helps make the group's structure transparent. A transparent, visible structure is always more empowering than a hidden, confusing structure. When unspoken rules become conscious agreements, we can choose whether or not to participate. When we know what the steps are needed in order to gain power, we can choose whether or not to take them. If we don't know, we can't make a choice. Even if power is handed to us, we might not recognize it or know how to make use of it. When the path to power is made clear, we can also challenge it if we feel it is restrictive or unfair.

Reclaiming, the spiritual network I helped to found, had a hard lesson around this. We began as a close-knit group of friends, operating by consensus but often making decisions informally. We grew into a collective, still small and close-knit. Some people were in the collective because they were doing real work for the organization, others were in simply because we liked them or because at some time in the past they had taken on central roles. Because we feared conflict, we had never agreed upon a way to get anyone out of the collective if they weren't doing a good job or were causing discord. As a result, we had become extremely wary of letting anybody new in. So many people who were doing major amounts of work were not in the collective.

Nonetheless, we had lots of energy and ambition. In the mid-1990s, we decided we wanted to try to get a building of our own in San Francisco as our headquarters. We held a large meeting, inviting lots of our allies and supporters. We expected to generate great enthusiasm and support. Instead, what we heard from people was something like this: "Why should we support you? We don't know who the collective is or how you got to be in it. We had no voice in choosing you. We don't know how you make decisions. If you want our support, you need to be transparent."

We were shocked. We'd had no idea that our warm, fuzzy circle which seemed so egalitarian to us looked so closed and insular from the outside. The meeting started us on a long process of soul-searching and restructuring, which culminated in the writing of our Principles of Unity, and the dissolving of the collective which was replaced by a more democratic council of spokespeople chosen by each working group. We never did get a building, but instead, we got a structure which allowed us to grow from a San Francisco collective to an expanded network of groups around the world.

A word of warning — a voice in decision-making should never mean control over the group's decisions. Social power can slip over into hierarchy and command if we are not careful. A group cannot grow and develop unless it balances the weight of even well-earned authority with openness and inclusiveness.

Money

In a hierarchy, money is often the biggest reward for power. And those who have money often wield more power, for they can control and allocate resources. Money is seen as good, and it confers value to those who have it.

In progressive groups, money is often seen as bad or tainted. Those who have it may feel guilty or ashamed. We often don't talk about it — most progressives are far more comfortable talking about sex than money. Wanting money, seeking money is a sign of a character flaw. Good people don't care about money.

And yet, our groups need money to flourish and survive. Sometimes we even make money, and questions of how to fairly divide it and compensate people for labor can become a deep source of conflict.

I find a useful way to think about money is to see it as neither good nor evil. Money is a facilitator — it makes other things possible. Money does confer power — the ability to get what you want done. But it should not be the marker of social power, nor should it determine formal power in a progressive organization. And money alone never confers power-from-within.

All-volunteer groups that eschew money are appropriate for many purposes. Indeed, small groups of committed volunteers are how most activism gets done, and many valuable things simply could not happen if people were all paid for their work.

Volunteer groups, however, tend to be time-limited. People who must make their livelihood elsewhere often have limited time and energy for unpaid labor. Volunteers are often ephemeral, as other stresses and interests may draw them away. An organization that depends on volunteers may lack continuity. Volunteers may be unskilled or less competent, and critiquing a volunteer may be difficult — when someone out of the goodness of their heart redoes your website for free, what do you say if you don't like the design?

When people have work and family responsibilities, their time and energy to volunteer is especially limited. For that reason, many activist groups tend to be composed of young people, who have fewer outside responsibilities and more fortitude to bear hardship and discomfort, and/or older people who may be retired and whose children are grown. People in the midst of building their careers and raising their families have less ability to get involved.

Some groups and collectives compensate everyone equally. An hour worked is an hour worked — whether that hour is spent scrubbing the floor or performing neurosurgery. At the Center for Alternative Technology in Wales, the director and founder gets paid the same as any other staff member. An equal pay scale can deflect envy, and build a sense of comradeship and shared power.

Other groups may define fairness differently. Is it fair for an untrained intern who is just beginning to be paid the same amount as a highly experienced person, who may create more value for the organization? Long-term workers or members have more of an investment in the success of a group. And if someone has invested years of their life in study and training to gain a higher level of skill, perhaps taken on huge debts or denied themselves other opportunities for earning, shouldn't they be compensated? Thus do unions advocate for pay increases according to seniority.

People also need something to look forward to in life. Why should I stick around, when any newcomer will be rewarded at my level? An equal pay scale may actually be insulting and disempowering to those who have the most to give. And such groups may notice that, over time, their most experienced and talented members move on.

These sticky money questions are a key example of conflicting good values that are hard to balance. We want equality, openness and accessibility, and we also want fairness, just compensation and long-term sustainability. How do we decide in which direction the balance should shift?

One question to ask is whether the work of a group is something people do as a sort of hobby or as a livelihood. Groups that offer extracurricular activities, that take place after work and on weekends or holidays or for a limited duration and demand only a part-time commitment, may work well on a volunteer basis.

Groups that require a larger commitment of time and energy may want to compensate at least some of their members. An equal pay scale has the advantage of eliminating envy and avoiding complex questions of relative worth. Where people are relatively equal in skills and experience, it can work well.

But when a group sustains itself over a long period of time, with new people coming in, when there are varied levels of training and skill and responsibility, a graduated pay scale may be more fair.

In recent years, we've seen pay scales in the corporate world that have grown to be widely unequal. In 1965, the average CEO earned 24 times the salary of the average worker. In 2005, that number had grown to 262 times as much as the average worker.[3] Private equity and hedge fund managers, meanwhile, (those folks who drove us into the economic meltdown of 2008) earned on an average

$657.5 million in 2006. That's more than 16,000 times the salary of the average full-time worker![4]

Clearly, such extreme differences are not consistent with the spirit of collaboration. When collectives and cooperatives do employ a differentiated scale, they keep the ratio much smaller. Mondragon, the cooperative in Spain founded in the 1930s, keeps its pay scale one-to-three.

For a graduated pay scale to be seen as fair, the group must also be clear about how people earn the higher rates of pay. Is higher pay earned by seniority? Or is it based on merit? If so, how is that merit determined? Who rates us, and by what scale are we judged? To whom can we appeal? If money is used to reward our contributions to the group, we must know how to earn those rewards and who will determine whether or not we get them.

TAKING RESPONSIBILITY

We've said that in a healthy group, power is balanced by responsibility. What exactly do we mean by that? *Responsibility* implies having both ability and obligation to act independently and make decisions, to respond to crises and to be accountable for the consequences of our actions. Some of the ways we demonstrate responsibility in our groups are:

Doing What We Say We'll Do, in a Competent and Timely Fashion

While a surly teenager might grudgingly wash the dishes and leave the pan full of greasy water in the sink and the pots undone, a responsible adult will complete

E
X
E
R
C
I
S
E

Questions About Rewards

- How do we reward people for their contributions to this group?
- What rewards do we personally receive for our contributions?
- Do we feel nurtured and appreciated?
- If not, what rewards would we like to receive?

- What is the differential between the most- and least-rewarded members of our group?
- Is this differential fair? Sustainable?
- Do highly skilled and experienced people remain in this group or move on? If they tend to cycle out of the group, why? Do they feel valued and rewarded?

the job by clearing the table, doing all the dishes, emptying the dishpan and scouring the sink.

Asking for Help and Guidance

Responsibility doesn't necessarily mean doing everything ourselves. Maybe I agreed to facilitate the meeting, but had no idea the major underlying conflict in the group was going to explode in the middle of it. Suddenly, I'm way over my head. I was prepared to run a simple meeting, not mediate an emotional firestorm. At that point, if I'm a responsible group member, I ask for help.

Passing on Tasks You Cannot Do

Sometimes we take on too much. Sometimes loss, tragedy or illness get in the way of fulfilling our tasks. A responsible person lets the group know in a timely fashion and asks to be relieved.

Making Sure Tasks Get Done by Others

Besides doing what we say we'll do, another level of responsibility is to make sure other tasks are getting done, to check in with people, to anticipate what needs to be happening and make sure it does.

Handling Crises When They Arise

When I take on responsibility for a project, I also take on responsibility for unexpected consequences or crises. If I'm the webmaster for the group, I need to jump in when the website gets hacked and fix the problem. If I put in the graywater system, I need to be willing to figure out why it's backing up and resolve the issue.

Planning, Strategizing and Looking Ahead

Responsibility for a project or a group means looking ahead, anticipating problems and taking steps to avoid them, thinking strategically about goals and how to reach them, planning for the long term as well as the short term.

RESPONSIBILITY REQUIRES POWER

When we ask people to take on responsibility, we need to make sure they have the power they need to do the job. The root meaning of the word *power* is ability. Empowering people does not mean handing them tasks they do not have the ability to fulfill. It might mean offering training, mentoring or skills sharing to develop those skills. I learned this lesson early on in activist circles, when we would sometimes call upon an unprepared or inexperienced person to facilitate a large or difficult meeting. After a few disastrous meetings, I realized that throwing a person into a situation where they are doomed to fail is not a form of empowerment. Facilitation is a skill that requires training and practice. Instead of pulling a facilitator at random from the crowd for a crucial meeting, we learned to create a facilitators' working group that would take on several related tasks: finding facilitators for meetings, setting agendas and offering trainings to develop a larger pool of skilled people.

When we ask people to take on responsibility, we must also invest them with authority and the trust to use it. Even the strictest of egalitarian collectives cannot oversee every single decision that must be made. I have in the past from time to time been in the unenviable position of trying to do media outreach for activist groups who refuse to give anyone the authority to speak in the name of the group. Their ideals are admirably egalitarian: everyone should speak for themselves, spokespeople often become media stars or may be perceived as leaders of a group that has no leaders.

The result, however, is crazy-making. The media collective can't articulate the positions or goals of the group, but they nonetheless have to write press releases, inform the media of events, respond to attacks and surprises and marshall public support for activists who may have been arrested or injured. They hold tremendous responsibility, but are not given the power to carry it out. The overriding message that comes across is, "This group doesn't trust anybody — even its own members. They can't find a single person they trust enough to speak for them. So why should I trust them?"

At least within our own groups, we can delegate the power we need to meet our responsibilities. That power might take several forms. It might mean the power to make day-to-day decisions, to spend funds, to set dates for events, to make statements for the group, to use the group's name, to write proposals, to decide where to plant the fruit trees.

Questions About Power and Responsibility

- Where do I take responsibility?
- Where do I abdicate responsibility to others?
- When I take on responsibility in this group, am I given the power and authority I need to be effective?

When we are delegated power, we must also know to whom we are accountable and how we are expected to show our accounts. This might be literal — what form do you want our receipts in and who keeps the overall books? Or it might be metaphoric. Who will be watching that news show, what do they expect us to say or not to say, who is going to tell me afterwards whether I did well or flopped? If I'm going to talk to the media, I'd like guidelines on what the group's message and values are, what things they might not want me to say and to whom I can go with questions.

LIMITS TO SOCIAL POWER

Healthy groups allow people to earn social power and be rewarded for their labor and commitment to the group. But healthy groups also put limits on social power — lest it reinforce privilege and turn into command and hierarchy.

Members who are privileged with more money or fewer life responsibilities may have more free time to devote to the group and so find it easier to gain power. Lucy, a single parent raising two kids alone on the salary of a teacher's aide may need to take a second job to pay the bills rather than devoting time to RootBound. Eli gains professionally from his association with RootBound, giving him added incentive to devote time and energy. Yet Lucy may still have creative ideas and a perspective that the community needs.

Eli, as founder and spokesperson, as someone who is on many committees and involved in many activities, might easily accrue so much social power that others would have no chance to have their ideas heard or their influence felt. While the most committed and hardest workers may gain power, they should never monopolize all the power. A group that wishes to grow and flourish must leave room for new voices.

Social power remains highest when you use it judiciously. If I throw my full weight into every argument, the respect people accord to me will rapidly disappear and be replaced by irritation and rebellion. In this way social power is something like the water I have stored in my water tank to last through the dry season. Some water is always flowing in, but during the summer, the flow may be reduced to a trickle. I have thousands of gallons stored — but if I draw them down too quickly or allow a leak to go unchecked, I may rapidly run out.

So, too, I may constantly be adding to my store of respect in small ways by things I do for the group. But if I start spending all that respect to get my way in every controversy, it will rapidly dwindle. And if I start to be perceived as someone who is trying to control the group, that store of respect can be quickly depleted.

There are many ways that a group can choose to place limits on social power. They may decide to limit areas of responsibility. If Rick Ragle is on the finance committee, the events committee, the outreach committee, the grounds committee and the meetings committee, how do I make a contribution if I don't happen to like Rick? Some people take on so much work for the group that they limit the possibilities for others to gain power. They may do this out of genuine love and care for the group, or they may have long-standing patterns of workaholism. For the health of the group and its members, responsibility as well as power should be distributed, not concentrated.

A group might decide to make a rule limiting the number of committees any one person can be on, or the areas of responsibility one person can undertake. In a healthy group, when Rick eagerly steps forward to take on yet another task, the group might say, "Whoa, Rick. Let's get someone else to do this — you've got enough on your plate."

DELEGATING POWER

"Hmmnff," I can hear Rick sniffing. "It's all very well to talk about limiting responsibility, but the reason I'm on all those committees is that nobody else is stepping up."

It's very common to hear people who do take on many responsibilities complain that others are not doing their share. Economists will cite the 80/20 rule, also known as the Pareto Principle or "the vital few and the trivial many": 20% of the inputs are responsible for 80% of the outputs.[5] Translated, it means that, in any given business, 80% of the results will be produced by 20% of the employees. In groups, 20% of the members are likely to do 80% of the work.

The Pareto Principle is an observation, not a law of nature. To build truly collaborative groups, we must challenge the pattern it represents. Imagine what our groups could accomplish if everyone worked at the level of that vital 20%! Surely we could save the world in record time, if instead of reducing most people to the role of the "trivial many," we could inspire each person to become part of the "vital all."

Delegation is an art. An empowering leader is often a skilled delegator, who recognizes that bringing other people into greater responsibility requires more than simply saying, "Do this!" Delegation may require mentoring, training, confidence building, information sharing. A healthy group encourages people to delegate responsibility and train others.

The time to train someone else to do your job is when you are still so in love with it that you can't imagine you would ever want to give it up. That's when you have the passion, enthusiasm and energy to train someone else. If you wait until you're tired of a job, you will be less effective as a teacher. Moreover, part of a group's security and sustainability comes from sharing information. If I'm the only one who has the password to the website and I get hit by a bus, what happens to the group's online presence?

How do we get people to take on more responsibility, so that power can be more widely shared, so that overworkers can relax and underworkers can be encouraged to make greater contributions? People may hang back because of their own lack of skill, knowledge, energy or confidence, but they may also face barriers that are hard to recognize when we're in the center of a group.

People May Not Feel That They Have the Authority to Act

Newcomers may be hesitant to take on too much responsibility in a group. They may feel the burden of the social power held by old-timers and fear to upset them or make mistakes. They might need to be formally empowered and mentored. Old-timers might pair up with a newcomer and make themselves available to answer questions or "sign off" on new ideas. The more explicit the power structure of a group, the easier it will be for new people to take on tasks and claim areas of responsibility.

People May Not Have the Information They Need to Act

Information is also power, and sometimes we hoard it even when we attempt to delegate. Information includes contacts, group history, history of the project and knowledge of the hidden undercurrents as well as general information. When a person is given a task, the group should ensure that they are also made privy to all the information they need to carry it out. If that information is not available, research and investigation may be the first part of the job in question.

People May Not Have the Skill, Knowledge or Experience to Do the Job

Sequoia TreeWarrior would love to work on RootBound's media team. He knows a lot about social media and is happily at home with Twitter and Facebook, but he's never done any kind of outreach to print, radio or TV. That's partly why the job appeals to him, because he wants to learn those skills, but he wouldn't know where to begin.

Groups can build in continuity and sustainability by mentoring, apprenticing and finding ways to train new people. They might offer trainings or skillshares for the whole group. Overworked Mary Mediamaven might welcome an intern that she can train in all the skills and nuances she's learned over time. RootBound might also send Sequoia and others to media trainings offered by other groups in the area. Building skills and capacity in their members also builds group allegiance and trust.

People May Not Have the Confidence They Need

To gain confidence, sometimes we must wrestle with a problem ourselves. Lucy has driven her teenage daughter Lila to dance practice twice a week for a month, but until she has to bike there herself, Lila won't truly learn the way. For someone else to gain confidence in a task I've been doing, I might need to step back and let them wrestle with it. I can offer support, but if I continue to take over each time they run into a snag, they will never learn to do it themselves.

HALLMARKS OF GROUP SANITY AROUND POWER AND RESPONSIBILITY

When power and responsibility are in balance, they create a strong Axis of Action. The group can move forward effectively to accomplish its mission. Individuals will feel empowered both to take on tasks and also to step back and let others have their turn. Group members will also be challenged to learn and grow.

Such a group will have:

- A clear structure for making decisions and an agreed-upon process
- Clear and transparent agreements about how people gain decision-making power
- A clear way for people to take on tasks and responsibilities
- Clear agreements about the scope of each member's authority to meet responsibilities
- Clear structures of accountability — who do people report back to? How, when and in what form is an accounting given?

- A group culture of appreciation and thanks to those who make contributions and take on tasks
- A culture of tending and mutual care for those holding responsibility
- A fair and transparent system of rewards
- Training and mentoring to help people step up to new responsibilities

When collaborative groups balance responsibility and power, when we empower our members to work passionately for the vision we hold and the goals we share, we can become far more effective at shifting the larger balance of power around us. We can become agents of change, challenging unfair and unequal power relations in society and providing a model of a more just and joyful way of working together.

CHAPTER 5

The Axis of Learning — Communication and Trust

THE SECOND AXIS

Outside the cafe, the day had grown dim. While Marta drifted from table to table, sampling conversations like a bee visiting a bed of flowers, Eli and Ella remained absorbed in her manuscript. When they finally looked up, twilight had fallen and dinner service was beginning. Marta caught their eye and returned.

"Shall we carry on this conversation over dinner?" she suggested.

"How about Indian food?" Ella said.

Together they strolled down University Avenue and found a table at a peaceful, intimate restaurant. Eli was unusually quiet throughout the walk, but over naan and samosas, he opened up.

"Power!" he said. "It all comes down to that. I should have known. I have too much power in RootBound. Because I'm the founder, and I'm a smart, good-looking, charismatic white male ..."

"Modest and humble," Ella broke in.

Eli bowed his head in her direction. "Winner of the Forty-fifth Annual Crow-Eating Contest in the East Bay Humility Sweepstakes. Why, I'll stake my humbleness against anyone else!"

"It's not as simple as too much power," Marta said. "Power is slippery, and the balance between responsibility and power is always a dynamic one. Perhaps you have too much power now that so many other responsibilities claim your time and attention, and you must look at ways to share that power more deeply. Perhaps others have too little power, and must step up. But most likely the heart of the problem is lack of clarity. There are so many different strands of power, visible and invisible, that no one knows how to disentangle them. Making the lines of power more clear will help you decide what to weave."

"You're saying that before we can reformulate our vision, we should deal with our power issues," Ella said. "Maybe we need a retreat for that. We could do some of the exercises you suggest in your writings, answer some of the questions. …"

"We'll do it!" Eli announced. "People will see that I really, truly do not want to hold onto power. I am so ready to let go … probably next week is too soon, but if we give a month's notice … I can put it out on the group listserv, and Marta, if you don't want to facilitate we can. …"

"Whoa," Marta stopped him. "Rein in those horses, before they run away with the chariot! Take a breath, and look back for a moment at my talisman."

She placed it on the center of the table between them. "What do you see?"

Eli and Ella stared for a long moment. Finally Ella spoke.

"The circle has two axes," she said.

"Exactly," Marta agreed. "Power and responsibility make up action — but action must be in relationship to communication and trust, which create the Axis of Learning."

At that moment, the waiter arrived with their curries, and Marta slipped the drawing back into its folder.

"Why learning?" Eli asked as he spread raita and chutney over his rice.

"Because miscommunication is at the heart of so many conflicts and misunderstandings. Clear communication is key to building trust, but most people have very poor communication skills."

"I've noticed that," Ella said dryly.

"So you're saying that we should do some communication training first, before we tackle the other issues?" Eli asked.

"Not merely training. To shift our style of communication, we must shift our worldview and our way of being. We must let go of winning and open up to learning — about ourselves, one another, our organization and its mission in the world."

"How do we do that?" Ella asked. "Will you help us?"

Marta nodded. "To begin with, I will invest trust in both of you, by sending you home with another chapter to read. Be very careful, for this is my only copy. When you've read it, let me know and we will meet again."

"Ummh, maybe I should meet you tomorrow instead when I can take the chapter and get it photocopied?" Eli suggested. "All kinds of things can happen. …"

Marta shook her head. "Take it now," she said. "I trust you, and I don't say that lightly or naively. I have every confidence that between the two of you — responsible adults who have successfully raised vulnerable children together — you can take care of one set of papers for a few days without losing or destroying them."

Ella smiled. "Is this part of the process?"

"You have invested trust in me, by sharing honestly your challenges and vulnerabilities. Now let me return some to you," Marta said. "Trust is powerful magic, for trust is the foundation of all else. Like any foundation, it must rest on the bedrock of accountability. Then you truly have something to build on."

Ella took the papers and placed them carefully in her bag. When the meal was done and they parted, she kept it firmly clutched under her arm, determined no purse-snatcher would grab the precious papers nor any accidental drop into a puddle stain them.

Back home, they climbed into bed together and passed the papers back and forth, reading avidly.

"This is exciting!" Eli exclaimed.

Ella smiled. "I can think of something else exciting we could do together in bed," she said.

Eli grinned. "Can you? Maybe we could practice some non-verbal communication skills together."

"Not on top of the papers!" Ella cried out in alarm.

COMMUNICATION IS KEY

Communication is the heart of any organization. As human beings, we are social animals, hard-wired to interact and communicate. As infants, we fix on other human faces, absorbing their expressions, looking for mirroring. When we, as adults, play with a baby, we have an instinctual urge to mimic the child's own facial expressions, to mirror their sounds, to respond to a smile with a smile of our own. Out of that primal communication, along with the non-verbal holding, cuddling and feeding a child receives, basic trust and connection arise.

With millions of years of evolutionary specialization in communication behind us, you'd think we would do it well. And yet too often in groups, old and ineffective patterns of communication generate conflict and hold us back from building trust and connection. Shifting our patterns of communication may be one of the most important changes we can make in all of our relationships.

COLLABORATION MEANS COMPLEXITY

In collectives, collaboratives and co-creative groups, communication is far more complex than in a hierarchy. Compare the charts below:

A hierarchy is a tree structure. If I'm a middle manager, I know to whom I report and who reports to me. In a well-run hierarchy, there is generally one proper path to send a piece of information up the ladder or to relay a decision down the chain.

A collaborative group is far more complex. It's a net, not a tree. We're often not clear who has the authority to make a decision, who needs to be consulted on an issue, who is informed of a problem and who has been left out of the loop. Probably the most common source of conflict around communication stems from people being left out — sometimes deliberately, often inadvertently. In a collaborative structure, it's much harder to keep track of who knows what.

Within our groups, we often form strong friendships and close working relations with certain people. That's one of the rewards of working collaboratively. However, it's very easy for friendship groups to toss around a new idea among themselves and come to a conclusion without ever consulting the rest of the group — again, sometimes deliberately, more often simply because those discussions are informal, and enthusiasm runs high. As Jo Freeman wrote more than 40 years ago in "The Tyranny of Structurelessness":

Hierarchical Communication Paths vs. Communication in Collaborative Groups.

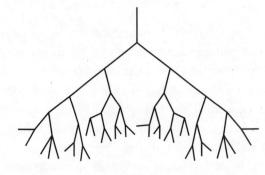

Hierarchy   Collaborative Group

At any small group meeting, anyone with a sharp eye and an acute ear can tell who is influencing whom. The members of a friendship group will relate more to each other than to other people. They listen more attentively and interrupt less. They repeat each other's points and give in amiably. The "outs" they tend to ignore or grapple with. The "outs" approval is not necessary for making a decision; however it is necessary for the "outs" to stay on good terms with the "ins." Of course, the lines are not as sharp as I have drawn them. They are nuances of interaction, not prewritten scripts. But they are discernible, and they do have their effect. Once one knows with whom it is important to check before a decision is made, and whose approval is the stamp of acceptance, one knows who is running things.[1]

Collectives and collaboratives can run smoothly — but to do so, they need to pay close attention to communication. When we make decisions or discuss new projects, we need to consider who should be consulted. Who must be part of the original planning? If we want buy-in from a particular group or demographic, we must include their representatives from the beginning, not just bring them in at the end as tokens. When we generate a new program, we must ask who will be affected and who will implement it, and include them in its creation. When decisions are made at a meeting, we need to ask who else needs to be informed and how that will happen. Paying rigorous attention to the questions below will forestall many conflicts down the road.

E X E R C I S E

Communication Questions

Before the meeting, ask:

- Whose ideas might benefit this project, who might have insights or perspectives that are important or enriching?
- Whose input must we have?
- Who is the project's strong advocate? Opponent?

- Who has vital information to present?
- Will the meeting represent the diversity we aim for?
- Who is most affected by it? Who has the most to lose or to gain?
- Whose opposition will keep it from going forward if they feel disrespected? (Work hard

C
O
N
T
.

to get those people into the room and in the meeting! Far better to argue out any conflicts face to face than to let them fester.)

• Who will carry out the decisions?

At the end of every meeting, ask:

• Who should be informed of the results of this meeting?

• Who is going to communicate the information, and how? By when?

• How will we know when that's done?

COMMUNICATION NORMS

We join groups hoping for friendship and trust. But we bring with us a set of unexamined norms that come from the larger culture, from our families, from our previous experiences, from the media and from the hierarchical structures we've all been exposed to.

Norms differ in different cultures, subcultures and classes. Trainer George Lakey, quoting ethnographer Thomas Kochman, discusses different cultural expectations in his book *Facilitating Group Learning*:

> Black culture prefers spirited, animated dialogue — argument — to get to the truth. Participants are expected to be right "out there" with their views, to take a stand, to show emotionally that they care, to listen to different views — discarding the points that were rendered invalid and coming right back with whatever pops up next. White culture prefers separating the person from the point of view, making statements in a more neutral and impersonal tone. Especially when an issue is controversial, whites often like to be low-key and blacks often like to be high-key.[2]

I come from a family where people yelled all the time. We yelled when we were angry, and we yelled when someone was in another room and we wanted them to hear. The yelling never spilled over into physical violence — my parents were social workers who didn't believe in spanking or corporal punishment. But when we got into arguments, they were loud arguments.

Contrast my expressive, emotive family with a passage from one of my favorite childrens' books, Arthur Ransome's *We Didn't Mean to Go to Sea*. After a series of accidents have set the children adrift in a friend's sailboat, 14-year-old Peter has managed to bring them safely across the North Sea in the teeth of a ferocious storm.

It had been a long time since they'd seen him, but Daddy had not changed a bit. He looked the same and he was the same, taking everything as it came, just as if it had been carefully planned that they were to cross the sea and meet him in a Dutch harbor. No one could have guessed from looking at him that it had been any sort of a surprise to him to look down from the deck of a Dutch liner at a little yacht coming in, and to see his son standing on the foredeck.[3]

Generalities about different cultures can shift into stereotypes, but they may contain a grain of truth. Some of us learn early on that emotions should be volubly expressed; others learn that they should be concealed. Some families yell, others press their lips together and suffer in silence. If we have a high degree of emotional intelligence, we learn to read the subtle cues. Peter knew his father was proud of him, although he never said so in words. But subtle cues can also be missed.

My grandparents were first-generation immigrants from the shtetls of Ukraine. My mother used to complain that, when she was a child, her mother's friends would never pay her a direct compliment. To praise a child was to invite bad luck, the "evil eye." Instead, they'd say, "Oy, she's so fat!" Her mother knew intuitively that this meant, "What a gorgeous, plump, healthy child!" Unfortunately, my mother didn't and just felt shamed.

Progressive groups may reject racism, classism and other forms of discrimination, but we may unconsciously pattern our group norms in ways that favor those of a certain class or ethnic background. When the norm favors a quiet, controlled level of emotional expression and someone yells, they can be perceived as completely out of line, even aggressive or abusive. On the other hand, when Jews, Italians and African Americans are happily arguing at the top of their lungs, they may retraumatize someone who comes from a family in which loud voices were followed by violence and abuse.

And of course, yelling can reinforce power-over and control. In my very first day on my very first job, working at a clothing store over the winter holidays when I was a teenager, I parked in the wrong spot, one reserved for the Big Boss. The Big Boss came in and yelled at the Manager. The Manager turned around and yelled at the Office Manager. She turned around and yelled at me. The right to yell is a perk of command.

How do we reconcile our different styles of communication? The first step is to examine our norms.

SPEECH, PRIVILEGE AND SOCIAL POWER

Those who hold social power in a group generally speak more than others and are listened to more attentively. And those who come from a background of privilege, who carry a sense of entitlement they may not even be consciously aware of, are more likely to speak up first and to take up more time in the conversation. Those who feel confident — perhaps because they are smart or articulate or well-educated — tend to speak more than those who don't.

None of these generalities are universal. We all know women who can out-talk any man, and bold, outspoken working-class folks who never hesitate to voice their opinions. Some people need to talk in order to know what they think. Others prefer to ruminate in silence. Nonetheless, groups that want to foster equality do well to pay attention to who speaks, how often and how long, and to challenge any communication norms that further privilege.

Patterns That Reinforce Privilege
Interrupting

In the consciousness-raising circles of the second wave of the feminist movement, we gave each woman a protected time in which to speak without being

---

EXERCISE

Questions About Communication Norms

- What style of communication did your family of origin use?
- What communication norms do you recognize in your ethnic group? The neighborhood you grew up in?
- What norms have we already developed as a group?
- Are they similar or different from the norms we each grew up with?

- How do we respond to people who might have different norms?
- Do our norms serve us well? Are there any norms we might want to replace with conscious agreements?
- Are there people our norms might exclude?

interrupted — because we had noticed that men constantly interrupted women. When someone interrupts us, we often cannot finish a thought or completely express it. Interruption can be a move of dominance: "What I have to say is more important than what you have to say."

Of course, there are cultural differences around interruption. I once gently chided a French student for jumping in and interrupting. "But Starhawk," she explained, "In France, that's how we show we are interested, by finishing each other's sentences."

Embroidering Over

In the women's quilting group to which Ella belongs, Stella Stitcher is often deeply resented for embroidering over other womens' work. She is by far the most skilled artist and embroiderer among us, and when someone else has done a section of a crazy quilt in awkward and hesitant stitches, she'll sometimes just cover it over with something better. No one denies her skill, but the women whose contributions are effaced resent very much her high-handedness.

We do the same thing, at times, in speech. Someone makes a point in a meeting, perhaps a bit hesitantly or awkwardly, and I repeat the same point in a way that seems more eloquent to me. Worse, I might preface my remarks by saying, "What Otto really meant to say was ..." Like dogs urinating over another's scent on a tree, we feel obligated to make our mark on every idea or project. The result is that other people feel disrespected, unseen and disempowered.

Taking Center Stage

When we hold social power, we can easily assume that we are entitled to speak for the group, to formulate its ideas and be its public face. When opportunities come along for public speaking or media attention, we may grab them thoughtlessly. In the group itself, we may subtly make ourselves the center of attention and discussion.

Appropriating Credit

In hierarchies, the secretary may write the report, but the boss gets the credit. The graduate student may do the research, but the professor gets cited as the author of the publication. In collaborative groups, we believe that everyone should receive credit for their work and ideas. Yet in the heat of discussion, we may forget to notice who came up with an idea. More often than not, someone who holds social power will get the credit. Those who hold less power are made invisible, and their contributions go unnoticed.

Opening up Participation

Differences of social power are always present in groups. But in collaborative groups, we want to hear everyone's ideas and opinions. We want people to feel seen, acknowledged and respected, to be fairly rewarded for their contributions. Here are seven key ways to mitigate the impact of privilege and social power:

1. Encourage the talkers to step back, to exercise discipline and allow time for quieter people to speak.
2. Encourage the quieter people to step forward, to speak first. At minimum, ask at least once in every meeting, "Can we hear from people who haven't yet spoken?"
3. Use processes that encourage respectful attention and listening. Agree not to interrupt one another, and hold people to that agreement.
4. Instead of embroidering over substandard work, give constructive critique, training, mentoring and support to improve the work.
5. Instead of rephrasing an unclear contribution, ask the person in a supportive way to clarify it themselves. "Let me see if I'm hearing you correctly — you're suggesting _____. Did I get that right?" That leaves the credit and the responsibility with the original speaker.
6. Take special care to credit people's ideas and contributions. If you are unfairly credited, you can say, "Thank you, but I want to note that _____ is the person who put forth that suggestion."
7. Make sure that opportunities to take the limelight are passed around. Offer training, support and mentoring so that less experienced people can learn the skills of public speaking and media work.

DYSFUNCTIONAL NORMS

Certain patterns of dysfunctional norms around communications come up again and again in collaborative groups. Most of them arise when we attempt to avoid dealing with conflict or disagreement directly. Some of them carry over from junior high school. We might expect conscious, progressive people to have put such behavior far behind us, but sadly, unless we examine it we often repeat it. Here's how to destroy a group:

Talk About People Behind Their Backs

Don't confront people directly or give people constructive feedback. Instead, complain about them to others.

Gossip

Bond with one person by dissing another. Online, you can spread gossip faster than ever and with less opportunity for people at a distance to ascertain its validity.

Spread Rumors, Especially Negative Rumors

Don't check them out first or bring them to the attention of the person they are about. Believe any negative rumors you hear, immediately, no matter what your prior experience has been with the person in question.

Scapegoat

Choose one person to pick on, to be the bottom of the pecking order. See if you can drive them out of the group. Whatever is wrong with the group is their fault!

Case-Build

Recruit others to your point of view. Present your case first and get them on your side before they have a chance to be influenced by another point of view. Demand that people choose sides.

Many of these dysfunctional patterns ultimately derive from a set of values, assumptions and strategies that Roger Schwarz, in *The Skilled Facilitator,* deems "The Unilateral Control Model."[4] Most of us operate from this model when we feel attacked or threatened. The core values that underlie the unilateral control model are:

- Achieve My Goal Through Unilateral Control: I try to get others to do what I want them to do.
- Win, Don't Lose: I am invested in winning the argument and/or achieving my own ends.
- Minimize Expressing Negative Feelings: Expressing emotion makes us vulnerable and may lead to loss of control.

- Act Rational: Decisions should be made on logic, not emotion — or at least, look like they are being made logically.

These values give rise to four core assumptions that most of us will recognize:

- I understand the situation, those who see it differently don't.
- I am right, those who disagree are wrong.
- I have pure motives; those who disagree have questionable motives.
- My feelings are justified — my feelings are caused by others' speech and actions, not by my own thoughts or assumptions.

Those values and assumptions lead to common strategies:

- Advocate for my position.
- Keep my reasoning private.
- Do not inquire into others' reasoning.
- Ease in — cushion and disguise my attempts to take control.
- Save face.

Some variation of the Unilateral Control Model may underlie many of the most dysfunctional patterns in our organizations. Although collaborative groups may be founded on expressed values of respect, empathy, compassion and cooperation, in practice we often revert to behavior that counteracts those values. We exhibit toxic patterns.

TOXIC PATTERNS
Toxic Gossip

Sharing news about one another is part of the healthful functioning of any group. "Groups gossip to define themselves," states Beatrice Briggs, who trains facilitators worldwide. "Outsiders and newcomers can read the visitors' guide, the employee handbook, the bylaws or the newsletter, but only insiders know, understand — or care about — the gossip. Our gossip partners are usually our closest friends. Tell me who you gossip with and what you gossip about and I will tell you where you are in the hierarchy of the group."[5]

Storyteller and Lucumi Priestess Luisah Teish says, "I define gossip as the discussion of another person's problems for entertainment. Vicious gossip takes a grain of truth and stretches it out of proportion, with the intention of slandering another's name and/or causing and furthering disruptions between people.

(I make a distinction between gossip and concerned conversation. Concerned conversation happens between members of an extended family. Its aim is to find solutions to problems, soothe feelings and to promote mutual laughter between members.)"[6]

Negative, false and malicious gossip is one of the most hurtful ways we betray each other. People come to a group looking for acceptance, warmth and community. They have their annoying habits — we all do. Instead of getting feedback and the opportunity to change, they become the subject of gossip. Sometimes "helpful" friends repeat the malicious gossip, which is hurtful. Other times they may never even hear the accusations, but sense the poisonous atmosphere, like an invisible, toxic gas. Or the gossip may go out online to dozens or hundreds of people who may never have met anyone involved.

Ursula is unhappy with the way Donna runs the community building committee. Instead of giving her direct and honest feedback, Ursula grumbles to Kristin, "She doesn't facilitate — she ignores my ideas and lets Edward talk on and on. I think she's got a crush on him. It's disgusting! He must be twice her age. And a married man! And he's not that good-looking — I can't imagine what she sees in him."

"She's not so young," Kristin sneers. "It's her biological clock — I've seen it again and again with women her age. Their hormones take over their judgment."

Before long, half the people in RootBound know — or think they know — that Edward and Donna are having an affair and that Donna is pregnant. Edward's wife catches a drift of the rumors and threatens divorce. Donna, a happy lesbian married to her long-term lover, comes home to a storm of accusations. The shaky community building committee receives a death blow, and any benefit it might have offered to RootBound is stillborn.

Gossip and rumor-mongering also leave us open to disruption. For political groups, infiltration and disinformation can be real concerns. Agents whose true agenda is the group's destruction may foment vicious rumors or spread unfounded accusations. Organizer Lisa Fithian wrote an account of the many destructive roles an FBI informant, Brandon Darby, played in Common Ground Relief in New Orleans after Hurricane Katrina.

In January 2007 I drove to New Orleans to pick up a friend who was kicked out of Common Ground by Brandon because she was a friend of mine. She was one of the coordinators at the St. Mary's site. Other relief work coordinators were leaving the organization and because of this Brandon accused me of coming to town to wage a coup against him.

Early the next morning one of his "assistants" called me, threatening me with lawsuits. Then I get a call telling me that Brandon told them that King told him that Scott and I were conspiring against him. Crazy shit, crazy COINTELPRO shit. At the same time Brandon began a purge of three long-time coordinators by demanding they turn in the keys and leave the premises. But this time even Brandon went too far. Malik (the group's founder) intervened and stopped the purge.[7]

Darby's destructive impact went far beyond gossip, to entrapment and disruption in many activist organizations. Fithian makes the point that if key activists had intervened to challenge his negative interpersonal behavior — or supported

EXERCISE

Changing the Pattern of Gossip

We are social animals, and the doings of other humans are endlessly fascinating to us. We all have some friends who are closer than others, and we all sometimes need to vent and complain about people. But we can also support one another in turning those complaints into constructive action.

When you feel attacked or wronged:

1. Ask yourself, "Is this actually any of my business? Why am I disturbed? Do I actually need to respond to this?"
2. Inquire about what actually happened, or about the person's motivations, before you make assumptions that rev up your anger or your sense of injury. To inquire is to ask questions in a neutral and non-accusatory way, to get all the relevant information out on the table. What actually happened? What are both sides of the story? What were people's intentions? When I inquire, I listen. I withhold judgment until I have heard all sides of the story.
3. Confront the person directly, and offer constructive critique.
4. Ask for help and support from other community members, including mediation, as needed.
5. Know what requests you want to make. What do you need in order to feel resolved?
6. Together come to new agreements.
7. Put those agreements into practice.

CONTINUED

When you hear a rumor or story about someone else's bad behavior or some act that disturbs you:

1. Remember that every story has at least two sides.

2. Ask yourself, "Is this actually any of my business?"

3. Inquire directly about what happened before leaping to judgment.

4. Support the person who feels injured in confronting the other party directly, with constructive criticism. Offer help finding mediation, if needed.

When someone brings negative gossip to you, ask:

1. Is this really any of our business? Do we need to respond? Why does this disturb you?

2. Have you inquired to find out what actually happened? Have we heard all sides of the issue? Can I support you in doing so?

3. What kind of support can I give you in directly and constructively confronting this person or situation?

4. If the gossiper is unwilling to directly engage with the person who is the subject of the gossip, change the subject. Refuse to engage. End the conversation. When someone tries to hook you in, don't get hooked. If your friend says, "I really shouldn't tell you this …." Respond, "I'm glad you recognize that. Let's talk about something else."

the women who did challenge him — he would have lost the credibility that allowed him to wreak even deeper harm.

The Internet can be fertile ground for character destruction. Public figures can be *swift-boated* — brought down by campaigns of lies. The term comes from the campaign to discredit 2004 Presidential candidate John Kerry by blatant lies claiming he never was part of combat operations in Vietnam that had earned him a hero's medals. Politicians, public servants and whistle-blowers are all subject to media lies and character assassination. In such a climate, groups that encourage gossip and rumor are ripe for destruction.

Put-downs and Shut-downs

Put-downs are terms of disrespect, of ridicule and humiliation. I use the term *shut-down* for a form of communication that, instead of opening up a topic and encouraging debate and healthy conflict, shuts it off. Shut-downs may be overt:

one of the drawbacks to yelling is that it often shuts down a conversation. But shut-downs can also be very subtle.

Marshall Rosenberg talks about the difference between a request and a demand.[8] A request is something you can say no to without paying a heavy emotional cost. A demand wrests a huge price for saying no. If I say to my partner, "Please, would you bring me a cup of coffee," he can say yes or no. If I say, "If you really loved me, you'd bring me a cup of coffee," he can't say no without admitting that he doesn't really love me.

Blaming and shaming serve as shut-downs. *Blaming* may hold people accountable for things far beyond the scope of their actions and not under their control: "You bought paper plates, and now old-growth forests are being clearcut!" Blaming imputes bad motives and generalizes from the action to attack the person: "You brought paper plates because you hate the Tree People and wanted to drive us out of the cooperative!"

Shaming also generalizes from the action to the person but goes far beyond true accountability or constructive feedback. If I say to an intern, "Relax your wrist and let the hammer swing," that's helpful feedback. If I say, "Good grief, did you never in your life pick up a hammer before? Your arm is as stiff as that block of wood! What — you're too good to do manual labor?" that's shaming.

Along with blaming and shaming goes *name-calling*. Racial and gender-based epithets, terms that disparage someone's sexual identity or ethnic group are clearly out of bounds in progressive circles. Nonetheless, even conscious people resort to name-calling, although the labels may be political or spiritual. "You're a scared liberal, that's why you object to my throwing a rock through the window of McDonalds." "You're a mindless thug, that's why you won't agree to a non-violence code." Or, in spiritual circles, we may hear, "You're functioning on a lower, material plane." "You're unevolved." "You're still trapped in the lower chakras."

Threats are another form of shut-down that we often employ when we attempt to assert control. We do need to hold one another accountable, and actions have consequences. But if I constantly invoke those consequences in interactions, I may shut down dissent and communication. "If you keep complaining, you'll undermine the group and you'll be responsible for destroying our work." "If I hear one more complaint, I'm calling a meeting to denounce you!"

We also shut one another down when, in the name of political correctness, we become language police, when we are constantly calling one another out for using the wrong terminology or forgetting the latest correct phrasing for an issue. Language is important, and a shift in language can represent a vitally important shift in consequence. There are some terms that should never be used in conscious circles of people committed to justice. But a *public correction,* no matter how well meant, humiliates the one who receives it. We should be careful and judicious in how many corrections we dish out.

Finally, another way to shut down dialogue is in how we *frame* an issue. "Frames are among the cognitive structures we think with," says linguist George Lakoff, who has written extensively on the frames we use in political discourse.[9] Frames are metaphors that tell us what to expect in a situation, what roles will be played and what values are being employed. A frame can be more emotionally powerful than the content of what is framed. Lakoff stresses that whoever controls the frame controls the argument. Consider what happens when a woman's right to terminate a pregnancy is framed as "murder." Or when cuts in government workers' earned retirement plans are framed as "pension reform." If progressives fall into the trap of disputing how much or little we need to "reform" the pensions people have worked for and counted on, we've already lost the argument.

When an issue is framed as a life-or-death dilemma, as a test of commitment or integrity, it's hard to have an open discussion. If we're arguing about whether to cut the weeds with a scythe or a weed-whacker, we could argue the pros and cons of each. But if your frame is "Every small decision is a test of our moral commitment to the environment," there's not much room for me to argue the merits of the weed-whacker without being branded as an anti-environmental lout. If my partner and I are arguing about which movie to go to, and my frame is "A compatible relationship means perfect agreement — if we can't agree then we shouldn't be together," there's not much room for my partner to prefer a Russian drama with subtitles over my choice of a light, romantic comedy.

Progressives tend to be morally driven people so integrity and consistency are important to us, and we have strong feelings and strict standards for how people should behave. Yet we live in a world that is not set up to further many of our goals and aims. We are constantly forced into compromises. We often do drive a car to get to the meeting about reducing our carbon footprint.

If we want to establish open and vibrant communication, we should take care not to frame every disagreement as a *moral test.* Instead, we should look for ways to frame our issues that encourage and support diversity and a wide variety of opinions and options. We might reframe the movie argument as, "A strong relationship can stand diversity — if we go see each others' preferred movies, we'll each stretch and grow." We might look at the weed-whacker debate as an opportunity to evaluate the trade-offs of time and energy vs. fossil fuels. Then we can hear all sides of the story.

Groupthink

When a group is filled with people who share similar opinions and backgrounds, when dissent is discouraged and information is carefully edited to support one point of view, groupthink is the result. *Groupthink* means that the group serves as reinforcement for its own point of view.

Pyracantha believes that eating meat is a moral sin. She surrounds herself with other vegans. They constantly confirm one another's opinions on the subject. They comb the Internet for studies confirming that a vegan diet is good for their health, and discard or discredit any information that challenges that view or presents different results. If someone admits to eating meat, they are denounced in the strongest possible terms. Pretty soon Pyracantha begins to believe that "everyone thinks" that meat-eating is a moral and political sin. If anyone tries to join her group, they are assumed to be a vegan. If not, they are rapidly excluded and shunned.

Groupthink limits our diversity, our collective intelligence and our ability to respond strategically. If we don't listen to those who disagree with us, we may miss important perspectives. If we continually reinforce and refine a position that gets more and more extreme, we may isolate ourselves and alienate potential allies.

If Pyracantha and her group decide to shut down a McDonalds, they might expect widespread support from "everyone" who presumably all know how bad fast food is. But if they try that in the heart of the inner city, instead of support they might meet incomprehension or outright attack from a different "everyone," the people who eat at McDonalds every day because that is the food they can afford and prefer.

To some extent, every group develops its own language — that's part of our human creativity. But when we forget that other people may not know the same language — that people who have not taken a permaculture design course may not understand what we mean by "stacking functions," that those who have never read anarchist literature may not be moved by the term "mutual aid" — we become ineffective communicators. Jargon is also the way elites consolidate and

Groupthink Brainstorm

Needed: A whiteboard or big sheets of paper, markers.

For five minutes, ask the group to complete these sentences as fast as they can, with whatever first pops into their heads. Scribes should record responses as rapidly as possible:

> Everyone thinks …
>
> Everyone knows …
>
> Everyone believes …

When the board is full of statements, give the group a few moments to read them over and observe them. Ask each person to pick one or two of their favorites.

Now, think of the opposite belief. How would it feel to look at the world through that lens?

Devil's Advocate Circle

For 10 to 20 minutes, discuss a group plan or project, but with each person speaking for those points of view opposite to the group's general beliefs. Notice how the energy feels, what emotions get stirred up, what new ideas surface.

Now stop, stand up and take a step forward, consciously stepping out of your role.

How did it feel to argue for that opposite belief? What did you notice about the group's energy? Have any new ideas or approaches surfaced? How does the energy of the group feel now?

---

guard power and information. When I was a graduate student in psychology, object relations theory was in vogue. I once wrote a paper and decided to present the theory in ordinary language, in part to find out if it really made sense. My teacher commented, "Excellent paper, but I wish you had presented object relations theory." I realized that without the jargon, she didn't recognize the theory.

FROM WINNING TO LEARNING

All of these dysfunctional norms reflect the overarching frame of the unilateral control model: the need to win, to advocate our own position, to avoid vulnerability. When we are caught in that model, we frame the group and the work as a contest or battle. We're in a constant duel between right and wrong, good and evil and must fight hard to protect ourselves and defend our positions.

Instead of war as our frame, we might shift to seeing our challenges in a frame of learning. Our goal is not to win, but to learn and grow, increasing our own capacity and deepening our connections. When we shift to a frame of learning, we can open up to others' points of view. Instead of contesting their ideas and trying to defeat them, we can give them a hearing and let them expand our understanding.

Theorists Peter Senge and Donald Schon apply systems theory to the management of businesses and corporations and advocate what they call "the learning organization."[10] By looking at whole systems, acknowledging our needs and drives for personal mastery, sharing a common vision and goals and examining our mental models and frames, we can learn as a team. Such organizations are nourishing to individuals and, ultimately, more effective in the world. While Senge and Schon work with conventional businesses, their ideas may apply even more to collaborative groups.

The learning frame underlies the norms and practices that can help us develop effective communication. We are not bound to continue destructive patterns of communication. When we recognize destructive norms, we can replace them with conscious agreements and new norms that work.

NORMS THAT WORK

Respectful Attention

We listen to each other with real interest. We give others our full attention. We may or may not agree, but we respect the person who is speaking and respect their efforts to contribute to the group.

Respectful attention in an age of constant stimulation also means taking our earbuds out and turning off the iPod, shutting off the cellphone during meetings or important conversations and protecting our communications from constant disruption and interruption.

Emotional and Practical Support

We give each other emotional support and, when appropriate, practical support in dealing with crises within and outside the group. We are willing to hear one another's doubts and fears as well as to celebrate our triumphs. We genuinely care about one another.

Learning and Inquiry

We approach disagreements in the spirit of inquiry. What can we learn from this? What information might this conflict be telling us? We test inferences and check out assumptions, willing to learn from one another. We can admit ignorance and confusion, and embrace the mystery of another's point of view.

Constructive Conflict

We don't hold back in advocating for our suggestions or arguing their merits, but we separate ideas from the people who hold them and don't stoop to personal attacks. We may not always succeed in persuading the group to our point of view. We yield gracefully and support others when the will of the group goes elsewhere. Constructive conflict actually makes a group far more interesting and lively. Meetings are full of debate and dissent, but with a ground of support and enthusiasm, that generates an atmosphere where ideas get sharpened and creativity flourishes.

Direct and Respectful Confrontation

When we have an issue, a problem or a conflict with someone, we confront them directly and respectfully, face to face or at least on the telephone, not online. We are willing to express our feelings and to listen. If we can't resolve the problem ourselves, we get help and mediation.

Constructive Critique

We learn to give and receive constructive critique.

Support for Growth

We support one another in learning, growing and making changes. We know that sometimes change takes time and repetition. We have patience with one another.

Mentoring, Training and Coaching

We offer one another mentoring, coaching and training when needed to help further one another's growth and development.

Energetic Support

We give each other energetic support. Even when we disagree, we're in some sense cheering each other on to develop our ideas, to bring forth our creativity, to make our best contribution to the group. A group where people are rooting for each other is a high-energy place to be. People will enjoy coming to meetings and leave feeling recharged and energized. Cheering for someone does not mean you always agree with their suggestions — it means you affirm their being, their courage in offering a suggestion, their creativity.

COMMUNICATION SKILLS AND TOOLS

When we seek to improve our group's communication, we need to develop and practice some core skills: giving and receiving feedback, testing assumptions and inferences and sharing our vulnerability.

Constructive Critique and Feed-forward

In the world of the arts, a constructive critique is a mark of respect. When an artist receives a thoughtful critique of her work, when a filmmaker gets "notes"

EXERCISE

Energetic Support Exercise

Stand in two lines. Ask people to reach across and shake hands with their partner. Tell them there are three ground rules: only interact with your partner, don't walk away from the interaction and no physical attacks.

Tell people: If you're on the line on the left, I want you to ground, center and find the anchor to your core self (see Chapter 1). Now, think of something you feel passionate about, an idea or a project that you'd like to invite your partner to join you in.

If you're in the line on the right, I'd like you to think about this saying attributed to Gandhi — that when you set out to change the world, first they ignore you, then they ridicule you, then they attack you — then you win. I want you to ignore, ridicule or attack your partner — but don't walk away from the interaction and don't physically attack.

When I say "Go," you'll begin, and when I hoot (ring a bell, blow a whistle, bang a drum), stop and freeze into silence. OK, go!

Let the exercise go for one to two minutes, then stop it.

Ask people to step forward, and consciously step out of their roles. Then switch roles and repeat the exercise.

After each side has had a chance to play both roles, stop and again ask people to step out of their roles. Take a few moments to debrief the exercise:

- How did it feel to be on each side?
- Were you able to stay grounded and anchored?
- Was anything your partner did effective at getting through the attack?
- How did it feel to be on the negative side?

CONTINUED

- Now ask people to shift one person down on the line and take new partners. This time the line on the left will again begin by grounding, centering and finding the anchor to core self. But now the line on the right is going to silently cheer for their ideas. You can use body language, gestures, but no sounds or words. Just imagine your partner is a football team, and you're cheering them on.

Again, when I say "Go," you'll begin, and when I hoot (ring a bell, blow a whistle, bang a drum), stop and freeze into silence. OK, go!

After one to two minutes, stop the exercise and change roles. Repeat.

Then debrief this part of the exercise:

- How did it feel to be cheered on?
- How did it feel to be cheering?
- What did you notice about the energy of the group? Your own energy?

- Sometimes we might actually feel uncomfortable with so much support. Did that come up for anyone?
- How would our group feel if we were offering this kind of energetic support to one another regularly?

Often, people find their creativity expanding and their ideas flowering in the sunlight of energetic support. Some people find that they rapidly run out of things to say: being listened to attentively, without being challenged, they feel heard and do not need to belabor their ideas. Others may find their original ideas expand. Generally people find this exercise enlivening and inspiring.

Variation: Repeat, but this time instead of just silently cheering, ask the supporting line to maintain the energy while asking supportive questions.[11]

on a screenplay, when a novelist gets a sensitive review of a new book, they know they are receiving a gift of time, care and attention. When a friend takes the time to tell me about an issue that is disturbing her, I know she cares about improving our relationship.

Here are criteria I use to distinguish constructive critique. Some of them came originally from artist Donald Engstrom, who started me thinking about the value of critique. Others come from my own experience both as a writer and creative artist and as a member of many groups.

1. The intention is to improve the work or the relationship.
2. A constructive critique is specific — both positive and negative critiques are most useful when they are as specific as possible. Not "That meeting sucked!"

but, "We really got off on a tangent about the cost of the new garden beds and the facilitator didn't get us back on course." Not "I adore your poem" but "I liked how you had five different creative ways to describe love, and none of them were imagery I'd heard before."

3. A constructive critique is timely. Not too soon — when the singer is stepping offstage from her heartfelt solo, still flushed with excitement, that's not the moment to tell her she was off-key in the second verse. But also not too late! The time to critique the architectural plan is while it's still a drawing, not after the concrete has been poured. I've literally had people say, "That terrible thing you said to me five years ago at the workshop — I never told you, and you probably don't even remember it." Right. And any chance that I might have learned from your criticism, apologized or healed our relationship is long gone.

4. A constructive critique is about something that can be changed, that the artist or friend has control over. Tell me you'd like me to be kinder, or to speak more slowly or to listen more, and I can do that. Tell me you'd like me to be smarter, taller or better looking, and we're both out of luck.

5. A constructive critique is given in private before it's given in public. If you tell me quietly, "You've got a piece of spinach in your teeth," I can remove it and I'll thank you for your helpfulness. If you shout out to a roomful of strangers, "Hey everybody, look at this — she's got spinach in her teeth," I'll feel shamed and attacked. Generally, any public critique risks being an occasion of shame and humiliation. An exception would be during a public feedback meeting, when everyone knows that critique is the purpose of the gathering and people are prepared to receive it.

6. In relationships, *feed-forward* is often more helpful than feedback.[12] Instead of telling people what they have been doing wrong, tell them how you want them to be right. Not "You slob — you never clean up your dishes after dinner," but, "One thing you could do that would help me feel great about living together is to do your dishes at night so, in the morning, I wake up to a clean kitchen."

7. A critique may need to be given more than once. Think about something you have tried to change and how long it took. So, have patience. Know that feedback sometimes must be repeated over and over, until new grooves are worn in our habitual patterns of behavior.

Receiving Feedback

Receiving feedback can be challenging. Even the most constructive critique can sting. We'd much rather be told a piece is wonderful than to be told where it doesn't work, however timely and specific the remark. But learning to receive and integrate criticism is a vital skill for any creative person or group member.

1. Try to stay energetically and emotionally neutral. Grounding, centering, using your anchor to your core self are especially helpful in giving and receiving feedback.
2. Just listen. Don't leap to defend yourself or your work. Even stupid, biased feedback is information. Give yourself time to take it in. Consciously choose to learn, rather than defend.
3. The best response is generally a simple thank you. Even when you've received negative feedback, you can thank the giver for the time, trouble and passion they've put into the critique.
4. If you really disagree, or if you're simply in a state where you can't take in one more utterance of either criticism or praise, the best response may be, "I'll

EXERCISE

Constructive Critique Practice

Movie Night

Pick a film — perhaps a documentary relevant to the group's work, perhaps just something fun that people want to watch. It could even be a children's movie that the group can watch together with their kids.

After it's over, imagine that the director, writer, producer or actors are standing in the front of the room and that you are their focus group, chosen to help them improve their work. Now, practice giving constructive critique — the more specific, the better. This exercise is very low risk and potentially lots of fun. The group will probably have the most fun if they pick a really bad movie!

Pairs Critique

In pairs, share a situation in which you have an issue with someone whom you would like to or need to critique. Review the guidelines for constructive critique and role-play the conversation. Partners can give each other constructive critique on how well they gave constructive critique. Help each other refine the scripts, and practice them.

think about that. I can't say right now whether I agree with your assessment, I need to let it sink in and mull it over. So I'll think about it."

5. Praise can be almost as hard to take in as blistering attacks. Praise is energy coming at you, so stay grounded, centered, remember to breathe and say thank you.

6. Some people will heap you with praise because they want something from you — whether that's energy or time or material resources or simply the added social power they believe will come from connection to someone they perceive as important. Notice your own feelings and energy level — and be aware that praise may cover up energy-siphoning. Again, staying grounded and centered will help you take in what is true and valuable and protect you from being drained.

Turning an Attack into a Critique

When we know what constitutes constructive critique, we can be more clear about when we're receiving the gift of thoughtful criticism and when we're under attack. We may sometimes be able to turn an attack into a thoughtful critique.

In ju-jitsu and other martial arts, a defender learns to use an attacker's momentum to throw her off balance. We can practice "criti-jitsu:" doing the same with a destructive critique or attack.

"You're an idiot!"

"What have I done or said that makes you believe I'm an idiot? Can you be specific? In what way would you like me to behave differently than I do?" (This only works if you are vigilant at keeping your tone neutral. Any hint of sarcasm and you're back into a fruitless argument.)

E
X
E
R
C
I
S
E

Criti-jitsu Practice

In pairs, share a time when someone has said something hurtful or attacking. Help each other discern whether there might be a way to shift that attack to a constructive critique. Some possibilities might be:

- Ask for specifics.
- Ask for it to come at an appropriate time.
- Ask what the critic's intent is.
- Ask the critic to suggest an appropriate structure or forum for raising the issue or making the critique.

THE LADDER OF INFERENCE

What happens far too often in relationships is that we leap up what organizational psychologists call *The Ladder of Inference*.[13]

Our trip up the ladder begins with an event — something that happens, words that are said, actions that are taken — "observable data: so self-evident that it would show up on a videotape recorder."[14]

> Rick Ragle is at a party at RootBound. He approaches Alice Vlack and when he's ten feet away, she turns away and walks off.

Step two: From the event, I select certain data that may fit my emotional state or unconscious expectations. While most writers assume that the data selection triggers emotion, I believe that the flood of emotion may determine what data we select. Either way, they go together.

> Rick feels rejected and hurt. From then on, the data he selects, the subsequent events he notices, are likely to confirm that feeling. He notices that later in the evening, Alice again abruptly leaves the room as he comes near. He doesn't notice that she is in and out many times, often turning away from conversations with others to bolt toward the bathroom.

Step three: I interpret the data through the lens of cultural and personal meaning.

> Now Rick interprets her behavior: "She's mad at me; she doesn't like me."

Step four: Meaning leads to assumptions.

> The assumption may be a low-level inference: "Alice saw me walking toward her and turned away deliberately." Or Rick may generalize to a higher-level inference: "She's still mad about the pool incident — can't anyone ever let that go? She doesn't understand how men relate — most likely she hates men!"

Rick may then marshall more data to back his assumptions, turning them into elaborate stories:

"She teaches Women's Studies, too. Aha — that proves it!" And one assumption triggers another: "She'll be against anything I might propose, just because I'm a man, and she hates me. She'll block me now at every turn in RootBound. She'll be part of that man-hating vendetta that's out to get me. I thought she was sort of cute, but really she's a dog. I don't belong here."

Step five: Assumptions give birth to conclusions.

"I need to get her off of the Planning Committee. If I can't do that, I'll quit. And no way am I going to support that child care budget she wants!"

Step six: Conclusions are reinforced by my overarching beliefs and stories.

"None of these granola types can deal with a real man." Those beliefs may tie into deep stories Rick carries from his childhood that define his sense of who he is in the world: "My mother never loved me, women don't love me, I'm not attractive," and into what he tells himself in order to defend against that primal sense of pain, "Screw them! A real woman would appreciate a real man. I don't need the rest of those vixen!"

Step seven: Beliefs lead me to take action.

At the end of the party, Rick corners Alice in the hallway as she's putting on her coat. "Go to hell, you stuck-up feminazi harpy!" he spits out, then leaves, slamming the door behind him. A stunned and bewildered Alice is left to climb her own ladder of inference.

Backing Down the Ladder Using Inquiry

Suppose Rick had been able to say to himself, "Whoa there, Ragle, back down!" Or perhaps a helpful friend might have been able to intervene. Had he gone back to the original event, he might have inquired about it instead of making a judgment.

To *inquire* is to ask questions from an open and neutral place, without forming a judgment beforehand. To inquire is to demonstrate trust. If Rick trusts Alice, he will hold open the possibility that there are many explanations for the behavior he witnessed.

Inquiry begins with the data, the event, what Rick saw or heard, with assumptions and emotions stripped away. "Alice," he might have said, "Twice tonight I noticed that you quickly left the room when I was walking over toward you. Is something going on?"

Alice might have said, "Rick, I've been scared of you ever since you pushed Edward into the pool. Stay away from me!" That might confirm some of Rick's worst fears, but at least the conflict will now be out in the open, where he has a chance to deal with it.

But Alice might also laugh and say, "Congratulate me, Rick. I'm two months pregnant. But no one seems to have told my morning sickness that it was supposed to happen in the morning, not all day and all night. Didn't you notice that I was running to the bathroom every 15 minutes all evening long?"

A true inquiry is open-ended, but it's easy to turn it into an accusation without meaning to. Note the subtle difference between asking, "Is something going on?" (which implies that it may or may not be) and "What's going on?" (which already assumes that something is).

The difference between inquiry and accusation may not lie in words at all, but in tone and body language. Consider the question, "Where were you last night?" Imagine it being asked by a friend who simply wants to know what you did for fun. Now imagine it being asked by the detective in a murder case. And now imagine it being asked by your life partner who has been up all night calling the morgue, the jail and every bar in town because you never came home.

Dare to Share Your Vulnerability

When your emotions are in full swing, when you are filled with hurt or anger or fear, stepping back to inquiry can be difficult. Maybe Rick cannot get back below step two. He's simply filled with too much emotion.

When someone shares a feeling, they are sharing their emotional truth. Feelings are neither valid nor invalid, they just are. Feelings don't have to be rational or justified. The assumptions

EXERCISE

Open-ended Questions

- Is something going on?
- What happened?
- What did I do or say that led you to believe _____?
- What's your take on the situation?
- I'm inferring _____, but I'd like to check that out with you and make sure that it's right.

and conclusions our feelings provoke may be invalid and just plain wrong, but the feelings themselves are real.

Feeling hurt, scared, sad or angry makes us vulnerable. Sharing that hurt can feel even more threatening and humiliating. We lose face. Maybe we're not the all-wise, ever-calm guide, the tough street-fighter, the powerful and successful person we're supposed to be. If someone has rejected us and hurt us — maybe we are not truly attractive or desirable.

Sharing our emotions is a risky business. It's far more comfortable to share our conclusions about the other person. Yelling "You're a vicious shrew!" feels far more powerful and satisfying than saying, "I feel terribly hurt by your behavior, and I'm afraid you don't like me!" But the first is likely to compound the hurt, while the second approach leaves an opening to gain new understanding and closeness.

So Rick might also have said to Alice, "When you turned and walked away as I walked toward you, I felt very hurt. I imagined that you were angry at me. Can you tell me what's going on?"

Even when someone's conclusions or actions are way off base, we can still affirm their feelings. "I'm so sorry that my actions caused you pain," Alice might say to Rick. She does not have to take responsibility for Rick's wrong conclusions, but by affirming his emotions, she shows that she has heard his distress and that she cares about the relationship. When we know our emotions are heard, we can more easily back down the ladder, away from our conclusions.

Non-violent Communication

Marshall Rosenberg encourages us to share both our feelings and our underlying needs with one another.[15] Non-violent communication has four steps: observation, feelings, needs and a request. "When you turned and walked away as I walked toward you," is Rick's observation. "I felt hurt," expresses his emotions. Were he to add his underlying needs, he might admit, "I need your friendship — it's important to me." His request might be, "Would you be willing to tell me what happened from your point of view, and to let me know if you are angry about something?"

Sharing emotions is not always appropriate. When we step out of our circles of equals back into the world of hierarchy, sharing feelings may leave us too vulnerable. Pyracantha Hazel was fired from her canvassing job with the Save All Trees Foundation because she continually tried to share her hurt feelings every time her grumpy supervisor snapped at her. The supervisor had the power to fire her and rid himself of an over-sensitive worker who was constantly demanding time he didn't have. And so he did.

GROUND RULES FOR EFFECTIVE COMMUNICATION

Roger Schor, in *The Skilled Facilitator,* offers nine rules for effective groups, which encompass many of the ideas above:

1. Test assumptions and inferences.
   The discussions above on backing down the ladder of inference are ways we might test assumptions.
2. Share all relevant information.
   Relevant information includes your own emotions and inferences, shared in order to test them, not to defend them.
3. Use specific examples and agree on what important words mean.
   Constructive critique is specific!
4. Explain your reasoning and intent.
   Share your own ladder of inference, or perhaps, your reasons and intentions for doing or saying what you did.

E
X
E
R
C
I
S
E

Non-violent Communication Practice

The non-violent communication formula can help us effectively share our emotions. We use I statements, speaking about what we noticed, felt and need, not blaming you statements: "When I noticed _____, I felt _____, because I need _____." We follow with a request — not a demand! Remember that a request is something someone can say no to without paying a huge price. "Would you be willing to _____."

In pairs, think of a difficult situation or a personal challenge. Help each other to formulate what you might say, using the non-violent communication script above. Role-play the situation and share feedback on how it felt to hear your partner's observations, feelings, needs and requests.

Pay special attention to how you formulate your request. How can you truly make it safe for someone to say no? How will you respond if they do say no? Practice!

Non-violent communication is taught worldwide, and groups can benefit greatly by more extensive training.

5. Focus on interests, not positions.

   Interests may be needs, goals, intentions, desires or fears. *Positions* are the conclusions you've reached about how to meet your needs. Sometimes your conclusions may lead to an impasse with another person, while simply sharing your needs and interests might lead to a mutual solution.

6. Combine advocacy and inquiry.

   Be open to learning. Inquire before you jump to conclusions. Advocate openly for your ideas and your point of view, but be open to learning from others.

7. Jointly design next steps and ways to test disagreements.

   Work together to find a mutually acceptable way to go forward.

8. Discuss undiscussable issues.

   Name the elephant in the room. Undiscussables are often our own emotions. Using the guidelines above can make it possible to address even highly charged issues sensitively and productively. Not addressing them will not make them go away.

9. Use a decision-making rule that generates the level of commitment needed.[16]

   Full consensus takes time and commitment and is worth pursuing for important matters. For minor decisions or procedural issues, a simple vote or a straw poll might be more effective. Don't spend half an hour trying to reach consensus on whether to take 45 minutes or an hour for lunch![17]

Let's look back at Ursula and Kristen, our toxic gossipers, and consider how they might apply these rules to their dissatisfaction with RootBound's Community Building Group.

Ursula observes that Donna Darling does not strongly facilitate the Community Building Group, and that Edward often takes up the bulk of the group's time. She might say:

"Donna, I'm noticing how much time Edward takes up in our meetings, and that you as the facilitator don't stop him. At our last meeting, I actually timed him and he spent 20 minutes talking about the carbon footprint of paper plates vs. machine- or hand-washed china dishes (Rule 3, Use specific examples). I'm feeling frustrated because I have things I'd like to contribute, and I don't often get the chance (Rule 2, Sharing all relevant information). I guess from that I'm inferring that you like him and don't want to confront him, but I'd like to ask you if I'm on the right track with that (Rule 1, Testing assumptions and Rule 8, Discuss undiscussables). I bring this up because I care about the work of the group, and I believe this is an issue because there are five others on the committee that may also have things to share. Our work will be strengthened if we are all more involved." (Rule 4, Explain your reasoning and intent)

Donna, using the ground rules, might respond, "Thanks for bringing this up directly. I feel sad that I haven't met my own expectations as a facilitator (Rule 2, Share all relevant information and Rule 8, Discuss undiscussables). When you ask if I 'like' Edward, I'm inferring that you mean romantically? Am I right in picking that up? (Rule 1, Test assumptions and Rule 3, Agree on exact meanings of words). I do like him as a person, but not in any romantic sense. But maybe I'm going easy on him because I see him as vulnerable ever since Rick pushed him into the pool (Rule 4, Explain reasoning and intent). It's hard for me to interrupt people, and maybe it's harder to interrupt men than women, in spite of my 15 years as a dedicated member of my feminist consciousness-raising group (Rule 2, Share all relevant information). How do you think we could best address this issue?"(Rule 7, Jointly design next steps)

Instead of spiraling into a destructive vortex of broken relationships, Ursula and Donna may both learn something from this interaction. Donna may become a better facilitator; Ursula may gain appreciation of the difficulties of running a meeting. The Community Building Group will be strengthened and, by confronting and working out their issues directly, will take one step closer to true community.

CONFIDENTIALITY AGREEMENTS

In some situations, *confidentiality* is necessary to create an atmosphere of safety and trust. Support groups, groups that center around people's personal feelings and vulnerabilities — for example, 12-step groups where people openly discuss their addictions — need confidentiality to function. I'm not going to share my deepest emotions, my most shameful episodes, my most intimate feelings, if I suspect they will become a topic of common gossip.

But in other situations, *transparency* is called for. If a group is secretive about how it makes decisions, how people get in and get out, how perks are distributed or how power is earned, it creates a breeding ground for resentment, disempowerment and dysfunction. And some secrets are truly toxic: for example, addiction, abuse, battering, child abuse and sexual assault. Many wrongs can only be carried out in an atmosphere of secrecy, and only openness and truth-telling can begin the process of healing.

Groups must be clear about what level of confidentiality and openness they decide is appropriate. Those agreements might change in different situations. Our group might be open most of the time — but we might decide that our annual retreat to deal with our inner process requires confidentiality.

Once agreements are made, they must be kept or trust is broken. Better not to have a confidentiality agreement at all than to make one and not honor it. If I know what I say will be an open field for gossip, I can choose to guard my tongue. But if I open my heart in good faith and then find out later that my secrets have become a joke for the rest of the group, I may suffer irreparable harm.

When considering issues of confidentiality, consider these questions:

- Who benefits if this secret is kept?
- Who benefits if this secret is revealed?
- What would I be able to share in this meeting if I know my words will be held in confidence?
- What would I be able to share if I knew this meeting would be on public record? [18]

Two Columns Exercise

In pairs, take a moment to share a time when you have been in conflict with someone and when you have employed some aspect of the Unilateral Control Model or one of the dysfunctional norms named above.

Take a sheet of paper, and draw a line down the center to make two columns. In the left-hand column, write down as accurately as possible what you said. In the right-hand column, write down what your thoughts were. Example: Ella responds to Patricia's announcement that she cannot make a crucial meeting.

Patricia: Oh by the way, I can't make that meeting on Saturday, something's come up. **Ella:** I'm sorry to hear that. Are you sure?	**Ella thinks:** What the hell do you mean, you can't make it? That meeting was set up to clear grievances, and you are the biggest complainer.

CONTINUED

Patricia: You all go ahead without me. It's fine.
Ella: I thought we'd all committed to doing some interpersonal work that day.

Ella thinks: Bitch! You're just trying to avoid having to deal with your problems or having people call you on your behavior. What a coward!

Patricia: You know I'm not much of a process-head.
Ella: Patricia, I have to say that I'm feeling like you don't keep your commitments to the group. I feel like the group is not important to you.
Patricia: That's not true! I've done every damn thing I ever said I'd do for this group — now I can't make one lousy meeting, and I have to take all this shit!
Ella: I'm just expressing my feelings about your choice to avoid this crucial meeting.

Ella thinks: This may cause her to go ballistic, but I have to speak my truth. I can't just sit back and fume — that's my pattern.

Ella thinks: There she goes again. Every time you call her on something, she just goes into attack mode. I can't work with her!

When both partners have had time to write out their columns, exchange them. Read them over, and see if you can identify moments when your partner slipped into dysfunctional patterns. Together write a new script, sharing more of the right-hand column and using some of the guidelines in this chapter (Ground Rules for Effective Communication or the Nonviolent Communication Practice). Then practice it.

Patricia: Oh by the way, I can't make that meeting on Saturday, something's come up.
Ella: What? Patricia, when I hear you say that, I feel frustrated, sad and deeply disappointed. I need for us to work on our group process in order to make this group function more effectively, and you are a key person in the group.
Patricia: You all go ahead without me. It's fine.
Ella: When you say, "Go ahead without me," I'm hearing a tone of dismissal in your voice. Am I getting that right?
Patricia: Maybe. You know I'm not much of a process-head. I don't like all these "delve into you deepest feelings" sessions.
Ella: What I'm hearing is that you don't feel they are important or productive. Can you be more specific about what you don't feel is valuable?

CONTINUED

Patricia: OK, I'll let you have it straight. I feel like the whole thing is a setup for people to gang up on me. I know I'm blunt and not always the most tactful person in the room, but that's who I am. If you don't like it, tough.

Ella: When you say that, Patricia, I feel frustrated and angry. I want to work with people who are open to hearing constructive critique. And I need to be able to express myself and be who I am. Would you be willing to listen to feedback from the group, if we are careful to keep to the rules of constructive critique?

Patricia: I'm not saying that I'm never willing to hear feedback — I just don't want to be ganged up on.

Ella: Do you have any suggestions on how we might structure the meeting so that you feel safe and that your voice can be heard?

FORMS OF COMMUNICATION

We live in an age in which wonderful new forms of communication are available to us as never before. We can send e-mails, set up listservs, hold virtual meetings online, organize with conference calls, webinars and Skype sessions. However, human beings evolved over millions of years in a world in which there was only one form of communication — face to face. We are sublimely equipped to read other peoples' body language, facial expressions and tones of voice. On a more subtle level, we sense energy. Psychologist Albert Mehrabian's studies suggest that only 7% of meaning comes through words, while 38% comes in the tone with which they are said, and 55% comes through facial expression and body language.

Face-to-face communication is important for groups. We bond more easily in one another's physical presence. Other forms of communication are useful, but they don't completely substitute for physical presence in real-time meetings. Yet we also live in an age in which much of work transcends place. We may be devoted to the idea of relocalization, but we organize around it nationally and globally. Our networks and our friendships are far-flung, and we cannot always meet in person.

Moreover, with climate change heating up the planet, many of us want to reduce our travel and our fossil fuel footprints. In a tumultuous economy, our groups often don't have the resources to support face-to-face meetings across long distances. When we can't meet in person, we must put extra care, thought and attention into making our online gatherings effective.

Groups can work together most easily online when they have first had a chance to meet face to face. Whenever possible, a group that meets virtually should try to arrange at least one foundational meeting in person. Once we have seen, touched and been in the presence of another person, we can picture her expressions and hear his voice even in cold words on a screen. Until we've done that, we may have great difficulty in feeling a sense of true connection. Shadowy virtual presences can easily become screens for our projections and fears.

Written communication is different from spoken communication. When we read a piece of writing, we don't necessarily hear the tone of voice or follow the intention of the writer. When we write, we don't necessarily know how our post will be read. Smiley faces and emoticons notwithstanding, there is no substitute for care and thought in written communication. When topics are controversial or emotional, be especially careful and thoughtful in what you write. Take a breath. Stop before you push that Send button, and reread what you've written. Try to imagine how your post might sound to someone who does not already know what you are trying to convey. Ask yourself, "Is there a worst-case interpretation someone could make of this?" When in doubt, ask a friend to review your message before you send it on.

Online communication is also never truly and reliably private. Most likely all of us have had the painful experience of dashing off a note to a friend — possibly one discussing in blunt terms someone else in the group — and then accidentally sending it to the entire group. But even communications we send privately might not remain so — the Wikileaks diplomatic scandals are a case in point. I've even had a private e-mail turn up as evidence in a court case. Guards at border crossings have been known to Google people or look them up on Facebook. So take care in what you put online: it may go places you never expected it to.

Online communication can be extremely useful. Here are a few guidelines to help them be most effective.

A Clear Intention

Listservs are most useful when their intention is clear. Is this an announcement-only listserv, a discussion forum, a friendship group, an organizing tool? How do people join it, and how do they leave?

Clear Guidelines on What Is and Is Not Appropriate to Post

Can I repost every political announcement that comes my way? Is this the place to denounce the bad behavior of one of the members? Can I ask for emotional support when my relationship falls apart? Can I ask for advice on a project or money to support an organization?

Here's an example of clear guidelines that have served one group well:

> This is a listserv for students who have completed an Earth Activist Training. We welcome your posts about permaculture, spirit and activism, and your sharing or questions about projects you are involved in. Traffic on this list tends to be light. You are welcome to post about anything you are actually involved in. Job announcements, grant opportunities, etc. are also welcome. When it comes to reposting political announcements, if you are actively involved in the campaign yourself, go ahead. But if it's just something that came across your desktop, no matter how vitally important, please don't pass it on here. We want to keep this list for projects we ourselves are doing. We welcome lively discussion and disagreement, but keep it on topic and please, no personal attacks.

Conflict Online

Conflicts simply cannot be resolved over e-mail or online. Let me say that again: conflicts simply cannot be resolved over e-mail or online. Attempts to resolve disputes online generally only make them worse. When people write, they tend to get more formal and rigid in their thinking, more huffy and self-righteous. When I'm writing, I can't see the person I'm writing to, and I don't know how my words affect them.

One guideline collaborative groups are strongly advised to adopt: discourage people from putting their personal conflicts online. Instead, ask them to meet face to face or at least to talk on the telephone or via Skype — in some form where they can hear and ideally also see one another. Encourage and support mediation if necessary. But do not use listservs or online forums as places to resolve personal conflicts.

If people do continue to use online forums for personal conflicts or to air grievances, the group may have a structural lack. Perhaps there is no appropriate forum in which grievances can be addressed or issues dealt with. If that proves to be the case, the group should look for ways to create structures for constructive critique and feedback. The discussion might shift from the personal conflict to problem-solving around the overall need for feedback and accountability.

Hold the Boundaries

Online groups may need someone who has the authority to enforce the guidelines. That might be the moderator of a listserv, who can if necessary remove a person from the list. It might be the group as a whole, who will step up and remind people that certain types of communication do not belong on the list. It might be someone charged with that specific task.

ACCOUNTABILITY

To invest trust, we need some way of knowing whether that trust is justified. We need to hold one another accountable and to build in structures of accountability to our groups. To be effective, groups that take on tasks must have some way of knowing that the work is getting done. Are people keeping commitments, doing what they said they would do? Are deadlines getting met? If not, who is picking up the pieces?

In collaborative groups, we need to consciously put in place mechanisms of reporting and accounting. Some of these might be:

Reports at Meetings

At each group meeting, we hear reports on every aspect of the project. We are collectively responsible for making sure it goes forward.

Reports Online

Online communication can be extremely useful for checking in on the progress of projects.

Individual Responsibility

One person might take on the responsibility for a certain task or aspect of organization. The Spanish term for this role is *responsable* — the responsible one. In Earth First circles, they call this person the "bottom liner" an oddly capitalist term for such a radical group — although it does a good job of conveying the sense of holding the ground on a project and leading from below. That individual may still report back to a larger circle.

The Buddy System

Responsables buddy up so that each has someone to report to, to go to for support or feedback and to take over if one person becomes incapacitated.

The Mentor System

More experienced folks take on training and providing oversight and support for newer bottom liners.

Diana Leafe Christian, who studied successful intentional communities around the world for her book *Creating a Life Together,* suggests that public accountability can be highly effective without blaming or shaming. "It's more difficult to forget or ignore responsibilities when they are publicly visible, when the 'community eye' is on us. People tend to want the appreciation of other people, and to experience ourselves as contributing to the group, not letting it down. Therefore, because other people are watching, the task tends to get done."[19] She recommends:

- Publicly taking on tasks at meetings and reviewing, at each meeting, what has been done — without using shaming or blaming language, but rather offering help and support to complete the undone tasks.
- Creating a publicly visible wall chart, showing the tasks to be done, who has committed to each and who has done them.
- Publicly thanking people and acknowledging when tasks have been completed.

WHAT DO WE MEASURE?

Patrick Lencioni, in *The Three Signs of a Miserable Job,* coined the term *immeasurement:* "Immeasurement essentially is an employee's lack of a clear means of assessing his or her progress or success on the job."[20]

Measurement is empowering when people themselves decide what aspects of their tasks to measure, and when what they measure is something that their own efforts can affect. A group planning an event might measure the number of tickets sold, the number of volunteers, the amount of money taken in. The media committee for a demonstration might decide to count the number of stories placed in newspapers, the number of radio interviews and TV news spots. The outreach committee might count the number of diverse groups that sign on to the coalition. A community garden might measure the pounds of produce given away or the number of bags of compost picked up on the community day.

Bookkeeping and Accounting

For groups that deal with money, keeping accurate and open books is a key aspect of accountability. Bookkeeping is a skill that must be taught, either in some formal program of education or by mentoring and apprenticeship. Especially when a group must account to the tax agencies or to funders for its finances, clear and well-kept accounts are vital to an organization's survival. Many groups who are otherwise completely composed of unpaid volunteers decide to hire a professional for this function.

Because money can be a highly charged issue, sloppy accounting creates a breeding ground for potentially virulent conflicts. Having clear rules and procedures can forestall bitter disputes and accusations that can divide or destroy a group. And for groups that do business, it can be a matter of survival.

Ryan Sarnataro worked at Rainbow Grocery, a worker-owned cooperative, shortly after it began back in the 1970s. Rainbow is now a thriving cooperative business, but it was nearly destroyed at one point in its growth when a bookkeeper was skimming funds. Many other collective food stores that started in the same period and a larger communal warehouse all went out of business, but Rainbow managed to survive. "We were lucky," Ryan says. "Embezzlers didn't embezzle so much they put us out of business. We had an old guy who came in and volunteered to help with the books — but he didn't want to rat out the bookkeeper. He kept talking about internal controls, but none of us had the background to figure out what he meant. But in his case, he didn't feel it would be right to say 'I feel the bookkeeper is embezzling' because the bookkeeper was cagey — he was falsifying records, and it was only later I could figure it out. Rainbow lucked out — it had a couple of us who cared about that stuff. Transparency is really important. You've got to be able to see through what people are doing. You've got to watch out for that bottom rung of bad actors who will take advantage."[21]

Accountability for Process

In collaborative groups, we want to get the work done, but we also care about how we treat one another in the process. We need accountability not just for the work itself, but for the quality of our relationships. Our goals may reflect not just what we want to accomplish, but how we want to do it.

Accordingly, we need to set aside time in meetings and/or create other means for feedback around our process and relationships as well as our tangible accomplishments.

At Meetings

Check-in time can be an opportunity for people to comment on how they are feeling about the work and the group as well as how their tasks are progressing. Meetings should include time at the end for evaluation and feedback, both on what got accomplished and how the meeting went.

Special Meetings

When lots of emotional tangles need to be sorted out, the group might schedule a retreat, a mediation or simply some special time to devote to process.

Online

While conflicts cannot be resolved online, groups that do much work online can use that forum to alert one another that something needs to be addressed and schedule a face-to-face meeting.

Mutual Coaching

Two or more group members might coach one another to help make changes in how they each deal with relationships. They can set times for check-ins, set their own goals and report back to one another.

E
X
E
R
C
I
S
E

Process Accountability Questions

- What do I feel I'm doing well in the group?
- Where am I feeling challenged around the group's work or process?
- Where do I need to step up more? What is my growing edge?

- In what ways do I help the group to function more effectively? In what ways do I generate conflict or discord?
- What kind of support do I need to be more effective in my communications?

Mentoring

The group might provide experienced mentors to newer people or provide the support and resources to find those mentors outside the group.

HOLDING SILENCE

"Silence is death" was at one time a slogan of the gay liberation movement, and sometimes it is. When silence conceals hurt, wrongdoing or abuse, it allows the abuse to continue and breeds shame in the victim. Silence in the face of injustice or oppression is collusion. And politicians have learned, to their sorrow, that silence in the face of a campaign of lies and attacks only encourages the opposition.

But sometimes silence is golden. When we are tempted to intervene in something that truly is not our business, silence can be strength.

We live in a world in which silence has become a rare luxury. We're surrounded by noise and inundated with sound, speech, entertainment and exhortation. We can walk through city streets or wild forests plugged into our own music box and receive phone calls on the tops of mountains. We need never be truly alone with our own thoughts.

Yet it is in solitude and silence that our deepest insights are born. We need to unplug sometimes, to listen to the birds and the wind and the rain. Even in groups and circles, sometimes the greatest intimacy can be found, not in speech, but in those moments when we sit silently together. A rapt silence is the gift a listener gives to a powerful story or an enchanting song. An engaged silence, a silence of deep listening and profound attention, may be the most healing response to those intense losses that no words can comfort.

We may win more respect by silence than by excessive talking. One year when I attended a Bioregional Congress held in Tepoztlan, Mexico, I had a horrible case of laryngitis. For several days, I could hardly utter a sound. To speak was such a painful effort that in the first five days I only contributed once or twice to meetings. To my surprise, the things I did say were listened to, repeated and many people came up and thanked me for my wisdom. Such wisdom as I have is usually diluted with lots of chatter. When the chatter was stilled, when I had to wrestle with every sentence, the few true pearls I had to offer were undimmed by the costume jewelry of constant pontification.

Groups function best when we make a discipline of balancing speech and silence. Those who hold social power, who feel entitled to speak on every topic, might make a practice of holding back. If something has been said before, you don't need to repeat it. If someone has expressed an idea with a bit of awkwardness, you don't need to step in and rephrase it for them more eloquently or tell the group what they really meant to say.

BUILDING TRUST

Trust and friendship are key rewards for working in collaborative groups. We join groups for two overriding sets of reasons: one because we care about the work or the subject matter the group addresses, the other because we hope for human connection. Groups are most effective at getting the work done when people enjoy one another's company and trust one another.

We build trust in a group through many sorts of communication. First, to trust one another we must know one another. We must have opportunities to share information, feelings, stories, to learn something about one another's lives outside the group project.

Small groups may meet this need by beginning meetings with a check-in, a short round where people get to catch each other up on their lives outside the group. At minimum, a check-in time may offer group members a chance to share anything that might be affecting their mood or focus at a meeting.

Larger groups may not have time for everyone to check in at every meeting. Business or work-focused groups may not feel that personal sharing at every meeting is appropriate. They may want to schedule a special retreat or a series of meetings where people can connect without the pressure of normal business. Or individuals may simply make an effort to connect informally with other group members, to ask about their lives outside the group and to show interest in their many facets as people.

Groups also bond by having fun together. Outings, field trips, hiking, camping, adventures such as river rafting or a ropes course, potlucks, dinners out, parties, garden days can all help a group know each other in ways that go beyond the business at hand. Reserved people who might not feel comfortable sharing in a meeting may open up on a hike or reveal a more flamboyant side at a party.

Hearing one another's personal stories can also help build trust. In a community where issues like money may become hot topics, we'll understand one another much better if we take time to tell our own stories about how our families of origin dealt with money and our own money history. In groups attempting to bridge differences of race, class, religion, gender or sexual orientation, taking time to share our own histories, our ancestor and family stories can build powerful bonds of understanding and trust.

Articulating a vision and shared values can also help build trust. When I know that the values I care about are important to others, that we share a picture of the world we want and are working toward common goals, I can trust my fellow members' intentions.

Shared work builds trust — or destroys it! When we take on projects together, when we observe how someone keeps their commitments and performs their tasks, we come to trust their word. Working together we may learn to trust another person's skills, knowledge or expertise — or perhaps, we might come to trust that they know their limitations and can ask for help when a task is beyond their capacities.

Trust is also built under fire. Times of crisis are when trust is tested. When we face danger together, when we come through a conflict or a difficult situation, when we show solidarity and look out for one another, we build trust. The TreePeople, who have locked arms while police attempted to drag them off platforms, who have stayed together through cold and wind and rain, brought one another food and comforted each other in jail have a level of trust and connection that is qualitatively different from the kind of bonds they may forge with the rest of RootBound.

Trust is also built by how we handle conflict within a group. Patrick Lencioni makes the point that trust is created not by avoiding conflict but by embracing it.[22] Open, passionate conflict around ideas creates excitement and trust — provided it does not descend into personal attack. When I know that others will stand up for their ideas, I can argue strongly for my point of view. When a group encourages open and respectful disagreement and debate, ideas are sharpened and potential flaws can be exposed.

Finally, trust is built by including the spirit, by sharing rituals and celebrations that honor our deepest, most sacred values, by creating opportunities to connect from the heart as well as the head. Spirituality is more than meditation, it can also lead us to action and is perhaps most profoundly expressed in service.[23] A moment of silence, a deep breath, a time for people to share the things they truly care about, a song, a poem, a dance break, a simple blessing over a shared meal can all bring people to touch that deeper level of commitment and care that inspires our greatest creativity.

CHAPTER 6

Leadership Roles for Leaderless Groups

WHAT THE BIRDS TEACH

Three days later, Ella and Eli met Marta at the tail end of one of her lectures on the Berkeley campus. They slipped into the large auditorium just before the end of class, and looked at the slide show Marta had onscreen, naming various types of leaders. Eli found himself grabbing for a non-existant notebook, reduced to tapping notes into an app on his smartphone.

When the class had cleared out, they met Marta at the door and offered her a ride back to her home.

"This was a brilliant chapter," Ella said, "But I can't tell you how relieved I am to give it back to you. I could hardly sleep at night, for fear the house would catch fire and destroy your only copy."

Marta just smiled. "You have justified my trust," she said, slipping the papers into her bag.

Together they strolled across the campus toward the lot where the Sterns had parked.

"I was interested in your leadership definitions," Eli said.

"Ah yes," Marta said. "And which kind of leader do you feel you are at RootBound?"

"I'm the type of leader that's trying not to be a leader but to get everyone else to step up," he said. "What do you call that?"

"Illusion," Marta said. "You cannot lead by avoiding your power or pretending it's not there. I'd like to see you own your authority."

"How can I own it when I'm trying to disown it?" Eli asked.

"Exactly," Marta said.

They walked on for a moment in silence, under a grove of acacias. As they passed, a flock of blackbirds rose up, squawking in indignation, wheeled in formation and flew off toward a further grove of trees.

Marta stopped.

"Observe the birds," she said. "What can we learn from them?"

"Not to stand under the acacias?" Eli suggested, wiping a white smear off his shoulder with his handkerchief.

"They don't seem to have issues about acting in unity," Ella said.

"Do you ever wonder how they do it?" Marta asked.

"Perhaps they have a Starling Commander who issues orders," Eli suggested. "OK, birds, we're going to rise up, bank to the left and fly to the next grove. Starlita, you'll be on my left flank — Blackie, you'll be on my right."

"No, don't you hear them always chattering?" Ella said. "They're doing Starling consensus. 'Oh oh — people are coming! I propose we fly off.' 'I have a clarifying question — do you mean, "fly off immediately" or wait until they get closer?'"

"I have a concern," Eli chimed in. "Define 'off.' How can we fly when we don't know where we're flying to?'"

Marta laughed. "Fortunately for the survival of starlingkind, they do neither. I'll tell you what happens — one has the impulse to go and takes off. The others see the movement and decide to follow. Suddenly, they are a flock. Is that not how you exercise leadership, Eli? You see a direction, head there yourself strongly and bring others along in your wake."

"I guess I do," Eli admitted.

"That's not a bad thing — it's a gift," Marta said. "Ella, you also have a gift. You are what I would call an affiliative leader. You bring people together, create harmony and good feelings in the group."

"Lately, not so much," Ella said sadly.

"But here's what we came to ask you," Eli said. "The board is pressing us to have a conflict resolution meeting, this coming Saturday. Would you be available, and willing, to facilitate it?"

"Personally, I'd rather put it off and do some of the other work you've suggested," Ella admitted. "But feelings are running so high — and because all of this is being argued out on the Internet lists, we've got people from all over pressuring us to do something. If we refuse, it looks like we're not responsive and just trying to sweep the issue under the rug."

"So you want to put my theories to the test?" Marta said.

"Please!" Eli and Ella said in unison.

"All right, then," Marta agreed. "But in return, I want you to do something for me."

"Anything!" Eli promised.

"I want you to look at this," Marta reached into her bag and drew out her class handout. "Answer these questions, consider your roles in RootBound and what roles are needed to bring the organization back to health."

On the sheet was another quartered circle, with small pictures of animals drawn in each section.

"Just as the talisman lays out qualities needed for group health, this mandala shows the roles associated with each direction," Marta said. "A group that functions well is never leaderless — just the opposite. It's 'leaderful' — but that leadership is fluid and takes on many different dimensions. The two of you fulfill some of these roles, but I'm sure there are others in RootBound who complement your strengths and who can be brought into this effort to renew the health of the community. Look this over, and by Saturday I'll expect you to have answered the questions and to come back with a list. Who in RootBound functions as a Crow, a Snake, a Grace, a Dragon or a Spider? How might their strengths be marshaled to move the community forward?"

ROLES IN COLLABORATIVE GROUPS

Collaborative groups share power, and healthy groups assure that their members have equal opportunity to earn social power. But equal does not mean identical. In collaborative groups, many different roles exist, including leadership roles of many kinds. Even when people hold equal formal power, they will still do different things, take on different kinds of responsibilities and function in different ways. This diversity can be a source of resilience or an arena of bitter conflict.

People with progressive, feminist or anarchist ideals may sometimes feel deeply uncomfortable with the concept of leadership. We tend to resist the domination of leaders in a command-and-control frame — as bosses, lords, generals that must be obeyed. The larger society around us, meanwhile, assumes that every group or endeavor must have someone in charge, or it will not function.

Collaborative groups may do away with power-over. In a collaborative group, no CEO may hold the formal power to hire or fire the others. There are no bosses and no masters. But collaborative groups still need people who take on tasks, who shoulder responsibilities, who keep an overview of group needs and tasks, who step out in front and say, "Let's go in this direction." All of these, and more, are aspects of what I call empowering leadership.

The role of an empowering leader is not to wield all the power in the group, but to spread it around, to create and defend a habitat where power-from-within can flourish in everyone. Empowering leaders do not command or issue orders. They lead by inspiration and persuasion.

> Instead of a chief, the Apaches had a *Nant'an* — a spiritual and cultural leader. The *Nant'an* led by example and held no coercive power. Tribal members followed the *Nant'an* because they wanted to, not because they had to. One of the most famous *Nant'ans* in history was Geronimo, who defended his people from the American forces for decades. Geronimo never commanded an army. Rather, he himself started fighting, and everyone around him joined in. The idea was, "If Geronimo is taking arms, maybe it's a good idea. Geronimo's been right in the past, so it makes sense to fight alongside him." You wanted to follow Geronimo? Then you followed Geronimo. You didn't want to follow him? Then you didn't. The power lay with each individual, you were free to do what you wanted. The phrase "you should" doesn't even exist in the Apache language. Coercion is a foreign concept.[1]

Picture a group of friends hiking through the woods. They may sit down at lunchtime and share food and conversation in a circle. But when they set off to climb a narrow and rocky path, they won't get far if they try to do it holding hands in a ring. Someone needs to step out in front and break trail. An empowering leader smoothes the path for others. An empowering leader might also take another position, step back from being trailbreaker and perhaps be the sweep at the back, making sure the slowest and weakest are not left behind.

Some creative projects are solitary, but many — from a dramatic production or a new community garden to challenging entrenched oppressive systems — can only be done together. That's why we form groups. So at times, we'll each be asking others to support our vision. And in turn, we will often be the support for others.

MULTIPLE LEADERSHIP ROLES

Collaborative groups do well to think of leadership not as a quality invested in particular persons, but as a set of roles and functions that we can each step into or back from.

Hierarchies have many formal roles and titles — CEO, General Manager, Line Producer — and generally those roles remain fixed.

Collaborative groups may also have formal roles: facilitator, treasurer, Compost Queen Extraordinaire. Often those roles circulate, particularly when they confer social power or potential power-over. The same person does not facilitate every meeting — we pass that task on because the facilitator potentially holds a great deal of power in the group. We recruit numerous people to speak to the media so that one person does not become identified as the voice of the group.

There are some exceptions. Specialized skills, such as bookkeeping and tasks that require experience or expertise, can only be circulated among those who have the necessary training and skill. For example, facilitating a large, tense meeting is not something that should be passed on to an inexperienced, new facilitator. If a group is committed to rotating roles, it must also commit to training and mentoring to help people develop the necessary abilities to carry out their tasks.

E
X
E
R
C
I
S
E

Questions About Formal Roles

- What are the formal leadership roles in your group?
- Who holds them?
- How do people acquire their roles? Do they volunteer? Are they elected or chosen?
- Do the roles rotate? If so, how are people trained or prepared to step into their new roles?

- If the roles don't rotate, how are they passed on?
- How do people train their successors?
- Are there any limits on how many roles people can hold at a given time?

Many groups are hybrids of collaborative and hierarchical structures. A group may function as a collective of equals, discover that to do its business it needs some form of legal tax status and incorporate as a non-profit with a board of directors. A department in a progressive university may make most decisions in common, even though the head of the department has the formal power in reserve to hire and fire her colleagues. Hybrid groups, too, may have a variety of formal roles. A nonprofit may be required to have, at minimum, a President, Secretary and Treasurer. A worker-owned cooperative that runs a grocery business may designate someone to keep the books, someone else to order the produce and a third person to take charge of dry goods.

CATALYSTS AND CHAMPIONS

Collaborative groups also have informal roles, and they are less clearly defined. Indeed, we may be unaware of the roles we are playing. Brafman and Beckstrom, in *The Starfish and the Spider,* identify two important informal roles in decentralized groups: the catalyst and the champion.[2]

The *catalyst* sets things in motion. Often the catalyst is an inspiring and/or charismatic person who fires up the group with creative ideas. A catalyst generally has a high degree of social power, earned or unearned, or both. They may have lots of street cred — the credibility that comes from hard experience, real or claimed. They may have written books or performed heroic or inspiring acts.

Eli and Ella were catalysts for RootBound. Their energy and enthusiasm got people fired up and enthused about the project. Eli also serves as a catalyst in many communities. He arrives, gives a talk and a workshop that draw out many people who have an interest in intentional communities and cohousing. He encourages them to link up and to form their own projects that will carry on after he is gone.

Catalysts are ephemeral. A catalyst might light the match, but she generally doesn't stick around to fan the flames or feed the fire. That role is played by the *champion.*

Champions are the organizers who make things happen. The champion is the powerhouse of a group, the one who pushes it through obstacles and defends it against enemies, external and internal. The champion puts sustained energy into the group. Without champions, no group or movement grows and expands.

I have often played the role of catalyst — writing books, making videos, coming into many locations to lead workshops and teach people everything from ritual to direct action to permaculture. But circles and rituals, campaigns and organic gardens do not spring up everywhere I go. Only where someone has stepped up to champion the work does it take root and grow into something lasting. When someone says, "I want to bring someone in to teach. I want to organize a workshop here. I want to start a circle. I want to make something happen," it does. As a catalyst, my books or my presence may ignite a longing for community, but the champion provides the kindling, the sticks and the logs that will feed the fire and allow it to warm a hearth.

These roles are informal and often go unrecognized and undefined. But collaborative groups and the larger social movements they are part of need both catalysts and champions.

THE MANDALA OF GROUP ROLES

In my earlier book *Truth or Dare,* I identified five key roles every group needs and placed them in a mandala that can be overlaid on the Talisman of Healthy Groups.[3] Graces, Dragons, Crows, Snakes and Spiders together weave an effective group.

The Axis of Action
South – Fire – Graces

Graces represent the enthusiasm and passion that we associate with fire — and fire is energy, the power and fuel that drives a group. Fire is also the hearth fire, and Graces are welcomers who bring people into the group and make them feel at home. For newcomers, they are the gracious hosts of the group. For old-timers, they generate the warmth and appreciation that comes with earned social power.

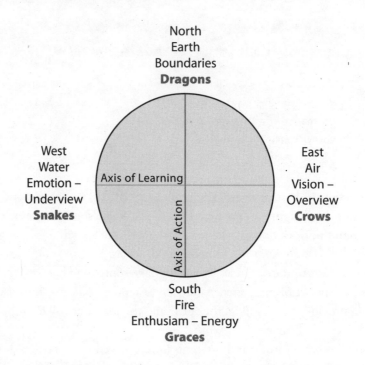

The Mandala of Group Roles

North – Earth – Dragons

Dragons are the group's *responsables*. They ground the group — that is, they hold the bottom line on responsibility, asking those hard questions like, "Do we have the resources to carry out this project? Who is going to actually do it?"

Dragons also champion the group as guardians and protectors. They may protect the group from intrusion or from breaking apart under its own centrifugal force. They guard the group's boundaries and manage the edges, those dynamic zones where the group's culture intersects the larger forces around it.

The Axis of Learning

East – Air – Crows

Crows are closest to what we generally think of as leaders. They keep an overview — what are our goals, and are we moving toward them? What might change in the future, and how do we adapt? What obstacles and unforeseen crises might we encounter, and how do we prepare? Who is keeping their commitments, and who is letting things slide? What's falling through the cracks?

Crows keep us on track by looking ahead. They keep account of what we've done and what we still need to do in order to reach our goals.

West – Water – Snakes

Snakes keep an underview. They watch the group's process and also help the group adopt practices and projects that build connections. They watch the patterns of emotion and communication in the group, and bring hidden conflicts up into the light. They challenge groupthink, keep watch on gossip and look at what is not being said or spoken about openly or directly.

Snakes may make people uncomfortable, and Snake is an uneasy role to fulfill. But in nature, snakes shed their skin and emerge, renewed. Groups, too, occasionally need to molt, shedding bad habits and old, ineffective patterns. Ultimately, snakes help build group trust by encouraging conflicts to be open instead of covert.

Center – Connection – Spiders

Spiders sit in the center of their webs, and from that position they can feel any movement in any part of the pattern. In groups, Spiders are the central connectors who watch the group's communications. They may set up avenues to communicate — listservs, aptly named websites, phone trees. They ask questions like, "Who needs to know about this decision? Who should be part of making it?"

Spiders may also be great connectors to people outside the group — the networkers that always know just the right person you should be in contact with.

These roles may be unspoken and informal. Some of us may be natural Graces, bringing bubbling enthusiasm and energy to all we do. Others may be born Snakes, always watching the emotions and seeing the underside, or Spiders who love nothing more than to link up people who share common interests. In collaborative groups, we can all be empowered to take on these various aspects of leadership without waiting for authority to be delegated.

A group may also find value in formalizing these roles. In Reclaiming rituals, we often designate a Crow or Crows to keep an overview of the flow. Graces welcome people and help those with special needs; for example, finding chairs for those who cannot stand for long periods of time or answering questions from newcomers. Dragons are the security people, who watch the edge of the circle and intervene when the drunk wanders in from further down the park or the police arrive and ask for the permit.

Taking on a formalized role may have a deep personal impact. When a group from our Pagan Cluster came to St. Paul in 2008 to protest the Republican National Convention, we planned a new moon ritual. A group of young people who were cycling from Milwaukee to St. Paul to join the protest had planned their arrival for the same park on the same evening. We decided to join forces, and asked them to be Dragons for our ritual.

The young cyclists were very taken with the idea of Dragons. On their trip, they made themselves dragon costumes and dragon headdresses. When they arrived, after riding for hundreds of miles, they sailed into the park and literally rode circles around us to establish the boundaries of the ritual circle. Throughout the ritual, they stood in witness, prepared to intervene if we were harassed by police, counterprotestors or bystanders.

Afterwards, Thistle, who had been our contact with the group, told me, "This was such a powerful experience for us. We spent a long time talking about what it means to be a Dragon, to hold that guardian energy. It felt really good to stand strong on the boundaries. And I think the discussion and process had a positive

E X E R C I S E

Mandala Role Experiment

Divide into pairs and discuss these questions:

- Which roles do you naturally tend to take on? In your life? In this group?
- Which roles are you less comfortable with, or less able at fulfilling?
- Which roles do you actively avoid?
- Which roles are filled in your group by someone?
- Are there any of these roles which are not filled?
- In your group, which roles confer social power?
- Which roles are likely to generate resistance or conflict?

For the next group meeting or project, commit yourself to taking on a role that feels uncomfortable to you, one which you would ordinarily not take. Share that decision with your partner, and ask for any support you feel you may need.

After the meeting or project, take time to check back in:

- How was the experience for you?
- What feelings came up?
- What did you notice or perceive in that role that you might otherwise have missed?
- What did you learn?

impact on our group dynamics. The effects will stay with us for a long time, I'm sure."[4]

SIX TYPES OF LEADERSHIP

Another way to look at leadership comes from Daniel Goleman, who pioneered the concept of emotional intelligence, collaborating with researchers Richard Boyatzis and Annie McKee.[5] They examine six types of leadership: the Visionary style, the Affiliative style, the Coaching style, the Democratic style, the Pacesetting style and the Commanding style. The authors compare them to the set of clubs in a golfer's bag — each style is useful under certain conditions, and each can be used well or badly.

The first four styles build group resonance, group harmony, connection and satisfaction.

Visionary

> I inspire people with a big vision and take the long view. I keep my eyes on the prize.

The Visionary can help us articulate our picture of the world we want, our sense of mission and purpose, our core values and our short and long-term goals — and identify the stakes, what is at risk if we fail.

The Visionary style is most needed when a group is beginning, when it must take a new direction or make changes in its mission or structure.

Coaching

> I bring out the best in each person. I help them develop their talents and strengths and overcome weaknesses.

The Coach cares about each individual, helps them identify and build on their skills and talents and to grow beyond their lacks. Coaches look for opportunities for others to develop and grow and to shine. Coaches encourage us to try new things and help cushion the fall when we stumble.

The Coaching style is most needed when individual group members need support or challenge in order to grow. When dealing with disturbed individuals or traumatized communities, one-on-one coaching may be far more effective than public exhortations or admonitions.

Affiliative

> I get groups of people to work together well and to bond in friendship.

The Affiliative leader is the team builder, bringing people together to work in concert toward a goal, building trust and creating an atmosphere of friendship and harmony in the group.

The Affiliative style is most needed when the group is in conflict, when it is undergoing stress or deep disagreements.

Democratic

> I listen to everybody and involve them in decisions that affect them. I welcome feedback and constructive criticism.

The Democratic leader creates an atmosphere of inclusiveness and open participation. The Democrat makes sure that all voices are heard and that power is not concentrated in one or a few hands.

While these four types of leadership tend to create resonance, if they fall out of balance they can each have their drawbacks.

Unbalanced Visionary

A Visionary leader may sometimes be so far ahead of the group and its resources that they shift from inspiring to overwhelming. Visionaries may need grounding and support from those whose strengths are in holding boundaries, respecting limits and keeping track of details.

Unbalanced Coaching

Coaches may err by sacrificing the needs of the group to the growth of the individual. Other team members may resent a Coach's special relationship with one individual. Coaches may need support from those who can watch the emotional balance of the whole.

Unbalanced Affiliative

Affiliative leaders may have trouble giving critical feedback, in holding boundaries or insisting on accountability. They may err on the side of being "nice" and condone behavior that actually undermines group harmony. Affiliatives need support from those who can give clear, constructive feedback, set boundaries and hold group members accountable.

Unbalanced Democratic

Democratic leaders may have trouble stepping into command when necessary. Sometimes decisions need to be made, and the group needs to push forward. Democratic leaders may need support from those who can push forward the group's momentum, make clear decisions and set directions.

The next two styles build group dissonance or disharmony, but also have their uses.

Pacesetting

I set a high bar and a fast pace — for myself, most of all.

Pacesetters drive the group to achieve more and complete tasks quickly. They take on big challenges and create the momentum we need to fulfill them — and can easily overwhelm lesser mortals and leave them panting in the dust.

The Pacesetting style is most useful when the group faces a big challenge, an emergency or a deadline. A strong Pacesetter can sometimes motivate a group to clear a big hurdle. But if workaholic, frantic pacesetting is the default mode, it's a sign that planning, forethought and self-care are lacking. Groups driven by Pacesetters often burn out.

Commanding

I take control. I give clear direction. I know what needs to be done, and I tell people what to do. I create order.

The Commanding style is a very familiar one. In collaborative groups, this style might be inappropriate, and group members who revert to it may face rebellion and resentment. However, in times of crisis or emergency, someone who takes command may save the group from disaster. When people are frightened, confused and unsure of what to do, someone with a strong idea of how to move forward can help mobilize the group and empower people to take action.

While these two leadership styles run the risk of creating resentment and disharmony, they can each have their positive side.

Positive Pacesetter

In a crisis, when a deadline looms, when we need to put shoulder to the wheel and work round the clock to get the job done, a good Pacesetter inspires by example. She does more than just manage and drive the work; she gets her own hands dirty, digs in and does it. Bouts of Pacesetting frenzy can energize a group and get it through moments of crisis.

Positive Commander

In an emergency, when adrenaline runs high, confusion often reigns supreme. People panic, forget what to do and can't find the relevant tools or information. Emergency services, armies and medical personnel are often organized in strict

E
X
E
R
C
I
S
E

Questions About Leadership Style

- Which of the six styles above do you tend to employ? Which are most comfortable for you?
- Which of the styles above are uncomfortable?
- What are your own strengths and weaknesses as a leader? Where are you effective, and where could you use support and/or constructive critique?
- Can you think of a time when you or someone else has used one of these styles effectively? What did they do? What impact did it have?
- Can you think of a group or organization that did effective work? Who were its leaders, and which of these styles did they employ?
- Which styles are most prevalent in your group?

Leadership Style Role-play

Take a pile of three-by-five cards, write one of the six styles on each of six cards, and leave the others blank. Shuffle them and pass them out so that no one sees anybody else's cards. Each person should then look at their own card and act out this role in one of the following scenarios (or something more appropriate to your group, if none of these fit).

- RootBound has discovered a structural flaw in the foundation of its community house, which will cost $50,000 to fix. A general meeting has been called to discuss what to do.
- Your city council has put out a request for proposals for groups who want to combine environmental education with job training for at risk youth.

CONTINUED

- You are a sustainability group that wants to create a new program.
- You are Transition Town Seaside, a group helping your coastal community come together to plan a low-carbon future. At your meeting, you are interrupted with the news that a devastating hurricane is about to hit.

Let the scenario develop for 15 to 30 minutes, then stop it and debrief:

- Who took leadership? In what way?
- Which styles of leadership did people employ? Did they do so in a balanced or imbalanced way?
- Which were effective? Less effective?
- What could have been done differently that might have been more effective?

Leadership Style Practice

Divide into pairs and discuss the questions about leadership styles above. For the next group meeting or project, commit yourself to taking on a style of leadership that feels uncomfortable to you, one which you would ordinarily not take, or choose one that you feel you would like to develop more fully. Share that decision with your partner, and ask for any support you feel you may need. After the meeting or project, take time to check back in:

- How was the experience for you?
- What feelings came up?
- Do you feel you used that style in a balanced or imbalanced way?
- What things did people do or say that pulled you toward imbalance?
- What did you notice or perceive, using that leadership style, that you might otherwise have missed?
- What did you learn?

command structures because they know that when anxiety is overwhelming, training, practice and clear lines of command are necessary.

But when the emergency or the danger is over, in a collaborative group the Commander steps back down. Those who like the position of Command aren't always eager to do so. Indeed, we see how governments can manufacture and sustain crises sometimes for decades or generations in order to justify more and more structures of control. The temporary wartime leader becomes institutionalized as the king.

In collaborative groups, we generally try to cultivate the first four aspects of leadership. We may from time to time step into the last two roles — indeed, to be effective we need to have them available to us. But we don't stay there long, if we're wise. As we grow into leadership, we can consciously develop our ability to employ the right style for the right need.

A PORTRAIT OF EMPOWERING LEADERSHIP

An empowering leader holds and serves a vision broad and deep enough to inspire others and allow them to take parts of it and make it their own. When Rob Hopkins founded the Transition Town movement, his vision was to take the insights of permaculture and ecological design and apply them on a local community level. That was a big vision, far too big for any one person to realize alone. Within it, there was room for many people to step up and realize their own creative ideas and pursue their interests — how to transform a vacant lot into a community garden, how to plant forest gardens in city parks, how to influence policy around water resources or investment in renewable energy. Rob's original vision called many people into their own power and leadership.

An empowering leader also helps the group develop a strategy — a plan for getting from here to there, with milestones and goals along the way.

An empowering leader is comfortable playing many roles and using the whole spectrum of leadership styles.

An empowering leader rarely uses Command mode. Most of the time, she leads by example and persuasion. But when Command is called for, an empowering leader will step forward and then step back into a more Democratic mode once the need has passed.

An empowering leader takes risks. In *Lord of the Rings,* the true leaders take the most dangerous position, leading the troops into battle. The evil lord Sauron and the corrupted Steward Denethor sit in safety, directing from behind.

Most of us are not subject to orc attacks in our daily group activities. The risks we take are those of failure, being seen badly by others, public humiliation, financial liability — and sometimes being stabbed in the back by our own group members. An empowering leader is willing to put themselves on the line for the group's mission.

An empowering leader also steps back. He doesn't hog the center or the spotlight, but is always looking for ways to share.

An empowering leader puts the needs of the group first. He thinks about how each of his actions will affect the group.

An empowering leader plans for succession. She trains her successors while she is still in love with doing a particular job and can't imagine that she'd ever want to step away from it.

An empowering leader practices good self-care. She takes on only those responsibilities she can fulfill joyfully, takes breaks and rests when she's tired. He looks after his own health and well-being, for he knows that sacrificing his basic needs will not truly serve either the group or himself over the long run.

All of this is, of course, the ideal. We can strive for it, but most of us will fall short in one way or another. An empowering leader makes mistakes. If she doesn't, she's probably not experimenting enough. An empowering leader is also a good learner, an experienced and willing apologizer, someone who can make amends and move on.

Keep Power Circulating

Power tends to concentrate, and even the most benevolent and empowering leader may unconsciously begin to hoard power over time. When power becomes permanent and static, the group often stagnates.

Collaborative groups need strategies for sharing power and developing leadership in all group members. To keep power circulating and flowing freely in the group, we can adopt a few key elements in our structure.

Limit the Accumulation of Power

We can make agreements that limit how much responsibility any one person can take on, how many committees they can join, for example, or how many aspects of a project they can coordinate. We can break big tasks into smaller roles and share them.

Share Roles and Responsibilities

Meetings typically are co-facilitated, so that a powerful role is shared. In Reclaiming, we co-teach our classes on Goddess spirituality, to model shared power, so that students get more than one perspective and so that no one person is seen as the spiritual guru. When roles can be shared, we can also reinforce one another's strengths and compensate for our weaknesses. A born Grace whose strengths are affiliative might look for a partner who is more of a boundary-setting Dragon.

Rotate Roles and Responsibilities

Many roles benefit by being rotated — for example, meeting facilitation. Some roles put people in center stage — media spokes, for example, or convener of a gathering. People who take on those roles get more attention — both positive and negative. Rotating them can spread both the praise and the blame around more fairly.

Other roles are more in the nature of chores that must be done — taking notes at meetings and distributing them, turning the compost, doing the dishes after the potluck. When they are shared, no one person is stuck with an unpopular task.

Train and Apprentice

Some roles require training and preparation: facilitating big meetings, keeping accurate books, propagating cuttings in the greenhouse. For the long-term growth of the group, we can create ways that people can learn, apprentice and be mentored in those skills. And when skills are needed by the group as a whole — for example, communication skills, consensus process skills — the group should devote resources to provide overall training for all its members. It will be well repaid over the long term by improvements in function and by hours and hours of fruitless arguments avoided!

Pass Power On

Because roles of power are fluid in collaborative groups, part of a leader's job is to sense when and how to pass the power on. Power circulates, and we can trust that, when we let go, others will take on the tasks and responsibilities, freeing us up to find new areas of interest and new challenges.

Let Go Gracefully

In a ritual, we often drum up a cone of power, bringing the group to a peak of excitement. Drummers, of course, love to speed up and go into a dramatic drum roll — but we discourage them from doing so because then they control the pacing and the buildup of energy (and often get it wrong). Instead, we teach them to hold a steady pace, listen to the group and follow the energy instead of driving it. As the cone rises, the drummers fade back until only voices are left. The voices raise the cone, because everyone has a voice, though not everyone has a drum.

When done right, no one consciously notices that the drumming has stopped, only that sound and energy fill the room with shared, ecstatic communion.

An empowering leader is like a drummer. She provides a steady beat around which a group can coalesce. He brings in new rhythms and riffs that set your feet dancing. If the leader/drummer drops out too abruptly, the group feels abandoned, adrift and may not have the skills or direction to continue. If the leader/drummer holds on too long, the group may begin to chafe and rebel.

Reclaiming began as a small collective in San Francisco. In the late 1980s, we were asked to teach a weeklong Witch Camp outside of Vancouver, British Columbia. For a few years, five to ten of us would come up to Canada and teach. We began training our successors early. Our original goal was to empower people locally to do their own rituals and seed their own community. But when we had trained enough teachers to carry on, we announced abruptly that we weren't coming back. By fiat, we declared that everyone who had taught or student taught at the camp was now a member of a new teachers' collective, and we left all decisions about the future up to them.

We were like drummers quitting suddenly, before the cone had begun to rise. Our pullback was abrupt, not gradual. In the name of empowerment, we took command and told people whom they should work with, without consulting them. We were determined to empower them, whether they liked it or not. But

---

E X E R C I S E

Stepping Back

How do you know when to step back, and how do you do it gracefully?

1. Make sure the baby knows how to swim before you drop it in the pool: does the group have the skills and tools it needs to continue?

2. Make sure that new leadership is ready and clear and/or that the group has a clear process for choosing leaders.

3. Train and mentor your successors. Involve the next generation of leadership in your decision and ask their advice on timing.

4. Step back gradually. In ritual, all the drums don't stop at once — they fade away, growing softer, one after another coming to silence, maybe one continuing a bit longer with a simple heartbeat. Remain available to help guide and support new leadership.

it didn't occur to us that they might want to be in charge of their own empowerment! It took the community many years to recover from our error.

BREAKFAST OF CHAMPIONS

Catalysts get lots of praise and adulation — and then skip town. But champions stick around, calling people to come to meetings, putting out the press releases, battling the opposition, goading everyone to greater efforts toward the mission.

In a perfect world, we'd appreciate, cherish and support our champions. But in co-creative groups, champions often come to grief. They become the subject of endless complaints and attacks; they receive little appreciation for all that drive and work. If they survive at all, they often find their enthusiasm diminished and their effectiveness undermined. Why does this happen? Well, here's one of Starhawk's Rules of Life:

People who make good organizers tend to have bossy personalities.

The very traits that make them champions make them eager to step into command roles or to set a pace that leaves others gasping. They're active, not passive. Rather than sit around and wait for something to happen, they'll make it happen. They have big enough egos to believe that their mission is vital and their purpose is righteous. They like control. They observe details and think ahead and plan carefully in order to maintain that control.

All of these are fine traits to have in a hierarchy, where you are expected to exercise control over others. But in a co-creative group, especially one with powerful ideals of equality, that tendency to control often leads to conflict with others.

The dance of stepping up and stepping back is difficult. No one does it perfectly, in a way that equally satisfies everyone. So there will always be someone who wants a leader to step back, perhaps far more quickly than she cares to or believes will truly help the group. Sometimes that person may covet the leader's role. At other times, he may himself have no intention of stepping up and actually doing the work. One person in Reclaiming once admitted to me that she had been trying to drive me out of the collective "Just to see if I can." Envy and jealousy sometimes masquerade as campaigns for equality. We may resent the social power someone else has accrued, fairly or unfairly. We may not believe in our own ability to earn the group's esteem, so we try to pull our rival down.

Of course, people may also have many valid reasons for fearing the concentration of power in the group or for criticizing those who take on leadership roles. If a champion or an organizer is at the center of every aspect of the group, then if you want to play you have to play with them. If Jane is on the Coordinating Committee, the Finance Committee and the Menu Committee, that doesn't leave much space in the group for Jane's heartbroken ex-lover.

Leaders do make mistakes. Champions may too easily slip into command mode or act in ways that hurt others. Many co-creative groups have no clear feedback structure for voicing these concerns. When there is no forum in which to voice issues or concerns in a constructive way, the result is a destructive pattern that plays out over and over again in groups: someone takes leadership and devotes an enormous amount of time, energy and commitment to a group or project. Someone else accuses them of hogging the center, flaunting power or privilege. Conflict arises, and the champion is attacked and eventually brought down. The conflict weakens the group and removes one of its most dedicated and hard-working members. The group never fully recovers and eventually dissolves.

EMPOWERMENT TO THE MIDLINE

Such groups suffer from a syndrome I call *empowerment to the midline*. We dedicate ourselves to empowering individuals, right up until the moment when someone actually begins to exercise power — defined simply as the ability to get what they want done. At that point, it's as if they've stepped over an invisible line that separates the oppressed from the oppressors. Suddenly this person we've worked so hard to help find a voice becomes the person everyone wants to speak out against.

I also call this pattern *empowerment to complain*. We focus our nurturing and attention on anyone who takes the position of victim and complains about leadership. Anyone who takes action or sets direction is suspect.

Unfortunately, this sort of empowerment is not very empowering. Nobody gets what they want, and often little or nothing gets done. True empowerment implies action. Complaining is not enough. Taking action means taking responsibility — suggesting, offering solutions and doing the work to implement them.

But in a group suffering from the empowerment to the midline syndrome, there's no zone of action, no autonomy, no scope for creativity. The group may have done away with the inequalities of leaders and followers, of some people being the stars and others relegated to mere extras. But they've done so by preventing anyone from having the power to act.

Here are some of unspoken assumptions behind the empowerment to the midline syndrome in progressive and collaborative groups.

1. People who have extraordinary skills, experience, levels of commitment or other resources or who take on big responsibilities — call them leaders — are always suspect. They are fair game for attack.

   The result is that no one feels truly safe in the group. There is no trust. No one is able to train, to mentor or pass on skills.

2. Leaders should never receive extra benefits, perks or rewards beyond the joy of the work itself, or they are exploiting others.

   In collaborative groups, we are often reacting against a larger system of hierarchy, in which higher levels of responsibility confer marks of status and collateral powers. We don't want to reproduce that sort of inequality. But we do want to allow people to earn fair rewards for their labors, marks of appreciation and respect. If a group continually sees its most experienced people drifting away or burning out, it may be a warning sign that this pattern is in force.

3. We must always sacrifice the needs, benefits and rewards of insiders to the needs of outsiders. Empowerment means always siding with the perceived victim or underdog.

   The group functions on power-under — people get their way by taking the position of victim. They gain social power, not by taking on responsibility, but by complaining about those who do. The complainers are not truly empowered to act, and those who do take action are undermined.

4. We refuse to acknowledge that people might have different levels of skill, experience, talent, commitment or responsibility, because to do so might affirm a hierarchy.

   The group is unable to make use of its members' skills and talents. We can't mentor and critique each other, we can't assess what skills and forms of responsibility are needed or are operative in a group and we can't set standards or hold one another accountable for meeting them.

In resisting the Authoritarian Father of patriarchy, we ask people to become the Selfless Mother of — gee, patriarchy. I had one of those life-changing moments of illumination when I realized that I had been perfectly prepared for taking leadership in leaderless feminist collectives by being raised as a girl in the 1950s. "Boys don't like girls who are smart," my mother said to me when I was six years old. We were, I believe, watching the Miss America pageant at the time, and she would occasionally sigh and say, "Maybe someday I'll see you up there!"

"Boys like girls who are sweet," she advised me.

I decided to try out her advice. I went back to school, and while I was always the smartest kid in the class — a young Hermione Granger — I learned to downplay my intelligence, not to answer every question, to conceal my straight As and bat my eyes. I soon had a string of boyfriends.

By the time I reached adulthood, I had decades of experience behind me in looking softer, sweeter and dumber than I really am. I had become an expert at subtly assessing others' ego strengths and making sure I propped them up. It was second nature to make sure I didn't threaten others — particularly men. I no longer even realized I was doing it — until the consciousness-raising group I joined in the early 1970s opened my eyes.

I want a world in which everyone has agency, in which we are all empowered to step into a zone of action. In truly empowering groups, our ideas can be supported by others and implemented to become reality. At times we support others' ideas, and at times we step up and others support us. We are not expected to be perfect, but are given the trust and charity to try new things, take risks, learn from our setbacks and own our mistakes.

LEADERSHIP AND ACCOUNTABILITY

Leaders must certainly be held accountable for their decisions and mistakes. Real abuse — deliberate, hurtful, humiliating or destructive behavior — should never be tolerated. How can we hold each other accountable in constructive ways that allow for both individuals and groups to grow in understanding and effectiveness?

The first step is to confront the belief that the problem is the person. "If we can just get Eli to step off the board, everything will be fine. Yeah, he founded the community, but it's time for him to get out of the way."

In the permaculture movement, we say "the problem is the solution." I often tell my students that I'm not sure if that's always true, but it always makes us look at the problem more creatively. To what problem is Eli's centrality the solution? Perhaps it's the lack of a structure that supports, encourages and challenges others to step up into greater responsibility. Anger and resentment at his perceived control might be the driving energy needed to create new structures of accountability.

Another way to look at it would be to ask, "In what way is the problem inherent in the structure?"

The problem in RootBound is not really Eli's arrogance or personality — it's the lack of structures for direct feedback and accountability. It's not the TreePeople staging a kitchen coup, it's that there's no way for people to constructively critique their cooking or ask for a different menu.

Changing people is hard. Think of your own efforts to change yourself! How many times have you told yourself to put down that cigarette or close the bag of chocolate chip cookies and walk away? You know that spending that 15 minutes on Facebook will make you late for work, but you still do it. You know that telling your daughter how you used to cook dinner every night for the family at her age, and wash the dishes afterwards, will not get her up off the couch to set the table, yet you still say it!

Changing the structures in which people operate is often much easier than changing people themselves. Just as a particular habitat will favor certain plants over others, group structure will favor certain behaviors. In a salt marsh, salt tolerant plants will have a competitive edge and will crowd out other plants. You can uproot all the sedges, but you won't grow roses unless you change the conditions of the soil.

In a group that allows vicious gossip, backbiting and attacks on leaders, people who thrive on negativity will have a competitive edge and eventually will drive out others who might prefer a different way of functioning. You can kick out the gossips, one by one, but unless you change the group norms and agreements, new attackers will simply take their places. But if you shift the group norms and structure so that negative gossip becomes a liability, people will either stop gossiping or leave.

Lack of structure creates a void where negative behaviors can flourish. If a group has no structure for constructive feedback, it will come in a negative form. If a group provides no structure for accountability, you can predict vicious attacks. If it keeps no financial records or any clear system of accounting, you can guarantee accusations of wrongdoing will arise, that can never be either proven or disproven.

To shift this pattern, we need to provide structures that favor the kinds of behavior we want. We need to develop group norms that both support those who step into leadership and hold them accountable in ways that respect their work and commitment. We need ways of giving constructive feedback.

Structures and norms also protect the group against infiltration and disruption — either by COINTELPRO Operations or by simple human craziness. Rumors, secrets, backstabbing, disinformation campaigns, entrapment and abuse thrive in a swampy habitat of murky secrets and mucky gossip. When we create positive structures of accountability and open feedback, when our communications are clear and when power is fairly and visibly earned, we create solid ground that is not easily undermined.

E X E R C I S E

Questions for Those Who Would Challenge Leadership

You can challenge leadership, you can even unseat the founder of an organization, but be aware that the campaign will be a costly one. It will be costly for you, if you fail. If you succeed, it will be costly for the group, if the target is shouldering a big workload, if she has support and friends or is a public face for the group. The campaign may diminish the group's effectiveness and make it lose face, perhaps even funding. You may attract supporters, but they may not trust you or like you. The overall level of trust in the group will be harmed and may take a long time to rebuild.

Before you embark on such a campaign — or if someone asks you to join in one, ask instead:

- Are we identifying X as the problem?
- What are the behaviors that bother us?
- Are there structures for feedback and accountability around those behaviors?
- If so, have we used them fully?

- If not, what structures might we create that would address this problem, not just around X, but for everybody?

If structures of accountability don't exist, wage your campaign to create them. You'll be seen as helpful, not harmful. You might even be able to enlist X's support. Once they are in place, you'll have the tool you need to address the disturbing behavior directly and constructively.

You might ask also:

- Is there someone ready to step into X's place and take on the work — not just the glory but the grunt work? Am I?
- What are the barriers to people taking on more work and responsibility? Are they internal barriers — lack of knowledge, information, skills or confidence that we can address through training and mentoring? If so, how do we put those structures in place?

- Or are they external barriers — people's lack of time, financial stress, other commitments? Are there ways we can address those? For example, providing child care at meetings?
- Do we have a group culture where people train their successors long before they are ready to step down?

If not, wage your campaign to begin building that culture. Start with yourself — are you training someone to take over your roles when you are ready to step down? Are you sharing skills and information? Once you lead by example, you can then urge others, including X, to do the same.

Is there a structure for mentoring our leadership? Perhaps your campaign could be waged to create a structure that offers mentorship and coaching to those who take on roles of power.

And remember, you always have the choice to start a new game. If X is at the center of the only game in town, play basketball instead of baseball. Start a project of your own, or another group where you can play more of a central role.

Questions to Ask When Your Leadership Is Challenged

Ask yourself or get a supportive friend to ask:

- Do I believe I'm being attacked?

Step back down the ladder of inference and ask:

- What behaviors, what are people doing or saying that I'm reacting to?
- How am I actually feeling: Scared? Hurt? Sad? Mad?

- Are there things I'm not seeing through this cloud of emotion?
- Am I selecting data — cherry-picking information, ignoring things that challenge my assumptions or stories?
- Am I getting feedback in a form that is destructive and unhelpful?
- Is there a kernel of truth in the destructive feedback that I should listen to?
- What information about the group and my behavior is this event giving me?
- Is there something about my style or way of working that I do need to change? What are my own irritating traits?

Ask for honest feedback from your friends and allies. Get the book *What Got You Here Won't Get You There* — read through the 21 annoying habits and the chapter on ways to get clear feedback.[6]

Hold your ground. Listen for the kernel of truth, but don't take in personal attacks. Don't retaliate, but also don't accept abuse. State your own boundaries, and hold them: "I'm open to hearing what specifically I've done or said that you want me to change. I'm not open to discussion when you start with 'asshole!'"

Don't attack yourself, internally or externally. You may have made mistakes — that's an inevitable aspect of taking risks and growing. But you have a right to expect appreciation and respect for what you have given to the group.

If it's warranted, apologize sincerely and enlist the group's support in helping you change.

CONTINUED

- Do I have support in the form of mentoring or mutual coaching? If not, can I create that structure for myself? Whom do I trust and respect that I can ask for feedback?
- Am I training my successors? If so, make that fact known to the group at large and let them know how people become one of those trainees. If not, begin.
- Do we have a structure for feedback and accountability? If not, can I exert leadership to create one? How would I like to receive feedback and show accountability?

Questions to Ask When You Observe an Attack

What do you do if you are watching someone else attack that bossy, ego-driven, controlling workhorse whom you also treasure as invaluable to the group? You and the other bystanders have enormous power — to shift the dialogue, to affirm the group's standards of behavior and boundaries, to use the conflict as a springboard to strengthen the group.

Shift the frame from the person to the structure (or lack thereof). Until structures exist for constructive feedback and true accountability, they can't be used.

- What structure of feedback and accountability are we missing? How do we create them?
- Do our leaders have mentors? If not, how can we encourage and create mentorship at all levels?
- How do we express our appreciation for the work X has done?

Apologizing

Apologizing is one of the great skills of leadership. We do make mistakes, and a true apology is one of the ways we make amends and let people know that we have heard their concerns and are open to change. A true, heartfelt apology can be part of our commitment to change and can help restore broken trust.

But too often, when people are asked to apologize, they instead defend their behavior and turn the apology into a not-so-subtle attack on the other person. "I'm sorry you felt hurt, but here's why I was entirely right in doing what I did."

Here are some guidelines for making a true apology.

A true apology is an "I" statement, not a "you" statement. "I'm sorry I hurt your feelings," not "I'm sorry you felt hurt." Or "I'm sorry my words or actions caused you pain."

A true apology makes the other person feel better, not worse.

Apology Practice

In pairs, share a situation in which you feel that you made a mistake or hurt somebody. Ask your partner to role-play that person. Ground, center and use your anchor to your core self.

Now, apologize. Ask your partner for feedback and, if necessary, restate your apology until it meets the criteria above. Then, practice it three times.

Notice how you feel. Ask your partner how she felt, and note how the energy shifts.

Then switch and do the same for your partner.

A true apology makes clear to the other person that you have heard their distress and concern. You may or may not agree with their assessment, but you have listened.

Less is more. A simple, sincere "I'm sorry" is better than a long, self-justifying explanation.

A true apology takes responsibility for our actions and commits to change.

Supporting Leadership

Most of us who have stepped into roles of leadership in collaborative groups get little training for the role. Often we have few if any role models and no one to turn to for help or guidance. No wonder conflict often erupts!

We may need to create our own structures for mentoring or coaching.

Ask for Mentoring

If we know someone whose judgment we trust, whose example inspires us or who has faced similar problems before us, we can ask them for help and mentoring. We might offer some form of exchange — whether of money or some other form of energy, in return.

Mentoring might be initiated by the person who wishes to be mentored. A group or a concerned friend might also suggest mentoring when problems around leadership erupt.

Mentoring can take place in person, by phone or online. I find that some kind of regular check-in time is more effective than an "as needed" schedule, because we don't always recognize those moments when we need help.

Create a Peer Coaching Agreement

We might not always have a wise mentor available, but the help and insight of a peer who is struggling with similar issues can also be invaluable. A different pair of eyes can see what we may miss — and we can return the favor. Coaching can be as simple as having a friend to whom we can send a draft of that blistering e-mail to review before we send it out. Coaching partners can practice many of these exercises together. As with mentoring, coaching can take place in many forms and situations.

A Peer Support Group

When many of us are struggling with similar issues, perhaps in the same community, perhaps in different groups, we can set up a peer support group to share our challenges and get feedback from multiple sources. Therapists, healers and educators often work with such groups, and they can be invaluable.

Inspiring Leadership

When we understand the dynamics of power, when we create structures that serve group communication and accountability, our groups can become arenas in which we all can step up into greater power.

In *leaderful* rather than leaderless groups, when we have big ideas, we can find friends who will help us carry them out. When others have creative visions, we can exercise our own power in supporting and amplifying their voices. Together we can create powerful zones of action where many people can become effective agents of change. All of us can be respected and rewarded for our contributions, supporting one another, not just to protest and complain, but to act, to confront, to create, to change and, ultimately, to transform the world around us.

CHAPTER 7

Group Conflict

THE CONFLICT RESOLUTION MEETING

A s Eli set up chairs Saturday morning in the dining hall for the conflict reso- lution meeting, he fought the urge to put ominous music on the stereo. If life were a movie, he thought, now would be the time for those minor chords and screeching violins signaling that the moment of truth was imminent. He just hoped Marta had more confidence that he felt.

As people began to arrive, they clumped into little groups, gossiping quietly with close friends but not speaking much to others and eyeing members of other factions suspiciously. The energy felt heavy and the mood grim.

Marta arrived early, smiling and carrying a large flip chart which Eli helped her set up. She seemed undismayed by the cheerless faces that greeted her and happily accepted a cup of coffee and a bagel from Donna Darling.

People slowly trickled in. The meeting was scheduled to start by 10 AM, and by 10:15 most people seemed to be in their places. Marta arranged the seats in a circle and sat against the wall, chart and easel by her side.

"Good morning," she said, "I've been asked here to facilitate this conflict resolution meeting, and I'd like to just tell you a bit about myself and ask for your agreement that I do this." Marta gave a very brief summary of her background. She chose to do this because she felt she might need to establish her credibility separate from her connection to Eli and Ella.

"I'd like to begin with introductions and a short question for you all. I'd like you to say your name and share one brief moment at RootBound that was joyful or wonderful for you. By brief — I'd like you to think Twitter or one of those two-line Facebook posts, not a full blog."

Light laughter greeted her, and the group began. Marta knew that this appreciative inquiry might take time, but she felt it was important to begin by reminding people of the good things they'd found at RootBound, to provide a positive basis for engaging with the conflict.

"I remember when Justin took his first solo swim in the pool," Andrew smiled fondly.

"I remember the day we used the community kitchen to cook a hundred meals for the antiwar protest," Elm contributed.

"I remember moving in day — the endless procession of boxes and how everyone helped with the big sofas," said Laura, one of the first members.

"Yes, and that grand piano that got stuck in the gate, and it took ten of us to shift it!" Joan smiled.

By the end of the round, the mood had lightened. People were looking each other in the eye, Marta noted, and some were smiling.

"I want to congratulate you," she said. "Not just in creating such a wonderful project and bringing it to birth. But I want to congratulate you for your conflicts. You have moved on from the honeymoon phase, and now you face the challenge of getting real. All groups have conflict — because groups are made of people and people are often stubborn, unreasonable and darn difficult to get along with. But they are also wonderful, and we can't do without them. So, learning to embrace, enjoy and do conflict well is a key task for any group that lasts. And I congratulate you for calling this meeting, and for your willingness to engage."

Marta then pulled out her first chart, which showed a neat, well-organized pyramid chart of a typical hierarchy.

"Here is the communication pattern of the groups we're used to," she said. "In a hierarchy, we know to whom we report and who reports to us. We can send a decision up the chain of command or down." As the group nodded, she pulled out a second chart. This one looked like a tangled web. "And here is a typical collaborative group," she said. Everyone laughed with recognition. "There are many different paths a message can go down, and often no one knows who is truly responsible for a decision."

Deftly, she led the group through a review of the Talisman of Healthy Groups and some basic approaches to clear communication.

"This is all very well," interrupted Betty Banjore, who was head of the Women's Committee and key author of their angry letter. "But we didn't come here for a workshop, no offense. We've got some serious conflicts to deal with. I represent the women of RootBound …"

"Not all the women!" interjected Magnolia of the TreePeople.

"A good quorum of the women," Betty went on undeterred. "We don't feel safe in this community when violence reigns! We want something done about it."

"I'll tell you what I want something done about," said Joan Springer in a voice that was rapidly rising. "To be honest, I don't give a damn about Rick shoving Edward in the pool. That's just guy behavior. But I absolutely don't feel safe when my little girl can be traumatized by vile, violent images in the mailbox."

"It's not the images that are violent, it's the culture of animal cruelty!" Pyracantha leapt to her feet.

"All right!" Marta spoke in a voice of command, realizing she was about to lose control of the meeting. "Tell me this, when you began building RootBound, what did you do first?"

There was a moment of silence.

"Poured the foundation?" Andrew suggested.

"Even before that," Marta said. "What does any good carpenter do when she comes to work? She lays out her tools. And that is what we have been doing. And now we are ready to go to work."

She fixed her eye first on Edward, then on Rick.

"Edward, Rick, before we take up your case with the whole group, I would like a chance to mediate between the two of you. Would you agree to that?" Both men nodded.

"But it's not just about them!" Betty was livid. "It's about all of us, and our sense of safety, and what we say is OK and not OK! I didn't take the day off to have this swept under the rug!"

Marta nodded. "I hear how important this issue is to you, Betty, and that it impacts your deepest, most basic sense of safety in this group. My intention is not to sweep it away, but to address it. We have this day together — at a certain time I will give you all work to do in small groups, and take Edward and Rick aside. Now, let me explain my reasoning. Although their conflict doesn't just involve them, if they are able to come to resolution I believe it will be a step forward in addressing those issues of safety for everyone. It is far, far easier for people in conflict to come to understanding when they do not have to save face or deal with all the complex dynamics of a large group. But I promise to bring the matter back before the end. Can you live with that?"

Betty nodded, somewhat reluctantly.

"So, let us begin with the affair of the mailbox — because that is something that everyone experienced. Joan, perhaps you'd like to begin and tell us what happened from your point of view. I'd ask you to start by just saying what happened, give us the picture as a video camera might have recorded it."

"I came home from a heavy shift at the hospital, where I'm a nurse," Joan said. "Jennie, my little girl, was sobbing on the couch. I couldn't get her to stop crying. I mean, she wasn't just like quietly shedding a few tears, she was in hysterics. Then she showed me these pictures she'd found in our mailbox. They were like — they were like an assault!"

"Let me back you down a step," Marta interjected. "What did you see in those pictures?"

"They were horrible," Joan said.

"I hear so much emotion," Marta said. "I can hear how deeply you and your daughter were affected. But tell me what you saw in the pictures?"

"Animals being tortured," Joan said. "Headless, skinless — who leaves these things where an innocent child can find them?"

Pyracantha started to speak, but Marta waved her silent.

"And how did you feel?" Marta asked Joan.

"Just awful. Sick. I felt like my daughter had been emotionally violated. I don't want those images in her mind."

"So, you felt sick. Disgusted. I guess I hear anger, too. Enraged that someone would leave these pictures for your daughter to find?"

"You bet!"

"I want to just stop there for a moment and give Pyracantha a chance to speak. Pyracantha, can you tell us what happened from your point of view."

"After the pool party, I just felt people were so ignorant and blind. ..."

"Let me just stop you. I do want to hear how you felt, but first tell me just what happened, as a camera might have recorded it."

"I have lots of animal rights literature and information that I distribute when I table on campus every Tuesday," Pyracantha said. "So I decided to share some of it with the community and slipped it into peoples' mailboxes. The next thing I knew, this crazy woman was waging a vendetta ...."

"Stop again, and tell me just what happened."

"Joan came to the TreePeople space. She yelled at Ailanthus and demanded we all leave RootBound."

"And how did you feel?"

"I felt like, that's what happens when you try to show a bunch of hypocrite liberals the real pain that underlies ..."

"Now, I'm going to stop you again, even though I very much want to hear what you have to say. But I'm hearing you shift into judgment, and I'd like to ask you to go back to feelings — you know, happy, sad, angry — and all the variations."

"I felt ... angry. And sad. And frustrated. Sad that people do such cruel things and won't look at them."

"Let's just take a moment, and sit with that sadness," Marta said. "I hear how much you care about the animals."

"I do. It breaks my heart to see them suffer."

Joan sniffed. "Well it breaks my heart to see my little girl suffer! And she's an animal, too!"

"I didn't mean to hurt Jennie," Pyracantha admitted. "I honestly didn't think about kids getting into the mail. I am sorry about that."

"Can you share what you were thinking?" Marta asks. "Give us your chain of reasoning. Show your work, as they say in math class."

"I was so frustrated after the picnic," Pyracantha said. "I felt like, people just don't see what's really going on, what their hot dogs really cost. I wanted to make them see."

"Whether they want to or not!" interjected Marion, Joan's partner.

"If you wait until they want to see, you'll wait forever because they don't!" Pyracantha countered.

"So you felt frustrated and unseen."

"I felt like my point of view was entirely discounted. 'We have a soy dog option' — well it's not about options! How would you feel if someone was torturing children right next to you and when you objected, they said, 'Oh it's OK because you can play volleyball with them over there while we keep on carving them up over here.'"

"You tortured my child!" Joan said.

Pyracantha fell silent.

"You know," Marta said, "I believe what we have here is a classic case of good vs. good."

"Whatever can you mean?" Betty asked.

"Most of the time, we're conditioned to think of conflict as good versus evil," Marta said. "But in groups like RootBound, more often we see conflicts between different values, good values, that bump up against each other. Pyracantha cares about the animals — and that's a good value. In fact, I'd bet it's one that we all share, although we may not all be vegans. Am I right?"

Around the room, heads nodded.

"And Joan and Marion care about protecting their child. That, too, is a good value, and again I believe it's one we'd all share. Am I right?" Heads nodded again, a shade more vigorously.

"Pyracantha, what are you feeling?"

"I'm feeling that people might say they care about animals, but they don't care very much if they still eat them."

"I would call that an assessment, not a feeling," Marta said. "I would guess that it's a somewhat accurate assessment, or rather, I would say that few people here care as strongly and passionately about the animals as you do. And how do you feel about that? ... remembering happy, sad, angry, mad ..."

"I feel sad," Pyracantha said. "So sad. And alone. Like if there's no room for me to express my opinions about the thing I care about most, I don't belong."

"Let's back up again," Marta said, "Because I just heard you jump to a conclusion that I'm not sure is correct. I'm hearing some very strong feedback from this community that one way you chose to advocate for your beliefs — putting the flyers in the mailboxes — was not effective and was even hurtful. Did you hear that?"

Pyracantha nodded again.

"And you feel?"

"Sad. Maybe ashamed. I really am sorry about Jennie," she looked up at Joan, tears in her eyes.

"But I have not yet heard anything that tells me there is no way at all you could advocate for your ideas here. Am I right? Can anyone imagine or suggest a way that Pyracantha could share her deepest concerns with you all?"

Donna Darling spoke up. "Pyracantha, I'm not a vegetarian, and I'm sorry if my offering you a soy dog seemed like it was trivializing your concern. I'd be very willing to hear some of your animal rights information, if, say, you wanted to give a presentation at some point. But I also teach little children, and I had the same concerns about the flyers in the mailbox — and I found some drifting around the play yard where kids might find them."

"I'd be willing to come to a presentation, for instance," Andrew Rick said. "Frankly, I think you'd be much more persuasive if you don't try to force opinions on people. It just creates resistance."

Others also chimed in to express their willingness to hear more on the issue.

"What do you hear?" Marta asked finally.

"I hear that people don't share my beliefs," said Pyracantha, "but they are willing to listen if I don't try to force my opinion."

"Can you live with that?" Marta asked.

"I don't know," Pyracantha said. "I can see that putting the flyers out didn't work, and I wouldn't do it again. But I don't know if I want to live the rest of my life in a community with people who don't share the thing that is most deeply important to me. I can do presentations to strangers, but in my home, maybe I want people who really care like I do."

"That's a decision that is truly up to you to make," Marta said. "I don't believe you can make people believe what you want them to believe or care about what you think they should care about. I do believe you have some very positive choices you can make: either to stay in RootBound and accept that others share many but not all of your values or to look for a community founded on the core value that is most important to you."

Pyracantha nodded.

"And you don't have to make that decision right now." Marta turned back to Joan and Marion. "And you, Joan and Marion, what do you need from the community now around this issue?"

"I've heard Pyracantha say she's sorry," Joan said. "I trust that she won't do it again. But I will say this — RootBound was never founded as a vegan community. But in our core mission statement, we say we're a family-friendly and child-friendly community, that the safety of children is one of our prime concerns. I want people to think about that — in terms of what you put out or leave lying around, whether it's animal rights propaganda or pornography or cans of used motor oil or whatever. Try to remember, people, that there are kids here!"

Around the circle, many heads nodded.

"Do we feel complete with this issue, now?" Marta asked. The circle nodded affirmation.

"Good. Then let's take a 15-minute break," Marta said. "When we come back, I'm going to ask you to work a bit in small groups, so let me give you the task now, because while you are doing it, I'm going to meet with Edward and Rick. I'd like you to each take ten minutes and write a list of what you think are RootBound's core values. Then, I'd like to you to join with three other people and compare your lists. See if you can synthesize them down to no more than ten altogether. Andrew, I see you have a big watch, will you keep time? You'll have half an hour in your groups, and then we'll break for lunch. We'll reconvene altogether after the lunch break."

TWO MODELS OF CONFLICT

Consider two farmers. One, Farmer Jones, runs her farm on strictly industrial lines. When bugs attack, she fights back with chemicals and pesticides that destroy beneficial insects along with the bad ones. The farm resembles a battleground, with strafed, dead earth and perpetual conflict.

Sometimes our groups are like Farmer Jones' fields, We unwittingly create conditions that give a competitive edge to people who thrive on destructive forms of conflict. When we try to fix the situation by removing the pests, we often do so with methods that kill off the good feelings and beneficial impulses of the group.

Now consider Farmer Smith. She's an organic farmer who knows that to grow healthy plants you must grow healthy soil. When Farmer Smith sees a leaf-munching bug, she doesn't break out the sprayer. Instead she asks, "Hmmn, what's out of balance? What information is this pest giving me? What can I change about the whole?"

Our groups can be more like Farmer Smith's fields. When we create the right ground conditions, when we set up structures, pay attention to communication and nurture the healthy aspects of our communities, we develop resilience. Conflict will still arise, but instead of becoming destructive, it may actually serve to strengthen the group.

Conflict is drama. There's no gripping story without conflict. Conflict is also information — it tells us something is lacking, something is out of balance. We can see conflict as a powerful opportunity for group learning. When we embrace conflict, our groups can become more exciting, more dynamic and more effective.

CONFLICT IS A NORMAL PHASE OF GROUP DEVELOPMENT

In 1965, psychologist Bruce Tuckman published a study of small group development that was to prove influential for decades, perhaps because of the catchy names he came up with for four stages that groups go through: forming, storming, norming and performing.[1]

My own formulation of the stages of group development, in *Truth or Dare*, uses the framework of the four elements linked to the four directions, equating to the four seasons and four times of day.[2]

In the East/Air stage, symbolizing sunrise and spring, the group begins. Inspired by new ideas, moved by a vision, people come together with fresh energy and enthusiasm; they define their mission and goals. Anything seems possible.

In the South/Fire stage, corresponding to noon and summer, the group gathers power. This can be a time of rapid expansion and growth, but it can also be a phase of conflict and struggle, of showdowns at High Noon as people jockey for power.

In the West/Water stage, which corresponds to twilight and autumn, the group reaps the harvest of its growth and struggles. Members may feel they've come through the fire together, and trust develops. People bond on an interpersonal level, which deepens the work.

In the North/Earth phase, corresponding to midnight and winter, the group strengthens its boundaries, accepts its limitations and grounds the vision in the hard, solid work that needs to get done. The trust which has been forged in the fires of conflict becomes the basis for achievement.

And, just as winter eventually turns to spring, the group's accomplishments often open up new horizons and give rise to a new vision. The cycle begins again.

Sometimes a group may need to redo certain stages. If we're not performing well together, perhaps our norms are not functional. We may need to struggle through some conflict and realign power or go back to the beginning and revisit our vision in order to create more effective ways of being together and a deeper trust.

EXERCISE

Questions About Stages of Group Development

- Which stages have your group gone through?
- Which stage is your group currently in?
- What challenges do you face in that stage?
- Are there any stages your group skipped or that may need to be redone?

GOOD VS. EVIL — GOOD VS. GOOD

We are acculturated to view conflict as Good vs. Evil. The sheriffs in the white hats battle the outlaws in the black hats. The good Americans battle the evil Nazis/Communists/terrorists. When we get into conflict, even with our friends and loved ones, we tend to frame the battle in the same way. We are each our own center of good, so those who oppose us must be evil.

But in collaborative groups, we often face conflicts that are not so polarized. We may have conflicting ideas about how to approach a problem. We may have a variety of creative solutions to an issue. We may each advocate for values we believe are important. We may each hold an important piece of a multifaceted truth.

Our conflicts are often Good vs. Good, and framing them in that way can help us resolve them creatively. Perhaps RootBound holds one set of values that say, "We should be as accessible as possible to people who don't have lots of money." It may also hold a set of values that say, "Whatever is worth doing is worth doing well. Quality and excellence count." And even a third set that says, "People should be paid for their work."

All of these are good values and important ones. However, they may be hard to realize all at the same time. If RootBound contracts to build a new unit, one set of decisions will lead to a cheaper, more affordable but lesser quality construction. Another set might lead to a cutting-edge, green building with all-natural materials, built by skilled craftspersons but costing much more. Neither course of action is evil — but if RootBound members frame the debate as black vs. white, the Affordablistas will be denouncing the vile, uncaring, arrogant snobs who want the natural bamboo flooring and the Qualitistas will be railing back at the cheap, shoddy, penny-pinching slobs who want to saddle the ecovillage with a cracker-box construction.

If, however, all can acknowledge that they are advocating for competing good values, they can look for a way in which the inherent dynamic tension can strengthen both visions. Are there ways the group can

Questions About Competing Values

When faced with a conflict, some of the questions a group can ask are:

- What values are at stake here?
- Are two or more values we hold dear in conflict? If so, how do we find a dynamic balance between them?

hold out for quality while holding down costs? Can they pay skilled construction workers fairly and use the energy of volunteers for less skilled jobs? Can those who have less money to pay for the unit contribute labor or some other form of energy?

Strategies for Balancing Competing Values

When we acknowledge a conflict of competing good values, there are often simple strategies that can offer a solution:

Turn Either/Or to Both/And

Is there a way we can do both? Might we be able to solicit donations from the makers of quality building materials for a low-cost unit as PR for them?

Alternate

The Qualitistas will build this unit, the Affordablistas will do the next.

Synthesize

We look at all aspects of building the unit, and decide on a few where quality must rule — the ones that might affect safety, health or the longevity of the building. For purely aesthetic concerns, we go the cheap route knowing that people can repaint the walls or put new faces on the cabinets later, when they get more money.

Think Creatively

We use natural building techniques in our new unit and cut costs by running a workshop that teaches the skills as participants work on our structure.

Conflicts of Taste

Collaborative groups that work on creative projects may also run into conflicts that have no good or evil inherent in them, but are questions of taste. What color should we paint the dining room at RootBound? Alice likes green, while Liam likes yellow. Or do we stick with a neutral off-white, which offends no one and inspires no one? Who decides?

Conflicts of taste can be extremely difficult to resolve, if only because there is no overriding reason for making one choice over another. When we recognize that there are no strong values at stake, but only preferences, we can defuse some of the heated arguments and look for creative solutions. The strategies above might work for many cases. Some other approaches might be:

Find out Who Really Cares

Often many people do not have strong opinions or much investment in an issue. Find out who does, and let them take charge of a project and work out any needed compromises.

Allocate Power with Responsibility

The person who puts out the newsletter decides what font to use. This works less well with decisions many people have to live with — like painting that dining room, but can be adapted. Perhaps the people who coordinate the kitchen and dining room cleanup might get a final say — but first we'll poll the whole community to exclude any colors that somebody actually hates.

Majority Rules

Choose several options and let people vote, going with the one that the majority like.

Reward Extraordinary Service

That unsung hera/o who coordinated all the volunteers for the work day — maybe she gets to decide what color to paint the hall?

Hold a Contest

The person who collects the most recycling, the child who is voted Most Helpful in the Garden — create a contest and let the winner decide.

Flip a Coin

MISUNDERSTANDINGS

Many of the conflicts that arise in collaborative groups are misunderstandings: hurt feelings, conflicts over something someone said or didn't say, annoyances and irritations. Most misunderstandings represent some failure in communication, and attending to the communication structures, norms and practices discussed in Chapter 5 will help prevent many fights. But even the most conscious group will occasionally experience breakdowns. Here are some of the most common:

Being Left Out of the Loop

Alice has said, several times in meetings, that she wants to be on the Events Planning Committee, but no one ever calls her.

Sometimes people are deliberately left out. Perhaps someone on the Events Committee does not like Alice and the committee does not want her to join. If so, they should tell her, hard as that might be, rather than simply avoiding her. Telling her might generate a different sort of conflict, but at least the issue will be out in the open and have some hope of resolution or transformation. And if people remember to use non-violent communication, to speak about their own feelings and needs and to make a clear request, they might be able to shift Alice's behavior.

But just as often, people are left out accidentally, because of the heightened complexity of communications in networks and collaborative groups. No one calls Alice simply because no one took on that responsibility and so her request never got on anyone's to-do list or because everyone assumes someone else is calling her. Rigorous attention to communication can help avoid many of these conflicts.

Communication can be a role the group assigns to one person, or it can become a regular part of meetings to say, "Who needs to be invited to the next one? Who is going to issue that invitation? Who needs to be informed of these decisions, and who is going to do that?" "By when, and how will we know it's been done?"

Accrued Irritation

Sometimes conflicts erupt because small irritations remain unaddressed over time and build up. If the group has no forum for feedback and does not develop a culture of direct communication and constructive critique, little annoyances can breed big conflicts. Create times and places where people can give one another constructive critique and feed-forward, practice giving feedback and encourage one another to do so.

Hurtful Words

We all say things, intentionally or unintentionally, that hurt other people. We all get our feelings hurt sometimes. When we feel hurt, rejected or scared, when someone acts disrespectfully toward us, we may lash out with words we later regret. When we hear words of judgment, accusation or dismissal, we may lash out in turn with anger that in turn generates more conflict.

Sex

In *Dreaming the Dark,* I proposed three rather cynical laws of small groups:

1. In any small group where people are involved sexually, sooner or later there will be problems.
2. In any small group where people are involved, sooner or later they will be involved sexually.
3. Small groups tend to break up.[3]

Sex is a wonderful thing, and passion and intimacy can be great energizers in a group. Much as we agree with the work of a group, often we join in the hopes of meeting that special someone to love, and when we do, our new-kindled love may set us on fire with passion for the work as well as the lover.

But intimate relationships can also pose challenges. When they are going well, when two people are enraptured with each other, they create an energetic knot within the group that may bind too tightly for anyone else to get in. Lovers may unintentionally exclude others from decisions or discussions and automatically support each other in any conflicts that erupt. Even if their behavior is exemplary, their very closeness can create envy in others.

Couples within groups might discuss how to open their attention to others and take special care to include others in discussions and creative sessions. We are not responsible for other people's jealousy, but couples might also want to consider whether they are unconsciously provoking envy by flaunting their affection or subtly taunting those who don't have partners.

But the greatest challenge for groups comes when couples break up. When two people have been the pillars of the community, their separation can crack the foundation. Close couples may represent parent figures for others in the group, and their divorce can restimulate the childhood pain of anyone who comes from a split family.

When we break up with someone we once loved, the pain and hurt we feel may be deeper than almost any other emotional pain we're likely to experience. Our basic sense of self may be wounded. We may be unable to continue working with our former partner. Any conflicts within the group will be amplified by our personal conflicts. We may try to force the other person out of the group or demand that the community take sides. If they don't we may feel hurt and betrayed, and our involvement with the group may wane.

We can't prevent people from falling in love or even in lust — nor would we want to. Love and pleasure are among the good things in life, and we want to affirm them. But we can be aware that the pain of intimate relationships can spill over into the larger group. When couples run into conflict, we can offer extra support — not by taking sides, but by supporting mediation and conflict transformation. If they truly can no longer work together, the group might help them divest from responsibilities or find new arenas of interest that will allow them some distance from one another. We can provide sympathetic ears and shoulders to cry on and also support our friends in moving on with their lives and finding new outlets for their energies.

Social power, earned or unearned, can also grant greater access to sex — more so for men than women, for men who hold power are sexy, whereas powerful women, decades of feminism notwithstanding, are still often seen as threatening. A high-status person may use their rank to pressure a lower-status person into sex: when the boss propositions the secretary, how can she say no? Conversely, a lower-status person may seek power by seducing a person of rank. The groupie may seduce the rock star, or Monica Lewinsky does the dirty with President Clinton in the Oval Office to gain status by association.

Collaboration is undermined when social power is not fairly earned or is unfairly wielded. Groups may wish to set some clear boundaries around the intersection of sex and power. For example, in Reclaiming, when we hold intensives in which some people are teachers — a role which confers high social power — we set a boundary that they do not get sexually involved with students during the course. If a true attraction develops, they can pursue it after the class. This prevents teachers from trading on the glamour of the role and also helps keep their attention on the work at hand. It protects vulnerable students, who may be tempted to enact old patterns stemming from earlier situations of abuse. It protects teachers from those who might be attracted to the role, not the person. And it forestalls the negative dynamics that arise in a group when the teacher is seen as favoring one student far above the others.

MEDIATING CONFLICT

There are thousands of books, programs and suggested processes for mediation, and professional mediators handle conflicts from divorce settlements to union negotiations. But mediation is also a skill we all should have, especially when we work collaboratively. The skills we develop in mediating the conflicts of others can also help us when we are embroiled in conflicts of our own. Mediating someone else's misunderstandings is generally much easier than transforming the conflicts we ourselves are embroiled in.

To be successful as a mediator, we are helped by understanding some key concepts.

Decoding Text and Subtext

When playwrights and screenwriters write dialogue, they know that people rarely express in words their entire range of feelings. When Ilsa walks into Rick's Café in *Casablanca*, he doesn't say, "Ilsa, I've been so terribly worried about you ever since you didn't show up for the train in Paris on the day the Germans marched in — I've felt hurt and rejected. I thought you loved me, but you betrayed me — now it's called into question my ability to believe in love. I carry that hurt with me and can't connect to another woman or risk another relationship. I've turned my back on the fight for freedom and withdrawn into cynicism and despair — and now, here you are! I feel wounded and enraged and hopeful and still desperately longing for you, and I love and hate you all at once!"

No, he says simply, "Not an easy day to forget ... the Germans wore gray, you wore blue." We feel all of the rest in the subtext of the scene.

Rick also attacks Ilsa: "Who did you leave me for, Lazlow, or were there others in between?" Again, that's the text, but Ilsa knows quite well the subtext is "You're a cheap whore who uses men for her entertainment and then drops them." She walks out — and we don't find out her side of the story for another third of the movie.

A skilled listener will name and validate the emotional subtext: "Rick, I hear that you feel frustrated, hurt, rejected and angry." Thank the Gods of Hollywood, there were no mediators or therapists sitting at Rick's bar! Great movie dialogue turns on subtext — *Casablanca* would lose its elegant sophistication if Rick directly expressed all he feels, or if Ilsa responded by validating his felt needs. But fun as it is to watch Humphrey Bogart clench his jaw with suppressed pain, it's not much fun to live it. Great movie dialogue is designed, after all, to generate conflict and drama, not to resolve it. In our personal relationships and our groups, being able to name feelings and create safety are important skills.

E
X
E
R
C
I
S
E

Text and Subtext: A Night at the Movies

Put on a DVD featuring a favorite emotional drama and take turns passing the clicker, pausing the film and speaking aloud the subtext of the scene as you perceive it.

Variation:

Reframe the dialogue using some of the communication guides given in Chapter 5. What tragedy might have been averted if Hamlet had been able to say to his mother, "Mom, when you remarried so abruptly, I felt hurt, frightened and angry because I need to know that you really love my father and didn't poison him. Would you be willing to tell me the truth about his death?"

What Movie Are We In?

Those of us who have raised teenagers know that often we and they live in very different realities. During that period I call The Sullen Years (roughly between 13 and 16, when they spend most of their waking hours sulking on the couch and texting their friends), teenagers endlessly replay *Cinderella*. You, ensconced happily in your own movie of some of the better scenes of *It's A Wonderful Life*, say brightly, "Cindy, how about helping me bake the holiday pies?" You're picturing a warm, cozy family scene with a smiling helper in a gingham apron rolling out the crusts. Cindy, meanwhile, gives out a deep, put-upon sigh, drags herself up from the clinkers where she's collapsed, exhausted, from the relentless amounts of thankless work you load upon her. She whines, "I washed the dishes last week. Why do I always have to do everything?"

The movies we are in, the stories we tell ourselves, can make transformation more difficult. Often we get cast in a role early in life, because of what we experience in our family of origin or because of dramatic or traumatic events. Ever after, when something or someone evokes similar emotions, suddenly we're back on the same screen. Just as hearing a few strains of "As Time Goes By" throws us into Rick's Café, a hurtful comment, an unintended slight, a stressful interaction can push us smack into the middle of our own horror movie.

When you're involved in a confusing conflict, in which the various parties can't even seem to agree on their picture of events, you may be in wildly different movies. When we are aware of the stories with which we most often frame our experiences, we can step out of them more easily and entertain alternate pictures of the world.

E
X
E
R
C
I
S
E

My Personal Movie

In pairs, share the answers to the following questions. Or, you can do this exercise alone, writing your reflections in a journal.

- As a child, were there particular stories, movies or fairy tales that you identified with?
- If the story of your life were a movie, a story or a fairy tale, what would it be?
- Are there any people or situations in your life right now that throw you into that story?
- What does the story tell you about your own sense of agency? Who holds power in your story?

- Can you think of a conflict or situation that you experienced through the lens of that story? How would your perception change if you changed the story? From, say, Cinderella to Jack the Giant Killer?
- Are there conflicts or situations that you are presently seeing through the lens of your story? How would your perception change if you changed the story to one in which you have greater agency?

When Is Mediation Appropriate?

Mediation is appropriate in cases of miscommunication or misunderstandings, to clear up hurt feelings and hurtful interactions. Mediation implies that we can find a win-win solution, that no one is either completely right or completely wrong and that both parties can come to share a mutual purpose.

Mediation is not appropriate in cases where people are accused of real wrongdoing — physical violence, theft, sexual assault or harassment, child neglect or abuse or other crimes. When real harm has been done to one person by another, right and wrong may need to be ascertained.

Some cases are not clear-cut. If Rick shoved Edward into the pool, was that a violent assault or an escalated misunderstanding? If Edward shouted, "I'll kill you, you overstuffed pompous idiot!" was that just trash-talk in anger or a criminal threat?

In doubtful cases, a group might begin with mediation with the understanding that they will progress to another level if the mediation fails to bring about reconciliation and restitution. Or, a group may decide to refer the matter to an Elders' Council or another structure to decide on the appropriate process.

Who Should Be in the Mediation?

The fewer the number of people, the easier it is to resolve or transform a conflict. The more people in the room, the harder it is to resolve. When other people are present, each party needs to save face in front of them and it's harder to admit fault. It's also a temptation to play to the jury, to swing other people to your side.

So, when two people have a conflict, a mediation is best performed for the two of them alone. Even when one person has a conflict with several members of a group, it may be helpful to split the issue into a series of one-on-one mediations. Often, when key players resolve their differences, other people can shift in response.

However, when an issue involves a group, one-on-one mediation may not be effective or appropriate. If I resolve my issue with Max and then go back to my team who are still angry at him, they may talk me out of the resolution. They may feel left out or shut out of the process and undermine it.

In any case, limiting the mediation to the people directly involved, perhaps with a limited number of allies from both sides, can often help move the process along. A second phase may be needed to involve the rest of the group.

The Seven Phases of Mediation

There are many schools of conflict resolution, transformation and mediation and hundreds of systems for intervening in conflicts. Below is my own approach to mediation, which involves seven phases.

1. A Safe Container

To feel safe in expressing vulnerability, people must know that they will be physically safe, that the mediator will intervene to prevent further hurt and that they will have a chance to tell their story and be heard. Generally, a mediator sets out agreements beforehand and asks both parties to consent to them.

To create a safe container, the mediator must find a place that is physically safe, comfortable and private. The setting should be neutral ground — not the home or office of either party. Time should be set aside for the mediation with no interruptions allowed. Cellphones should be turned off and/or left outside the room. Kids should be instructed to leave Mommy alone or be placed under the care of a sympathetic friend.

Confidentiality is often one aspect of safety. We cannot open up and show our vulnerability if we fear that our intimate revelations will become a subject of gossip outside the mediation or open us to further attacks. Generally a mediator will ask both parties to agree that what is said in the mediation will not be repeated outside, unless both parties give permission. However, if one or more parties cannot be trusted to keep confidentiality, it is better not to have the agreement than to have it violated.

Agreements are part of creating safety, but an equally important part is coming to a clear, mutual purpose for the mediation. Part of creating the container is finding an intention all parties can support. Why are we having this mediation? What's at stake? Do we want to improve our relationship? Improve the functioning of the group? Become more effective? Do we want an amicable divorce?

If we're honest, most of us engage in conflict with one overall desire: winning. Winning might mean walking away with some prized object or perk, with money or a position of power, or it might simply mean getting the other party to admit that our point of view is right and they are wrong.

But such intentions do not result in successful resolutions. A skilled mediator might address those conscious or unconscious hopes at the beginning, and ask people if they are willing to let them go in favor of an intention that can create safety for all concerned: finding a way to transform the situation so that everyone gets something they need and want, finding a way to work together in the future more effectively or transforming the situation to find the best outcome for all concerned.

2. Getting the Information Out

We need to know what happened, what was said, what was felt, what inferences and assumptions were made, what consequences ensued, all the relevant information. This includes bringing forth the subtext and emotional context and finding out which movie each party is in. What are people feeling? How are they framing those emotions? Which ladders of inference are they climbing, and what assumptions are they making? What chains of reasoning are they using? What values are at stake?

It can be tricky to get people to share the information in ways that don't simply pile on the hurt. A skilled mediator will have a toolbox of processes to use that can encourage people to express the full range of emotions and information in ways that can lead to transformation and don't simply compound injuries.

3. Getting People to Listen

Much of mediation involves getting people to listen to one another on multiple levels, to subtext as well as text, emotions as well as words. And the other half is making sure each party knows they have been heard.

A common mediation tool is to ask each party to repeat back what they heard from the other party and then to ask the first speaker if the paraphrasing is accurate, insuring that they feel heard. Participants might be asked to change seats and speak the other person's lines or to write out the story of what happened from the other person's point of view.

Hearing is not the same as *agreeing with*. Listening will not necessarily lead to agreement. It will, however, lead to deepened understanding. Some form of active listening is part of every mediation.

4. Reframing the Information and Shifting Positions

When the information is out on the table and heard, a skilled mediator can help reframe the situation in ways that open up positive and creative outcomes. Reframing might involve identifying the competing stories, the different movies each party is in, and then finding a way to tell a new tale. It may mean naming the conflicting good vs. good values at stake and agreeing to seek a dynamic balance.

Skilled mediators may help the parties in conflict identify their own assumptions and inferences and separate them from the factual accounts of what happened. They may ask the parties in conflict to share their own chains of reasoning, to test out their assumptions, back down their ladders of inference and identify their own stories or movies.

Again, a successful mediation may not lead to agreement. Most often, people in conflict will not come to agreement on their interpretations of the events of the past — but they can hopefully come to understand the other party's perspective and concerns. They may or may not permanently shift their stories of the past, but they can come to agree on a new story for the future.

5. Taking Responsibility

For a mediation to be successful, each party must take responsibility for their part of the conflict. Generally, that involves some form of apology. An apology is a statement of sincere regret, coupled with an intention to change in the future.

Beyond a simple apology, amends may be called for. Amends are actions we take to set right what has gone wrong, to mend hurts and redress grievances. A public apology may be a form of amends: "I'll write a note to the listserv in which

I apologize to you for the hurtful things I posted, and to the group for misusing the forum." It may also involve tangible reparations: "I'll pay for replacing that window my kid broke with her softball."

Part of taking responsibility is also making a request of the other party. Marshall Rosenberg, the originator of Nonviolent Communication, defines a request as something you can say no to without paying a huge emotional or tangible price.[4] To make a request is to be vulnerable and to demonstrate trust. "I'm sorry that I didn't realize I'd hurt your feelings. In the future, I'll check in with you when I sense discomfort, and I would ask you, next time you feel hurt by me, to tell me directly and immediately."

6. Agreements to Go Forward

While people may never agree on what happened, they may more easily come to agree on how they want to go forward together. What movie do we now want to step into together? How do we want to treat each other? How can we avoid repeating the patterns that led to the hurt? What structures might the group lack that this conflict illuminates? What do we want to tell the larger community about their agreements?

A successful mediation will culminate in a set of shared agreements. Here's an example of agreements from a mediation between two friends who have long-standing conflicts about how to appropriately raise concerns on the group listserv:

> Our listserv can be a useful forum for discussion and to some extent serve as a virtual meeting ground. However, written communication is very different from face-to-face communication, and nuances and tone are much harder to read.
>
> • Remember that posts will be read in the context of what has been going on before and what history you have with each other. If you are raising an issue which you feel someone might take personally, especially if you have a history of conflict or problematic communication, alert them privately before you put something out publicly. We will strive to focus on the issues raised and refrain from personalizing.
> • Misunderstandings and painful communications will inevitably happen, no matter how sensitive we are. If we are hurt, confused, unsure or angered by something one of us has written, we agree to call each

other up, meet face to face or at least e-mail each other privately to check our assumptions. We will strive to assume positive intent and refrain from public accusations or personal attacks. If we have a disagreement, we will deal with it directly and not use the listserv as a court of appeal.

- When we want to raise an issue or open a discussion, we will start from an open, neutral place, asking, "What do you think?" rather than stating what we think the other person's position is.
- We will avoid using loaded terms and will try to keep discussions about issues and structures, not individuals.
- We will remember that we have a lot of history together and a lot of love for each other and that we are allies on far more things than we are divided about.

7. Follow-up

How will we know these agreements are kept? What will happen if they are violated? Do we want to check in with one another or with the mediator periodically? Change takes time and repetition. Often we make attempts to change, slip back and need to be nudged, reminded or prodded to try again. A successful mediation will include a plan for follow-up and accountability.

Accountability does not mean punishment or coercion — which can actually undercut the success of a mediation. But it does mean having a community or a mentor to whom you report your successes, your mistakes, your efforts at change. The success of groups like Alcoholics Anonymous rests on their structure of a regular meeting, which creates a community of accountability. They also build in mentoring by assigning members a peer sponsor who offers guidance and who becomes another agent of accountability.

Tools for Mediation

The Box

At the beginning of the mediation, talk about our natural human urges to win, to be right, to make the other person look bad. Ask people to take a moment to think honestly about what their own hidden agendas might be. Assure them that no one else need know what they are, and ask them to write them down. Give them no more than ten minutes to do so.

Bring out the box — any type of box big enough to hold the papers, as long as it has a lid that will close. Ask the parties involved if they are willing to place those hidden agendas in the box and suspend them for the time of the mediation. Have them fold them up and write their names on the outside, and assure them that when the mediation is over, they can take them back if they wish. Ask each person to physically place their paper in the box, close it and set it aside.

Active Listening

Active listening means listening with full attention, to both text and subtext. When we listen actively, we are focused on the other person, striving to understand rather than formulating our comeback.

One party begins, telling a bit of their story while the other party listens. The mediator should set a strict time limit — no more than five minutes — and assure the second party that they will get their turn.

When the time is up, the mediator asks party number two to paraphrase in their own words what they heard and the emotions they sensed.

Party number one is then asked whether the response seems accurate to them, is given a chance to correct it and is asked to confirm that they feel heard.

Then party number two is given the same amount of time to speak, and party number one reflects back, with two correcting and confirming that their side has been heard.

Each party will get multiple turns in the course of a mediation. The mediator directs the process and makes sure time is allocated fairly, intervening to stop any destructive attacks.

Telling the Other Story

Each party is given a set amount of time — generally, ten to fifteen minutes — to write out the story of what has gone wrong as they believe the other party would tell it.

At the end of the time, each party reads what they've written aloud, and the mediator employs active listening techniques for them to test the validity. Alternatively, they may exchange papers and read each other's versions.

Using this technique gives everyone the challenge of shifting perspective. It may also reveal where each side misconstrues the other's position or, at times, that each side understands the other better than they thought.

Alternate version: Instead of writing, have the parties switch chairs and tell the story verbally from the other point of view.

Another Movie

Challenge the parties to tell the story of what's happened as if it were a particular movie, a fairy tale, a drama. How does this shift if it's *Romeo and Juliet*? What if it's *Lord of the Rings*? The point of this exercise is not to reach agreement, but to pry people out of their rigid belief that their story is The Truth — and to awaken creativity and humor.

The New Story

What's the new story we want to be telling, about our group, our community, our world? Can we shape it together around our mutual goals and purposes? What would it look like if we succeed with this project?

Every good story involves conflict, so how can our conflict strengthen the plot?

Backing Down the Ladder

Rick Ross, in *The Fifth Discipline Fieldbook,* identifies five steps for backing oneself or another down the ladder:

1. Identify the conclusions someone is making.
2. Ask for the data that led to the conclusions.
3. Inquire into the reasoning that connects data and conclusion.
4. Infer a possible belief or assumption.
5. State your inference and test it with the person.[5]

"Rick assaulted me" is not a neutral statement: it already embodies meaning, judgment and a specific frame. The data that led to the conclusions would be an account of what happened, as a video recorder might have captured it. "Rick yelled at me; I yelled at him; he shoved me into the pool," is closer.

Each side will likely have a very different version. From Rick's point of view, this is what happened: "I was distressed about the paper plates and told Edward so. He started yelling and came toward me. I put out my hands to protect myself and tried to push him back. He stumbled and fell into the pool."

My own approach, generally, is to start from the bottom rung and go up the ladder, beginning with a neutral description of events, then identifying the emotions and feelings that lead to data selection, assumptions, stories and conclusions.

What Happened?

People sometimes need help at this point to separate factual information from judgment. "She insulted me," is a judgment. "She got up when I sat down next to her at the community dinner and walked away" is factual information. The mediator should intervene when judgments come up and gently guide each party back to what they saw, heard and directly experienced.

How Did You Feel When It Happened?

The mediator might need to gently remind people what feelings are: happy, sad, scared, mad, hurt — not judgments. "I felt hurt," is a feeling. "I felt that you're a cold, uncaring boor," is a judgment. The mediator might also reaffirm that feelings just are — they don't have to be valid or invalid, justified or not. If we feel something, that's our reality.

What Assumptions Did You Make?

What meaning did you place on what happened? Here's where we want to bring out the judgments and the stories. "I thought she's mad at me because my kids always leave the front yard in a mess and she wants to drive me out of the cohousing block." "He hates me because he's jealous that I'm an attorney and he's just a bicycle messenger." At this stage, the important thing is to bring forth the underlying story, not to challenge it.

Ask Open Questions

The mediator should help each party formulate an open question that comes from a place of inquiry. Open questions refer to the facts or events without already including a judgment or an assumption. Examples of open questions might be: "What's going on with you?" "How do you feel about me?" "Are you mad about something?"

A formula that often works well is: "When you _____ (stick to facts of the event), I felt (a feeling term here, not a judgment) and I assumed _____. Is that true?" For example, "When you got up just after I sat down, I felt hurt, and I assumed that you were angry at me. Is that right?"

Using active listening, have the first party ask their questions. When they receive answers, ask them to paraphrase and repeat them back.

The mediator must decide whether to bring each party through these steps one at a time, or whether to shift more quickly between them, asking each in turn for their view of what happened, what they felt and what assumptions they made. Sticking with one side at a time builds momentum and coherence, but if the second party is too tense to listen they may lose trust that their side will be heard. Going first is also a position of power: the first speaker may set the frame for the discussion in spite of the mediator's efforts to keep the field open. If time is an issue, giving a large chunk of time to the first speaker may end up taking away time needed for both sides to be fairly aired.

Reframing

When both sides have aired and questioned their assumptions, the mediation can shift into a new phase — of reframing the events, telling a different story, taking responsibility, formulating apologies, creating a new story or coming to new agreements.

Tools for Change Mediation Script

Margo Adair and Bill Aal, of Tools for Change, have put many of these steps together into a script for mediations:

1. State the particular common mission and values which are affected by the current circumstances (what is at stake).
2. When ... (observable behavior/event) happened,
3. I felt ... (emotion only e.g. sad, angry)
4. Because I think the consequence is/ has been ... (your evaluation of the impact on your shared mission and/or how the event is contrary to your shared values. It is good to describe what in your experience has caused you to draw this conclusion).
5. I know that I also contributed to the situation by ... (acknowledge how you personally contributed to the problem by what you did or neglected to do).
6. I value ... (the positive side of the situation and/or how the person(s) makes positive contribution(s)).
7. I would like ... (what action or alternative policy you would like). Because I believe this would serve our mission by ...

8. I will ... (what you are willing to do to contribute to resolution) so that ... (anticipated improvement that this will make in the situation).[6]

The Fishbowl

Fishbowl is a term for a process where some people talk while others witness. There are several different ways to use this process in mediation or simply in group discussion:

Pair in the Bowl

The parties in conflict sit in the middle, others sit in a circle around them. They dialogue — or a mediator guides them through an active listening or other process, while the circle witnesses. Later, witnesses can be asked to reflect back what they heard from each side.

Group in the Bowl

When a subgroup of a larger community is in conflict, the parties most engaged can sit in the center and be guided through a mediation process while the circle witnesses and later reflects back.

Open-seated Fishbowl

The group in the center can have an open seat, where people from the circle can step in and add their comments or reflections, and then step back out. The group in the center can also be more fluid, with people staying in for a short time, then stepping out to leave room for others' comments.

Specified Group in the Center

The center can be opened for people who share a certain experience or identity or who hold a particular view around which the group as a whole may be polarized. I've used it, for example, in mediating between the "peace people" and the anarchists in a community organizing to oppose the war in Iraq. The anarchists got into the center and talked about their experiences in that community. They stepped back and witnessed as the "peace people" moved into center to talk about their experiences. Sitting, listening and witnessing, each side began to hear the other and to see them as people, not just annoying political factions. Afterwards, they broke into pairs to talk. The result was not agreement on every point, but a strengthened ability to work together to form a common strategy that both sides could carry out.

When Someone Won't Accept Mediation

One of the most vexing problems in groups occurs when people are in conflict and refuse to mediate or simply avoid mediation. There are several approaches a group can take:

Create More Safety

Avoidance may be a signal that the person in question does not feel safe. A mediator or ally can help them explore their fears and assumptions and find agreements and approaches that can give them confidence that they will be heard, respected and protected.

Create Prior Agreements

Ideally, long before conflict erupts a group will make an agreement to seek mediation when warranted. Then people can be held accountable to that agreement.

Social Pressure

When a conflict is affecting the group, when an individual is complaining but not confronting, friends and allies can encourage, chide and if necessary insist that they directly engage with the other party. Allies can be helpful in arranging mediation, being go-betweens to set up time, spaces and mediators and, if necessary, contribute to material support if a mediator must be paid. Consistent pressure combined with support from the group will generally bring most people to the table. If not, the group should hold solidarity around its commitment to open and direct process and make clear that further complaints, grumbling or charges will not be given air time or supported until a direct mediation takes place.

Beneficent Coercion

If membership in the group is contingent on keeping agreements, and those agreements include willingness to directly engage in conflict and to engage in mediation when necessary, then someone who refuses to mediate may be asked to leave the group. Pay, rewards or other benefits can be made contingent on accepting mediation. Coercion is not a popular option in most collaborative groups, but it has its moments when, judiciously applied, it can move a group into more productive functioning.

MARTA MEDIATES BETWEEN RICK AND EDWARD

Here's a transcript of Marta's mediation between Rick and Edward.

Creating the Container

Marta: Welcome, Edward and Rick. Please, take a chair and make yourselves comfortable. I'd like to start by setting some basic agreements, if that's OK with you? (They nod.)

First, that you agree to my facilitating this meeting, which gives me license to direct the proceedings, to interrupt if necessary and to guide the process. In return, I will agree to be as fair and impartial as is humanly possible, to protect both of you from sustained attacks and to intervene to maintain safety and an atmosphere of respect. Do you agree? (Again, they nod.)

Also, I'd like us to agree that the intent of this mediation is to help repair the breach in the community that came from the incidents at the picnic and to find ways that the two of you can live in the same community and work together, when necessary. I don't guarantee that you will come to agree on your interpretations of the past, but my goal is to make it possible for you to go forward into the future. Can you agree to that?

(Nods again.)

And finally, I'd like to ask us to agree that what we say here will be confidential. The purpose of this agreement is to allow for safety, so that you can each speak freely. At the end, we will determine together what to say to the community. Can you agree to that? If so and, to affirm all the agreements, I'd like to hear you say yes.

Rick: Yes.

Edward: Yes.

Getting the Information Out/Getting Them Both to Listen

Marta: Now, I'd like to start by hearing from each of you your account of what happened. By that I mean — if you were a video camera recording the scene, what would you have seen. Edward, why don't you begin?

Edward: Well, we were trying to have a nice community building event, and then Rick assaulted me.

Marta: Edward, I'm sure that's true to what you felt and experienced, but again, can you just tell me the specific acts or words, as a camera might record them?

Edward: He started yelling and screaming abuse at me, and then he pushed me into the pool. That's an assault, legally. I could have had him arrested.

Marta: When you say "abuse," can you say more specifically what he was shouting?

Edward: I don't remember the words, more the tone and volume.

Marta: And how did you feel?

Edward: I felt threatened.

Marta: "Threatened" — I would call that more of an assumption or a conclusion, that Rick was threatening you in some way.

Edward: He was. He pushed me into the damn pool.

Marta: But what was your emotion? Scared? Angry?

Edward: Scared. I was frightened of him ... he was out of control. And that made me mad! I'd worked hard to make that picnic a success. I didn't deserve that shit!

Marta: Rick, in a moment I'm going to give you your turn. But first, I'd like you to repeat back to Edward what you heard him say, both the content and the emotion.

Rick: I heard him say that I assaulted him, which I have to say is a way over-blown picture ....

Marta: (interrupting) You will have your turn to make your case. But now I'm asking you to repeat back the specifics of what Edward said happened, and how he felt.

Rick: Edward said I yelled and screamed at him and pushed him into the pool. And he felt scared and angry.

Marta: Edward, does that sound like what you said? Has Rick heard you?

Edward: Yeah, I guess so.

Marta: Rick, tell me what happened from your point of view.

Rick: I got to the picnic. I'd been looking forward to it — I'd been feeling for a while that RootBound needed some more juice in the community department, that we were losing our connections and becoming just another suburban development. Then I got there — and there was one of the TreePeople in tears, and I saw the paper plates. I guess I went sort of ballistic.

Marta: "Ballistic?" Is that an emotion or a judgment? Can you say specifically what you said or did?

Rick: I got mad, and I began to express my opinion very loudly. OK, to yell and scream. But I've said from the beginning, every meeting or every event we've ever had — let's not create waste! We have a whole goddamned dining room full of cups and plates, why in the name of creation do we need to waste paper?

Marta: I'm hearing your chain of reasoning, your inner dialogue. And you felt?

Rick: Mad! Angry! Frustrated! Unheard! Hell, those TreePeople kids, they risk their lives defending the trees. I've patched them up a dozen times — the least we can do is …

Marta: (interrupting) Please, Rick, I want to hear the feelings.

Rick: It felt like a slap in the face.

Marta: That's a powerful image, but not an emotion.

Rick: I told you. Mad. Frustrated. Ignored.

Marta: "Ignored" — that's a perception about what others have done or not done. But what's the emotion underneath it?

Rick: Why it's — I guess it's — hopeless.

Marta: Hopeless. Whew, that's a powerful emotion. I'd like to just sit with that for a moment, to acknowledge it and give it space. (After a beat) Edward, can you repeat back what you've heard so far from Rick?

Edward: Rick came to the gathering — he was looking forward to it. Then he saw Pyracantha crying, and the paper plates, and he got mad and started to yell and shout, because underneath he felt hopeless.

Marta: Rick, does that sound right to you? Do you feel that Edward has heard you?

Rick: (nodding). The ice caps are melting, the temperature's rising, we don't know what kind of godforsaken world we're leaving to our kids, and no one's doing anything about it. Now I come into my own community, where we're supposed to be a model of a different way, and what do I find?

Marta: Rick, I hear you sharing your chain of reasoning that reinforced your anger and hopelessness. But before we go there, I'd like to finish your account of what happened.

Rick: Edward came at me, and I put out my hands to stop him. I didn't mean to push him into the pool — he just kind of bounced off my hands, stumbled and fell.

(Marta gives him a long, intense look.)

OK, maybe there was a bit of spring in my wrists.

Marta: And you felt?

Rick: Mad. Maybe a bit scared. Edward's a big guy — he probably outweighs me by 50 pounds. I didn't know what he was going to do.

Edward: I was just trying to calm you down!

Marta: Edward, can you just repeat back again what you heard Rick say?

Edward: He's just making excuses for assaulting me. (at Marta's frown) OK, he saw me coming toward him, he felt mad and scared, so he put out his hands to defend himself and gave me a push.

Marta: Rick, is that accurate?

Rick: Close enough.

Reframing

Marta: OK, now one thing I'm hearing from both of you is that there were some cherished values at stake. Edward, you were acting out of a deep sense of care for the community, wanting to make an occasion where people could come together. And Rick, you were feeling the whole weight of the environmental movement, all the frustration and despair about climate change.

Edward: Hey, I care about the environment! I'm a solar engineer, for God's sake! Those plates were more than 50% recycled!

Rick: There's still the carbon footprint of making them!

Edward: What about the carbon footprint of transporting the water to wash the china!

Marta: I don't think the argument is really about the china. I think it's about values, and I suspect they are values that actually you both hold. So Rick, with your permission I'd like to walk you back down your ladder of inference and see if we can discern what those values are.

Rick: I'm game.

Marta: So, you came, you saw the paper plates, you felt a rush of emotion, anger, frustration, hopelessness … and you made some assumptions. Can you identify them?

Rick: I guess I assumed that someone on the committee didn't give a damn about the environment. And that they were deliberately trying to goad the TreePeople, with the meat and the paper plates.

Marta: Would you be willing to test that assumption?

Rick: How?

Marta: Here's the formula, you say, "When X happened, I felt Y, and I assumed Z. Is that right?"

Rick: When I saw the paper plates, I felt angry and hopeless. I assumed that you didn't care about the forests that the TreePeople spend their lives defending, and that you were deliberately trying to diss them. Am I right?

Marta: Edward, I'd like to suggest that feelings are feelings — they don't have to be right, wrong or appropriate — they just are. The assumptions and the conclusions that arise from our feelings, however, may be wrong or right.

Edward: I can see how you would feel mad, frustrated and even hopeless, Rick. I often feel hopeless, myself, about the environment — and about the community. But I do care about the forests and about climate change, even though I might make different choices sometimes than you would. And I certainly didn't intend to cause distress to the TreePeople or to you. If I had known how strongly you felt, I would have gone with the dining room china.

Marta: Edward, do you want to say more about your own chain of reasoning?

Edward: I wanted it to be a happy, joyful, community building event. I thought maybe just this once, we'd use the paper plates to give us a vacation from doing the dishes or worrying about who was going to do the dishes. And when Edward started yelling, I guess I also felt angry and hopeless. I assumed that he cared more about his rigid ideals than about the community, or he wouldn't have started screaming. I guess I assumed that he was trying to undermine the whole process.

Marta: Can you say that directly to him?

Edward: Rick, when you started yelling, I felt scared, mad, hopeless and disappointed. I assumed that you didn't care much about the community and had no investment in the picnic being a success. Was I right?

Rick: I guess I can understand how you might have felt that way, but no, you're wrong. I do care about the community. I didn't mean to wreck the picnic. I'm sorry for that.

Taking Responsibility

Marta: Rick, do you want to say more?

Rick: I'm sorry I pushed you into the pool. That was wrong of me. It was out of line, to take it into the physical.

Marta: Edward, can you repeat that back?

Edward: I hear that you're sorry you pushed me, and you admit that it was wrong. I accept the apology.

Marta: I'm hearing that you both share some powerful, common values. You both care about the environment, and you both care about the community. How do you think this incident has affected the community?

Rick: Very negatively. Now everyone hates me.

Edward: It's made it much harder to bring the community together. People have really splintered around it. And some of them have taken it places that I never wanted it to go.

Marta: How do you feel about it?

Rick: Guilty. Ashamed. I know I have a problem with anger, sometimes. I'm not proud of it.

Edward: I feel sort of guilty, too, although rationally I know I don't have anything to feel guilty about. And — frustrated. Some people are making such a big deal out of this — I mean, it is a big deal, but not that big a deal. Guys fight. Sometimes we get physical. I've been known to take a swing at someone. It's wrong — but it's not like a capital crime.

Rick: Thanks.

Marta: What do you think you could do to shift the community's energy and perceptions around this?

Edward: I think just knowing we had a mediation will help.

Rick: I feel like I should make a public apology, maybe when we come back from the break. And in the newsletter.

Marta: Are there any other amends you'd like to ask for, Edward?

Edward: (smiling) I think it would be poetic justice if you do my dishwashing shifts for the next month.

Rick: (grinning) Seems only fair.

Agreements to Go Forward

Marta: So, I'm hearing that Rick will make a public apology when we resume, and in the newsletter, and will do Edward's dishwashing shifts for a month. Is there anything else we need in order to move forward?

Edward: Rick, would you consider some kind of anger management group or training? Or maybe some counseling or therapy around it?

Rick: I've been thinking about it for a long time. I guess this incident shows me I really need it.

Edward: Actually, I've been thinking for a while that it might be good to bring the men in the community together, to talk about how we handle our anger and emotions. I used to belong to a men's group, back in the 1990s, and it really gave me a lot of support. Would you be willing to help me start that?

Rick: (surprised and delighted) You're on, bro! And if we do that together, I think it will help repair some of the rifts in the community.

Edward: And undercut the "Get Rick" vendetta!

Marta: So, we have agreed that Rick will make a public apology, will do Edward's dish shifts for a month, will seek counseling around anger management and that the two of you together will start a men's circle in RootBound. Is there anything else?

Rick: What do we tell the community about this? And how?

Edward: I think we can just tell them that we had a successful mediation, that we have resolved our issues and are looking forward to working together on creating the men's group. In your apology, you can mention the amends and the counseling. And I personally will never buy another paper plate as long as I live!

Rick: Sounds good!

Follow-up

Marta: So, when will you do all this? And how will you know it's done?

Rick: I'll speak to the group when we reconvene. I'll send a note to the newsletter tomorrow. Edward, I'd be happy to show you the draft.

Edward: Great!

Marta: Do you feel a need for any further mediation, or does this seem complete?

Edward: I feel complete. Thank you so much!

Rick: Me too!

Marta: So, what have we learned?

Rick: I've learned that my anger issues affect not just me, but the whole community. I've got to learn to handle it differently.

Edward: I've learned that my size can be intimidating, even when I'm not intending it to be. Not that I'm saying I deserved to be pushed into the pool. And that anger can cover hopelessness and despair.

Marta: I've learned, once again, that bitter conflicts can arise even between people who share common values. But that when they can be dealt with honestly and openly, creativity is unleashed. Thank you both for your willingness to be honest and vulnerable.

Rick: Thank you for helping me find a way back into community!

Edward: Thanks for relieving me of dish duty for a month!

Wrongdoing

Mediation is appropriate, as we've noted, for misunderstandings or miscommunication. But what happens when someone is accused of real wrongdoing: misappropriating funds, sexual harassment or abuse, physical violence, lying, spying and other forms of behavior that endanger individuals and the group? Mediation may not be a strong enough response to such behavior. Indeed, it may actually condone such behavior by implying that the perpetrator and the victim are both at fault.

When a real line has been crossed, a different process is necessary. Most often in our collaborative groups, we don't discuss those lines until an incident happens. The boundaries are assumed: we don't think to tell new members, "Don't murder anyone, don't physically assault people you disagree with, please don't engage in cannibalism or grave robbing or put poisonous substances into the dish you bring to the potluck, and we'd strongly prefer that you don't embezzle the group's funds, either."

Nonetheless, at some point in a group's formation, it may be useful to discuss the lines, ideally, before mayhem occurs. Below are some basic boundaries:

People have the Right to be Physically Safe

No one deserves to be assaulted or physically harmed. You can have an annoying personality, you can irritate people, you can wear that too-short skirt and still you don't deserve to be physically harmed, raped or injured.

Yes means Yes, No means No and Stop means Stop

People have the right to say yes and the right to say no or stop at any time, and have their wishes respected.

People Have a Right to Set Their Own Boundaries

And those rights should be respected — whether they are around their person, their time, their resources or their money.

DRUGS AND ALCOHOL

Harmful actions are often associated with drugs and alcohol which lower our inhibitions and reduce our control. Drugs can be enlightening, and alcohol can be pleasurable and relaxing, but for people who have trouble with either, they can open the gates to disaster.

Some groups set clear and rigid boundaries: no illegal drugs or alcohol. Others set no boundaries at all, and the group culture may even encourage drinking or drug use. Many groups set no obvious limits but carry an unspoken expectation that it is fine to drink, but not to show up obviously drunk; OK to get high, but not so high that it's incapacitating.

It's simpler to set and hold a clear boundary than a fuzzy one. "No drugs or alcohol" is easy to understand and to enforce, while "Not too much alcohol" is far more subjective. However, those rigid boundaries may not be appropriate for every group. Again, this is a subject that deserves group consideration before problems arise.

DUE PROCESS

In the criminal justice system, *due process* refers to a set of rights that protect the accused. Those of us who fight for social justice are often strong critics of the courts and legal system. We point out the many injustices that the system perpetrates. Groups with anti-authoritarian ideals may refuse on principle to call in the police or take legal action for any reason. Collaborative groups often prefer to

EXERCISE

Boundary Questions

- What are some of your individual boundaries? What are some lines which, for you, cannot be crossed?
- What boundaries are appropriate for the group to set?
- What boundaries do we draw around sexuality? How do we differentiate between mutual seduction and sexual harassment?

- What are our boundaries around the use of intoxicants? Smoking?
- Are there different boundaries we set for people who hold different roles? For example — that workshop teachers do not get sexually involved with students during a training.
- How do we ensure accountability around money?

settle their differences themselves and to create their own forms of justice when wrongdoing occurs.

But sometimes our homemade methods of justice may prove unfair. Delfina Vannucci and Richard Singer in *Come Hell or High Water* describe the unfortunate patterns they've seen when groups respond to accusations with gossip and hearsay.

> Many of us rightly condemn the injustices of the societies in which we live, but then we fail to turn that same scrutiny and skepticism onto our own activist organizations and anti-authoritarian collectives. Do we accord one another at least the rights that are written into the United States system of justice? ... Or are we even more authoritarian and less just whenever we condone the wholesale condemnation of people and behaviors we may not even know firsthand, and when we fail to establish fair procedures to air grievances and resolve conflicts?[7]

Due process refers to a set of basic human rights which many generations have fought for, going back to the days of the Magna Carta and beyond. Here are some of key aspects of due process:

- A person is innocent until proven guilty.
- The accused has the rights to know what the charges are against them, who brings those charges, to confront their accusers, to present a defense and to have an advocate.
- The accused has the right to a speedy and public trial and to be present at it.
- The accused has the right to a jury of their peers — to be judged by neutral people who do not have a personal stake in the outcome.

For centuries, people have struggled to free themselves from closed-door trials conducted by secret tribunals, from biased, corrupt judges and indefinite imprisonment. One of the most alarming setbacks to the cause of liberty has been the reinstatement of so many of these practices in the so-called War on Terror. How ironic that many of the very activists who stand strong against the CIA's secret renditions and the torturous conditions at Guantanamo may fail to provide their own comrades with due process in their own circles. We pass on rumors and grievances without verifying them. We judge cases where we are best friends or worst enemies of the parties involved.

When hurt feelings or miscommunication is all that's involved, such judgments may still do harm. But when accusations of real wrongdoing are made and accepted without a fair and open process, they can destroy lives.

What does due process look like in a collaborative group, when someone is accused of harmful acts?

- *Innocent until proven guilty:*
When we hear a story or an accusation against someone, we remember that it may or may not reflect the truth. We withhold judgment and do not pass the story on until we hear both sides and undertake some process to ascertain the truth.

- *The accused has the rights to know what the charges are against them, who brings those charges, to confront their accusers, to present a defense and to have an advocate:*
When someone is accused of serious wrongdoing, they get a fair hearing. They are told that the accusation has been made, by whom, and a face-to-face meeting is arranged with supportive help for both sides.

- *A speedy and public trial and a jury of their peers:*
A jury of peers originally protected the commoners from being tried by nobles — and undoubtedly assured the nobles that they would not be tried by resentful commoners. In collaborative groups, a jury of one's peers might mean simply a circle of neutral friends and community members who are not directly involved in the issue at hand. A speedy and public trial might translate into a timely chance for accused and accusers to directly confront each other, with community witness and support.

Confronting someone who has harmed us can be a terrifying and traumatic experience, and we often want to shelter a victim from that stress. However, confrontation with the right support can also be healing and transformative.

In the feminist movement of the 1970s and 1980s, we took a strong stand for believing victims of rape, abuse and sexual assault, in reaction to centuries of silencing of women. Before the feminist movement brought attention to rape and abuse as social issues, not just personal tragedies, rape victims were routinely shamed and traumatized by their interactions with police and courts.

Because we had to fight so hard for women to be believed at all, we often took the line that any charge of rape or sexual assault must be true. However, over time many of us began to realize that this position led sometimes to abuse of another kind. In the height of the ritual abuse scares, innocent people were at times convicted of horrific crimes, and lives were ruined.

Collaborative groups rarely have to deal with such serious charges. If they do, the situation has moved beyond the scope of what a group can deal with internally. Progressive groups are often reluctant to turn to the authorities, but when child abuse or severe violence is involved, the safety of the potential victims must take top priority. The justice system can be biased and unfair — however, it also includes many checks and balances to assure fairness. Support can be offered the accused in many ways — from bail money to jail visits to help securing good legal representation.

But most situations that we deal with are much murkier. Not "He jumped me, tied me up and dragged me into the bushes," but "He won't stop making suggestive remarks even when I've turned him down." Not "She's starving her child in the basement," but "She yelled at my kid and whacked him on the butt!" Not "He stole hundreds of millions of dollars in investment money through his Ponzi scheme," but "He 'borrows' $20 from the pot whenever he gets short, but doesn't pay it back."

STRUCTURES FOR ADDRESSING WRONGDOING

Collaborative groups do not have the resources to impanel a jury and hold a full trial. What can we do to respect individual rights and also redress real harm?

A collaborative group needs some sort of process or structure to deal with cases of wrongdoing. There are many models for that structure, but all of them require investing some individual or group with the authority to investigate facts, hear the case, make judgments and enforce them.

A Standing Ethics Committee

A few people are chosen to be part of a standing committee that can be convened in cases of harm or ethical wrongdoing. This model has the advantage that a structure is already in place and does not have to be created during the tension and stress when a situation develops. It has the disadvantage, however, that its very existence may encourage people to wage vendettas and escalate grievances. And when authority is permanently invested in the people on the committee, they acquire power that may shift the balance in the group away from collectivity.

A Standing Pool

Rather than a set committee, a group can identify a pool of people who have skills in mediation and dispute resolution and can be called upon at need.

An Elders Circle

When a case of wrongdoing surfaces, both parties agree on a number of elders who are invested with the authority to decide what to do, how to ensure due process, how to determine the facts in the case, what amends should be made and how the resolution will be followed up.

The Elders Circle model has the advantage of flexibility. It can be composed of people who are present and available, and because it exists only temporarily, no one accrues authority permanently. It has the disadvantage that it requires agreement from both parties and their willingness to participate. "Elders" do not have to be older — they are chosen for their fairness and discernment, which may or may not grow with age. The group may prefer a different name for this circle.

A Discernment Circle

When both parties do not agree, or when the wronged party is unsure of how to proceed with a grievance or unclear on who authored the harm, or when someone is involved with an ongoing conflict that does not seem to resolve, she may call a Discernment Circle: a group of elders in whom she invests the authority to hear the situation and recommend a course of action.

A Discernment Circle is not a trial-in-absentia of an accused wrongdoer. It's a chance for someone who feels hurt or victimized to wrestle with their own emotions, receive support and decide on what the next steps should be. It is most effective when it is more than a cheering squad for grievances, when its members are objective and help the aggrieved person examine her own assumptions and inferences. While it has no authority over the accused, it can recommend a course of action to bring about a fair hearing or to ask for amends.

When Authority Exists

Many of the groups we work in are hybrids of collectivity and formal authority. I work in many collectives, and I also teach courses in which I am the acknowledged leader and organizer. When I hold that role, I also hold the authority and responsibility to assure the safety of the group and to maintain the conditions that make it possible for the group to carry out its functions. At times, I've had to ask individuals to leave when their presence either damaged the group's ability to function or posed a danger to themselves or others. When we do hold formal power, it is imperative that we be willing to step up and use it, when necessary, to protect the group.

Restorative Justice

One of the most inspiring and helpful frameworks for dealing with wrongdoing comes from the restorative justice movement.[8] Restorative justice developed out of programs in the 1970s to bring together offenders and victims for encounters, but it draws on many sources, including indigenous practices of council and peacemaking. While the criminal justice system is based on punishment and retribution, restorative justice sees crime as a breach in the community and seeks to restore safety, trust and community well-being.

Today, the restorative justice movement has spread around the globe and is included as an alternative in many criminal justice systems. Over many years of practice and experience, the restorative justice movement has synthesized key principles:

1. Crime causes harm and justice should focus on repairing that harm.
2. The people most affected by the crime should participate in its resolution.
3. The responsibility of the government is to maintain order, and of the community is to build peace.[9]

Some of the key features of the movement are:

1. Opportunity for Encounter

Restorative justice emphasizes direct encounters between victims and offenders. These may take place in many forms, from letters, one-on-one mediated encounters, family circles or community circles in which all who are affected by the crime come together.

2. Emphasis on Making Amends

Amends may be suggested by a *sentencing circle* or come from an agreement between victim and perpetrator. The intent of the amends is to repair the harm done, by offering a sincere apology and committing to changed behavior and by making restitution in some form, which could be monetary or through labor or service.

3. The Goal of Reintegration of Victims and Offenders

While the criminal justice system removes offenders from the community, restorative justice seeks to reintegrate them so that they may become productive members who can make contributions to the greater good. It has a focus on healing the victims and generosity toward offenders, with the result of a far lower rate of recidivism than conventional systems.

4. Inclusion of Victims and Offenders in the Program

Both victims and offenders are involved in the process of encounter and restitution. Victims are given support, and offenders are faced with hearing the human pain and seeing the direct results of their actions.

The restorative justice movement is a great resource for collaborative groups seeking to establish fair and compassionate procedures for resolving serious breaches of community trust. Applying the principles, learning from decades of experience and seeking training and mentoring can help wean us away from unhealthy patterns of trial-by-gossip and conflict avoidance.

CONFLICT CAN BE CONSTRUCTIVE

When we embrace conflict instead of fearing and dodging it, when we apply what we know about power and communication, mediation and transformation, when we approach our disagreements in the spirit of learning and compassion, then our conflicts can actually strengthen our group. When we can wrestle with competing ideas and values and retain our love and respect for one another, we grow stronger and deepen our trust. When we assure due process and, fairness and confront wrongdoing in the spirit of reconciliation and restoration, we can learn and grow from even the worst blows to community. As we become more skillful at resolving our internal disputes, we can strengthen our effectiveness in confronting the wrongs of the larger society and modeling more just and compassionate ways of beings.

CHAPTER 8

Dealing with Difficult People

AND THE DRAMA CONTINUES ...

When RootBound reconvened after lunch, everyone seemed more relaxed. The mood was friendly and open. Pyracantha had spied Jennie playing on the swing set, had gone over to her and apologized personally for sending the pictures that had upset her so deeply. They had had a long talk about animals, and Pyracantha found Jennie, at least, was very interested in everything she had to say.

Marta felt hopeful as the people settled into the circle. Edward and Rick sat together, and when the session began, Rick stood up.

"First, I want to apologize to all of you," he said. "I was very wrong to take my argument with Edward into the physical. I've apologized to him and offered to make amends — in part by doing his dish shifts for the next month! But I also want to apologize to all of you. My actions created a rupture in the community and undermined our ability to renew our enthusiasm and spirit, which I care about deeply. I feel very bad about that, and I would ask any or all of you for suggestions of any way I can help to repair the damage.

"One thing Edward and I talked about is our need, as men, to deal with our anger issues. We've agreed to form a men's group together, here at RootBound, to offer one another some support and some challenges, and we invite the other men to join us."

His statement was greeted by lots of smiles and a smattering of applause. But Marta noted a few faces that still looked unconvinced.

"Hmnph," Betty snorted. "Typical guy behavior. They yell, they scream, they bash each other — then suddenly they're the best of friends."

"Well, that is kinda how we are," Edward admitted. "But I feel resolved with Rick. I know he's learned from the incident, and so have I. I don't think we'll have to deal with any more bashing."

"Well, what about the rest of us?" Betty said. "What about the women?"

"Oh come on, Betty," Marion said. "I'd say the women here could bash it up with the best of 'em, if we so choose. Haven't you ever lost it? I'll best there's a slapped face or two, at least, in your closet if we started to dig."

"That's not the point," Betty said. "The point is, how do we establish some ground rules of safety as a community?"

"Good point," said Marta. "What agreements would you suggest?"

Betty thought for a moment. "I suggest we put a statement into our operating agreements that we do not tolerate physical or verbal violence as a way of settling disputes."

Around the circle, Marta saw many heads nod.

"Define 'verbal violence,'" Acacia challenged.

"We will get to that," Marta said. "But perhaps at a later meeting. I'd like to take up your suggestion as a proposal, Betty, which I understand must be circulated to the membership and brought up for consensus at the next general meeting. Am I right?"

"That's right. But it seems like a lot of bureaucracy for this," Betty grumbled.

"I would, however, like to ask the group if we agree to the broad sense of the proposal?" Marta went on. "Can I see a thumbs-up if you do?"

Around the circle, thumbs pointed to the sky.

"Betty, let me ask, are you feeling safer now?" Marta asked.

"I guess so."

"Is there anything more you'd like to request of the group around safety issues?"

Betty shook her head. "I feel done."

"Anyone?" Marta asked. "This is the moment to raise your issues, while we're all here and can address them."

No one spoke. For some reason, Marta still felt a bit uneasy. She gave it one more try. "This is your chance." She waited: silence.

"All right, then," Marta said. "We've worked through some conflicts here today. In our last hour, I'd like to bring you back to the question I raised about core values. …"

The day ended on a positive note. Eli and Ella were jubilant.

"You are a magician," Eli told Marta, as they celebrated with another delicious Indian dinner.

"A good Witch!" Ella smiled. "I feel hopeful about RootBound again!"

"I do too," Marta said. "But my instincts are telling me that we're not out of the woods yet."

And indeed, although the energy had greatly shifted at RootBound, something strange seemed to still be in the air. Eli noted certain groups of people seemed to be avoiding him, mostly a core of friends connected to Andrew Bagly, a newer member who edited an alternative online news blog. Andrew had always been friendly to Eli, but now Eli noticed a definite sense of chill.

More worrisome, Eli ran into his old friend Arman Butler at a meeting.

"Hey Eli, how 'ya doin'?" Arman asked with an expression of concern. "You OK?"

"Yeah, sure, why wouldn't I be?" Eli asked.

"The stories I hear … I hear there's a mess at RootBound."

"There's conflict, sure — what community doesn't have conflict? But I wouldn't call it a mess. In fact, I think we've made some great strides in dealing with it."

"So, the gossip isn't true? Kind of a shame — some great drama, what with violent assaults, dead animals left in mailboxes, kids terrorized and, of course, the cover-ups. …"

"What?" Eli was outraged.

"You ever thought of marketing RootBound as a reality TV show?"

"Who'd you hear this from?" Eli demanded.

"Here and there," Arman shrugged. "I don't remember … could have been at that meeting with Bagly."

"I'll kill him! I'll break his legs!" Eli sputtered to Ella that night.

"Better do it quick, before we consense on that anti-violence statement," Ella suggested. Their mood was not improved when Arman sent Eli a link to Bagly's blog, which featured a blistering article entitled "Community Cover-up: What Happens When Ideals Go Bad." While the post mentioned no names, it was clearly directed at RootBound.

"This may be just the chance you've been waiting for to practice your good communication skills," Ella suggested.

Eli approached Andrew in RootBound's parking lot the next morning.

"Andrew, can I talk to you for a minute?" Eli said. "Some gossip has reached my ears, attributed to you, and I wanted to check it out."

"I don't gossip," Andrew said. "If you listen to gossip, that's your problem."

"But I gather from your blog that you're not happy with the resolution of the pool incident. Am I right about that?"

"What's to be happy about? Typical male patriarchal bonding behavior. Two guys rough each other up, then collude to bury the whole thing. Then they're all buddy-buddy. And the solution — we're all supposed to go grunting off in the woods, beating drums and finding our Inner Man! I don't think so. And you — you just let it all go down so you can be the fair-haired boy, making your big bucks from touting your oh-so-great community. Let me be honest with you — the whole thing makes me sick!"

Eli was shaken. "But Andrew, you didn't say a word at the time!"

"What was the point? It was clear that everyone wanted to bury the whole thing. There wasn't any room for disagreement."

"That's not true!" Eli objected. "Marta asked at least three times if anyone …"

"Oh Marta, the great Marta. Marta the Martyr! Marta the deal-broker!"

Remember your tools, Eli told himself. Non-violent communication. Listening. Empathy. He took a deep breath.

"Andrew, when I saw your blog and heard the rumors you're credited with spreading, I felt hurt, angry and blindsided …."

"You know what?" Andrew interrupted. "I don't give a shit what you feel!" He stalked off.

"Now what do we do?" Eli and Ella were back at Au Coquelet with Marta.

Marta reached for a napkin and drew a new version of her Talisman.

"Here's a protective charm," she said. "Employ it, give him room to change or shift the group norms so that he has incentive to leave if he is unwilling to change. And recognize what you can and cannot control. You can discourage gossip within your own group. You can't control what others say about you behind your back. You can only prove them wrong by surviving and thriving."

Marta smiled, stood up and told them she was late for a meeting. Only after she'd left did they discover another packet of papers she'd quietly tucked into Ella's bag.

RECOGNIZING DIFFICULT PEOPLE

We can have the ideal group structure, clear visions, goals and boundaries, great conflict resolution agreements, impeccable communication skills and excellent meeting facilitation, and some people will still be cranky, ornery, fussy, mean, sad, unsatisfied, manipulative, stormy, whiny and downright difficult. Who are these people? Well, they are us, some of the time. Difficult people are not a breed apart. Even I — gifted with nearly saintly patience, compassion and understanding — have been known to snap at people, yell, throw things, slam doors and storm out of meetings — and that's on my good days!

Nonetheless, some people are consistently, chronically difficult to deal with. In the context of this chapter, I mean people who have patterns of behavior and interaction and/or communication styles that cause continual distress and conflict. Many times, they are also gifted, wonderful and important contributors to the group, but sometimes a person's difficulties can be such that they overwhelm the group's capacity for support. They may undermine or even destroy the group. Collaborative groups need strategies to protect themselves and to take the steps that will be most truly supportive of such people.

AVOIDING A TELESCOPIC VIEW

When we look at patterns and try to make sense of problematic behavior, we also need to be careful not to become wedded to what management consultant Bill Wiersma calls "a telescopic vision." It's as if we saw the person through the narrow field of a telescope "focusing tightly on their blemishes, to the exclusion of everything else. The resulting narrow view soon defines the other person by his or her flaws, producing an uncomplimentary caricature of sorts that is devoid of positive aspects of character ....

When people are viewed telescopically, they are often trapped in expected behaviors — unable to change the view or perception others have of them and often continuing to fulfill their observers' predictions about their behavior. Likewise, the people holding the telescopic views become ineffective, as they are unable to nurture or to bring out the very tendencies in others that would break the cycle. Caught in ever-spiraling cycles of unwanted behavior, both parties lose."[1]

When a teacher defines a child as a delinquent-in-the-making, he is likely to treat her angrily and harshly. She becomes angry in response and acts out, confirming his opinion. She may have unsuspected talents and abilities that will never be realized because the teacher's efforts all go into attempts to control her and punish her bad behavior, not to bring out her gifts.

CREATING SUPPORT FOR CHANGE

When we set out to change ingrained patterns, our own or others, we need help. Counseling, professional life coaching, self-help groups such as Alcoholics Anonymous or other 12-step programs as well as many forms of traditional and non-traditional therapy can all be enormously helpful. We didn't develop our dysfunctional patterns in isolation, and we can't cure them in isolation. Some form of structured support from another human being is vital.

Groups can also help members by encouraging mentoring and peer coaching. A mentor is someone who is invested with the authority to offer constructive critiques, set challenges and suggest new areas of growth. Generally a mentor is someone who has a level of skill and experience we aspire to and is willing to take on the responsibility of guiding our growth.

A peer coach is a more level relationship. When we peer coach each other, we form a bond and share our vulnerabilities, our hopes and our challenges. We agree to give each other honest, constructive feedback, to challenge one another to stretch our growing edges and to report back regularly to one another.

Marshall Goldsmith, in his article on peer coaching, describes how he works with a friend who commits to asking him a series of questions every day. He reciprocates by asking his friend his own set.[2] He suggests the following exercise:

E
X
E
R
C
I
S
E
Support for Change Coaching Questions

Think of some of the key areas of your life in which you are trying to make changes or maintain beneficial practices. They might include your work, your creative projects, your relationships, your family and your health. Write out your own list of daily questions, and recruit a friend to ask them of you. Or, write them in your journal and make a practice of asking and answering them yourself.

WHY ARE PEOPLE DIFFICULT?

Sometimes we find people difficult simply because their personality styles or cultural norms don't fit our expectations. Other people may be angry or traumatized, suffering from an acute loss or chronically in a state of depression. People may have conditions that undermine their ability to participate in a group: mental illness or addiction to alcohol or drugs. Some may have agendas that run counter to the good of the group — for personal gain, for power, for attention. Political groups who contest the power of the system may need to contend with infiltrators or undercover police agents.

TRAUMA AND POWER-UNDER

We live in a society in which trauma is epidemic. Judith Herman defines *trauma* as follows: "Traumatic events overwhelm the ordinary systems of care that give people a sense of control, connection, and meaning … they overwhelm the ordinary human adaptations to life. …"[3]

Trauma comes in varying degrees. *First degree trauma* might be the assault, the damage or pain that we suffer ourselves. We are the ones being beaten. *Second degree trauma* comes from witnessing the beating. We might not suffer the physical pain or harm, but when we empathize with the victim and especially when we are helpless to take action or alleviate the suffering, we may suffer deep emotional wounds. *Third degree trauma* might be hearing about a traumatic incident, reading about it or imagining it. Any of us who listen to the news or watch TV experience this sort of low-level trauma almost continually.

Trauma shatters our energy field — our physical, emotional, psychic and energetic field of protection. When our ordinary ways of coping no longer serve, we may shut down our capacities to feel and empathize. Perhaps we cannot escape physically from an abusive situation, so instead, we remove ourselves emotionally and psychically. Once closed down, our emotions may remain frozen, and we may find it hard to experience joy and pleasure.

Conversely, trauma can also make us hyper-alert, always wary of a new injury about to happen, seeing danger whether or not it exists. That shutdown state can alternate with periods in which we relive and reexperience the trauma, through nightmares, through flashbacks or through times of depression and overwhelming grief and sadness. Trauma survivors often feel guilty or ashamed, even though they were not the ones who perpetrated the act of violence.

After a trauma, we may have trouble reestablishing our physical and emotional baseline. We may crawl into bed and sleep for days — or be unable to sleep. We might stuff ourselves with food — or find ourselves without an appetite, unable to stomach our usual meals. We may crave company or withdraw into isolation. We may be unable to speak about the event — or unable to stop talking about it.

Trauma can also leave us with overwhelming rage. Steve Wineman calls that helpless anger *power-under*. "We find it in our own tendencies to demonize the oppressor, in our susceptibilities to infighting and splintering, and in the imposing difficulties we repeatedly encounter in our efforts to build coalitions and to forge a kind of unity that can house multiple identities and honor the integrity of our experiences of oppression."[4]

Grief and trauma leave us less than usually competent and organized. Simple tasks may seem overwhelming. Our culture expects people to be competent, on game and efficient at all times. We are allocated little, if any, time to mourn or grieve after a loss. But trauma takes time to integrate, and grief takes time to heal. Many cultures have mourning traditions that determine what you can do, wear or celebrate for months or years after a severe loss. They understand that losing a loved one makes us, in some sense, a different person, and we need time to integrate that change.

Supporting One Another through Grief and Trauma

A caring community can support people through grief, loss and trauma in many ways. When a group has a culture of active listening and emotional sharing, we can become healers for one another in times of grief and stress.

Admit Your Ignorance

People respond differently to trauma, and there is no one course of action that is right for everyone. Since the essence of trauma is helplessness, we cannot undo its damage by making survivors even more helpless, by telling them what they should do or feel.

Listen

We can make ourselves available to listen, actively, empathetically, hearing emotions as well as content. We don't have to fix the situation or relieve the pain. Indeed, we cannot. A good listener is a witness, not a problem-solver or an advice-giver.

Advocate

We can help the trauma survivor find appropriate support and services — legal or medical help, if needed — and offer practical support.

Protect

Just as a wounded lamb will attract vultures and ravens, a trauma may attract those who feed on emotional drama for their own needs. Sometimes the greatest service we can offer a trauma victim is to simply ward off those who think they know best or want to pry open the wounds.

Do the Dishes

Someone who quietly cleans the house or fixes a nourishing meal is offering care and concern in tangible ways that can sometimes create a healing and supportive atmosphere more effectively than the most eloquent words.

Do Not Blame the Victim

Trauma arouses our deepest feelings of guilt and shame. Do not reinforce them by implying the event was in some way the fault of the survivor — even if, deep in your heart, you believe that's true. No one deserves to be assaulted — even if they have an annoying personality or made a stupid remark. No one deserves to be raped, even if they were wearing a short skirt or walking down a dark street. Shame and guilt are normal responses to trauma, but not valid assessments. The blame and shame belong to the perpetrator.

Don't Tear Open the Wound

The aftermath of trauma is not the time for cathartic therapies, nor is it the moment to open up the deepest emotional wounds of childhood. Experienced trauma counselors do not encourage survivors to relive the events or reexperience the pain directly, but rather to create some distance and control, as if events were happening on an imaginary movie screen. Well-meaning friends who push for a catharsis without skills or a safe container risk doing enormous harm.

Encourage Creative Integration

Writing, drawing, singing or dancing are acts of power. When we create, we take control, if only of the words on a page. When a trauma survivor is ready, creative expression can help counter helplessness and further integration and healing.

Support Strength and Resilience

When someone has suffered a trauma, they need to be supported for their strength, honored for the choices that have helped them survive, reminded that they are resilient and that they can recover and that they will feel joy, love, hope and self-confidence again.

See the Person as Whole

Instead of incessantly focusing on the traumatic event, we can engage in conversation about their work, their hobbies, their family, their favorite activities, even their favorite musical group or sports team — not as a way of avoiding the incident, but as a way of asserting that they have a life beyond the trauma, and that they will return to life.

BORDERLINE BEHAVIOR

Some responses to trauma become fixed in ways that are seriously debilitating and even life-threatening. Trauma can lead to suicide, drug or alcohol addiction, disease or severe, prolonged mental illness. It can also become ingrained in those personality traits that are so difficult to deal with.

> In the last 15 years there has been increasing recognition in the mental health field that severe trauma is a primary antecedent of "borderline personality disorder" .... The need to identify a proximate villain, the splitting of their world into sharply defined figures of benevolence and malevolence, their utter conviction that they are being acted upon and victimized, their patterns of self-abuse, and their chronic expression of powerless rage all are indicators of unhealed trauma.[5]

Borderline personality disorder is a psychological term for a pattern of behavior that can be extremely difficult for groups to deal with. Someone with borderline personality disorder may exhibit intense rage triggered by minor incidents, often when boundaries are set or perhaps by some form of rejection or abandonment. Another aspect of the pattern is *splitting*: either/or, black/white thinking, putting people on a pedestal only to knock them down again, dividing the group into factions or attempting to split up couples or friendships. We need not collude with destructive actions, but we can be less reactive and more compassionate if we understand that unhealed trauma may lie behind these actions. As always, good communication skills are our best defense.

POST-TRAUMATIC STRESS

When the normal symptoms of trauma do not abate over time, if months after the trauma the survivor is still not able to carry on with life, they may be suffering from post-traumatic stress.

Some warning signs might be changes in sleeping or eating habits that persist over time, alcohol or drug addiction, severe depression or isolation. Loving friends might pay special attention to trauma survivors, making sure they don't just drop out of sight or disappear without being noticed.

When trauma becomes post-traumatic stress, a caring community will intervene to get skilled and experienced help in a safe and protected setting. Community members might find a skilled trauma counselor and arrange for financial support to help pay for therapy. They might advocate with the insurance company to get psychiatric help. Although many of us have strong critiques of the mental health services and are reluctant to hospitalize people, sometimes medication or hospitalization can literally mean the difference between life and death.

HOW TRAUMA PLAYS OUT IN GROUPS
Horizontal Violence

When we can't strike back at those who are truly harming us, we often lash out at those we can reach. We yell at our lover because we can't yell at the boss.

In groups, we may fight even the most minor conflict to the death. We attack our fellow group members with all the unexpressed rage that really belongs to the perpetrators of violence. In our minds, we are always fighting for our lives. Just as enraged dogs will attack one another with no regard for their relative size, we lose sight of real power differentials and may demolish a group member with a blast of anger without realizing that we have shifted from victim of abuse to abuser.

Horizontal Violence Strategies

1. Friends don't let friends abuse one another. A group that sets healthy boundaries and standards for behavior needs to hold one another accountable for keeping them.
2. Offer constructive critique and honest feedback.
3. Collective intervention: Others in the group can support one another to tell the raging group member that their behavior is not acceptable. Couple this with:

4. Good cop/bad cop: While one or more group members set and hold clear boundaries, another might offer help and support to find counseling, coaching or mediation.

5. Mentoring: Assigning the offending person a mentor can provide long-term encouragement to both change behavior and look at deeper patterns.

The Perpetual Victim

Some people cling to the role of victim, claiming center stage. Whatever issue or drama erups somehow always ends up being about them. Their patterns may originate from deep hurt and trauma and we can feel sympathy, but colluding with them is not helpful either to the person or the group. Fruitless efforts to appease them can drain the group's energy and undermine its effectiveness.

When we are caught up in the role of victim, our speech and actions reflect our sense of powerlessness. To regain our sense of empowerment, we might begin by challenging the inherent assumptions in our words and practicing alternative framings and affirmations.

Blaming

Statement: "You made me feel …"

Assumptions: I am at the mercy of other people's speech and actions. I am helpless to do anything but respond to how others treat me.

Alternate suggestion: I choose how to respond to other people's statements and assessments. I can choose what to take in and what to discard. My feelings are real and valid, but I can move through them quickly and separate them from my own assumptions and other people's judgments.

Blurting

Statement: "I have to speak my truth."

Translation: I'm about to blurt out something hurtful in the most blunt way possible.

Assumptions: Truth is uncomfortable, painful and festering. My feelings and perceptions are The Truth, and I must get it out just as I might vomit up a bad meal, regardless of consequences.

Alternate suggestion: I choose to speak my truth, using all my sensitivity, wisdom and skill so that I can be clearly heard and effective.

Bleating

Statement: "I'm being silenced."

Assumption: If people actually heard me, they would agree with me. So if they don't agree with me, they are shutting me down.

Alternate suggestion: I can advocate for my own perspective — whether or not others agree — and respect their right to differ. I do not need anyone's permission to advocate for myself.

Strategies for Transforming the Role of Victim

1. Clear, fair and transparent ways that people can earn power in the group will provide constructive alternatives to victimization.
2. Structures and practice of constructive critique can provide positive channels for complaints.
3. Encourage responsibility with questions like: What would you suggest to make the situation different? What structures would you like to see in place that would help us address your needs and concerns?

EXERCISE

Victim Coaching Suggestions

A good coach will tell us the truth and call us on our dysfunctional patterns, with questions like:

- How did this situation become about you? What if you weren't at center, how might that feel?
- What benefits are you getting from playing this particular role?
- How might the situation shift if you felt you had power?

I Choose Exercise

You can do this in pairs or as a journal exercise. Think of a situation in which you tell yourself, "I have to …" "I have to get out of bed and go to work." "I have to keep Pondweed happy or she might leave the group."

Notice how your body feels when you say "I have to." Notice what you feel energetically and emotionally.

What would it feel like to change "I have to …" to "I choose to …"? "I choose to get up and go to work" "I choose to make Pondweed happy." How does changing the phrase change your own sense of power and self-esteem? Perhaps you choose to go to work in order to support yourself in comfort and independence. What other options become apparent once you acknowledge your own power to choose?

Reversing the Vortex of Victimhood

In collaborative groups with a social conscience, we hold compassion and sympathy for victims of violence and oppression. At times, that sympathy can lead us to subtly favor the position of victim. People are awarded social power because of their victimization or their identity as part of an oppressed group. But this is not true, earned social power. Rather than supporting people's resilience and strength, we lock them into their victim identities.

For example, we may try to control the environment to remove any possible triggers.

For survivors of sexual assault or abuse, even innocent, unwanted touch may stimulate intense memories or rage. An alcoholic might be triggered to drink by seeing wine passed around in a ritual. Some groups make rules: "No touching, even affectionate hugging, without asking first." "No drinking."

At times, those rules may be useful. In Reclaiming, for example, our public rituals and gathering are clean and sober — both to support those who are in recovery from addiction, but also because that rule tends to discourage those people who think a ritual is just a chance to party. This sets a serious tone and intention.

At other times, rules may perpetuate a survivor's sense of victimization instead of calling forth their resilience. Instead of prohibiting all hugging and touch, the group might instead say, "How can we support you to set your own boundaries and take responsibility for your own level of comfort?" That might mean a strong commitment from the group that it is OK for someone to say, "Please don't hug me, I don't like it." Or it might mean support to find help in desensitizing that trigger, so that the person can begin to enjoy the bonding and affection of the group.

CLASHING STYLES AND NORMS

Some people are difficult because their style or personality simply clashes with our own.

Puppies are noisy, loud, friendly and exuberant. When they like you, they bound all over you, and if they are large, can even knock you down. When they are threatened or scared, they bark.

EXERCISE

Questions About Personal Style

- What personal expressive styles did your parents have? Other members of your family of origin?
- What styles were approved of and rewarded in the culture you grew up in?
- How was a person of your age, gender or background expected to behave?
- Do you fit those expectations? How have they served you or done you disservice?

The Pie Exercise

Draw a circle that represents the group's time and energy. Now draw the slice of the pie that represents the amount of time, space and energy you take up. Share it with your coach, and ask for feedback. Is your perception accurate? If you take up a lot of time and space, what can you do to make space for others? Make a clear commitment, for example, "I will wait to volunteer my opinion at meetings until at least two other people have spoken." Check back with your coach to discuss what happens.

If you take up little space, what prevents you from stepping forward and claiming your fair share? Are the barriers in the group, in yourself or both? Some helpful coaching questions might be:

- Are there opinions, ideas or insights you are not voicing? Why? What is the group losing because of your silence?
- What risks would you be taking by voicing more of your thoughts?
- What would it be like to be more central in the group? What emotions come up when you imagine it?
- What messages did you receive in the past that contribute to your silence now? Can you give that voice a face, a name and hold some dialogue with it.

Personal Style Coaching Suggestions

Consider some of these questions:

- Whose personal style do you feel most comfortable with in the group?
- Whose style or personality clashes with yours? How?
- Is there any feedback you could give to that person or requests you could make that would make it easier to work together?
- Are there ways you are willing to modify your own style in order to better work together?

Cats, in contrast, are wary, quiet and contained. They size you up silently, and if they like you, they may rub against your ankles or issue a soft purr. If they dislike you, they may hiss or scratch, but mostly they simply go away.

Some people behave more like puppies, others like cats, and when they meet in a group, their different styles may clash just as real dogs and cats often do. Brash, boisterous, outgoing people add energy and zest to a group, but they may also take up a lot of the available space. Quieter, more introverted people may be unwilling to fight for space or simply get exhausted. But they, too, may have valuable insights and skills that the group needs.

These differences may be purely personal, but they may also be rooted in class or cultural norms. People who grew up in poor or oppressed communities may have internalized, early on, the message that if they want recognition, they need to stake their claim and defend it vigorously. People from upper- or middle-class backgrounds or other ethnic cultures may have internalized a very different message. When recognition is assumed, demanding it may seem rude and uncouth.

Agreements and processes that help equalize participation can also help assure that each person gets space and recognition.

PATTERNS OF REACTION

Beyond class and cultural norms, there are personality styles that may further the group's health or dysfunction. In *Truth or Dare,* I suggested that all of us are to some extent formed by a society rooted in punishment and force, one that does not truly value our inherent worth. We may be appreciated for our achievements, lauded for our looks, our wealth or our hard work, but every day we encounter a thousand messages telling us that we are not worthy, not valued for simply being who we are. We internalize the voice of society, the inner authority, critic, boss or self-hater, as novelist Doris Lessing defines it. And, I suggested, we respond to that self-hater in four basic ways:

Comply	Withdraw
Rebel	Manipulate[6]

Each of these strategies arises as a way we protect ourselves, possibly even save our own lives. They may each offer some positive benefits, but each can also have its shadow side. All of us probably employ each of these strategies at various times, but some people are most drawn to one or the other.

Comply
The Pernicious Perfectionist

When we comply with the internalized self-hater, we may become the Good Girl or Good Boy who is always trying to please or the perfectionist Boss who holds high standards. High expectations can be a mark of self-esteem: I think enough of my skill and professionalism as a writer to make sure anything I put out into the world reflects my best efforts. But the Shadow Side of the Perfectionist is the Vicious Critic, who holds us to impossible standards which can perpetuate a sense of continual failure. In groups, we may become fault-finders, always complaining, rarely if ever praising anyone but always noting what went wrong.

When confronted with the Pernicious Perfectionist, whether within or without, our basic strategy should be to transform her into a helpful critic, a careful editor or a useful overseer.

Strategies for Transforming Perfectionists
Create Safe Structures for Constructive Critique

When a group has clear channels for feedback and a culture that trains people and encourages constructive critique, we can direct the Vicious Critic to voice criticism at an appropriate time and setting where it can be heard and valued. Often there is some truth in the barbs of the most annoying nitpicker, and creating a forum for evaluation and specific feedback can help move the work toward a higher standard of excellence.

Encourage Responsibility

Constant criticism can be a way people attempt to gain status and social power. In a healthy group, power comes with responsibility. Sandra is always complaining about the mess in the RootBound toolshed, among many other things. Instead of listening to her ongoing rant about everyone else's lack of consideration, the group could say, "Great you organize the toolshed, and we empower you to come up with a way to make sure it stays organized and the tools get maintained."

Put the Perfectionist to Work

Need someone to proofread the newsletter? Or to go over the books and make sure the accounting is correct? Got some painstaking job requiring meticulous

EXERCISE

Perfectionist Coaching Suggestions

Ask your coach to keep track of the number of critical remarks you make in a meeting or the amount of time you take up on a critical rant. Then, ask your coach to ration you to a limited number of criticisms or a set number of minutes per meeting. You might arrange for a signal if you go overtime.

Alternatively, you might earn each critical remark with two expressions of praise and appreciation.

For really strong inner critics, counseling, life coaching or therapy can be enormously helpful.

care? That's where the Perfectionists comes into their own, and putting them to work can allow them to gain respect and social power through their positive contributions rather than their negative critique.

The Appeaser

The Appeaser tries to make everyone happy, worries over anyone's distress and has trouble setting boundaries or holding people accountable. The positive aspect of Appeasing would be Peacemaking — mediating, listening and helping people come to understand one another. But an Inimical Appeaser gives way when she shouldn't. Rather than hurt someone's feelings, she may allow them to hurt the group, draining its energies and resources. An Appeaser and a Pernicious Critic together make a lethal combination, with the Appeaser eternally trying and failing to make the Critic happy.

An Inimical Appeaser can learn to be comfortable with conflict and transform into a Peacemaker, with conscious group support.

Strategies for Transforming Appeasers

Embrace Constructive Conflict

Conflict becomes safe in a group that encourages open disagreements and strong arguments about ideas and plans, while discouraging personal attack. When the group is comfortable with differences of opinion, the Appeaser can relax and may even develop strong opinions of her own.

Create Safe Structures for Conflict Resolution

Clear structures for conflict resolution and a group culture that encourages directness, that offers training in mediation and skilled support for people in conflict can relieve the Appeaser from the self-imposed duty of eternal peacemaking.

Create Clear Structures of Accountability

When the group has clear ways to hold people accountable, the onus is removed from potential appeasers.

Rebel

The Reactive Rebel

Rebellion is good for the soul. In the face of oppression and injustice, standing up and saying No!, shouting, marching, taking to the streets and tearing down the prison walls are acts of liberation.

But some of us have the Rebel so ingrained that we respond with belligerent obstruction to any exercise of authority, unearned or earned. In a group, we might viciously attack the leadership, whether or not they deserve it. When confronted with the Rebel, we can attempt to harness that passionate fire to ignite our movements and direct that oppositional energy against our real opponents.

Strategies for Transforming Rebels

Clear Structures of Power

When the lines of power are clear and transparent, when people know how decision-making power and social power are earned in the group, then the Rebel finds little fuel for the pyre he might wish to erect for those he perceives as leaders.

Clear Channels for Constructive Critique

Forums for feedback and a group culture that teaches and practices constructive critique can help a Rebel channel that anger into specific and helpful criticism.

Encourage Responsibility

Ask the Rebel to step up and take responsibility instead of simply attacking the leadership. At minimum, she should be challenged to make constructive suggestions for change. Even better, put her in charge of tasks and get her to organize projects.

EXERCISE

Appeaser Coaching Suggestions

Encourage the Appeaser to work with the Two Columns Exercise in Chapter 5. Ask him to keep an account of times he tries to placate and make nice and to write down what he was actually thinking. Together construct some scripts that would allow the Appeaser to express more of his real thoughts and feelings, to check out his assumptions and share his own chains of reasoning. Practice them.

The Terrible Tyrant

"Meet the new boss, same as the old boss!" The Who

While it may seem an odd choice to place the Tyrant under Rebellion, think of all the revolutions that have led to the establishment, not of libratory and empowering systems of governance, but of new authoritarian regimes. When we are possessed by the Rebel and we gain power, we often wield it harshly. If our models of power have always been authoritarian, we may simply not know any other way to behave. We struggle for control, without realizing that we've shifted from being the victim to being the bully.

The Tyrant and the Rebel both hold the potential to transform into Empowering Leaders. But to make that happen, the group must set and hold clear boundaries and expectations, forming a united front.

Strategies for Transforming Tyrants
Direct, Constructive Feedback

Too often a group will complain endlessly about a Tyrant behind his back, but never say directly what behavior offends them. The rules of constructive critique can help us confront tyrannical behavior in a positive way.

Behavior Shaping

When our poodle was a puppy, we had a professional dog trainer come to teach us how to train her. She taught us the new approach to dog training: behavior shaping. Instead of punishing the puppy when she did something wrong, we rewarded her whenever she made a move in the direction of doing something right. So, if we said "sit" and she twitched her hindquarters, she got praise. The next time, if she lowered them, she also got praise.

Rather than complaining about the Tyrant's bad behavior, reward any move she makes toward sensitive, empowering leadership. "Betty, when you speak to me in that softer voice, I really hear your emotion and your vulnerability, and that makes me feel so close to you and so much more open to your ideas."

Group Solidarity

Tyrants have been overthrown by groups of ordinary people standing together and saying, "This is unacceptable." Collaborative groups can offer consistent, constructive critique and hold leaders and organizers accountable for the standards of behavior they expect.

Mentoring

Sometimes people wield power tyrannically simply because they don't have any other models for how to be. Mentoring a Tyrant can help provide regular feedback, constructive suggestions for change and a sympathetic person to discuss issues with before taking action. Tyrants may have great passion, organizational skills and valuable commitment to the group, and mentoring can help to bring them out.

Withdraw
The Unlovely Underminer

Grumbling, mumbling, sniping without directly confronting, posting snide critiques on the Internet but not coming to the mediation, not finishing tasks, leaving

---

E X E R C I S E

Tyrant Coaching Suggestions

Think of a time when you have reverted to yelling, screaming, laying down the law, speaking in the Voice of Dad. What were you feeling? With your coach, take time to identify the emotions and the vulnerability that might have underlain your outburst.

Now, together create a script for directly expressing that vulnerability and asking for support. What might you have said? How might it have been received?

What might you say in the future in a similar situation? Practice!

key work undone and undermining the work of others — all of these are passive-aggressive forms of behavior, ways people withdraw from open conflict while continuing to seek power.

A group culture that discourages undermining, expects direct confrontation when people are in conflict and where the norm is energetic support are your best defenses against the Underminer. Again, our goal is to transform the Underminer into someone who can openly advocate for their positions and offer constructive critique directly.

Strategies for Transforming Underminers

Create More Safety for Open Disagreement

Develop a culture of constructive conflict, and encourage and challenge people to fight their battles openly.

Draw out the Fire

At times, bringing the attack out into the open can help to transform a mumbled snipe into a constructive critique. "I'm sorry, Pondweed, I couldn't hear you clearly. But you sound distressed. What's the problem? Can you give me some specific examples?"

Practice Constructive Critique

Creating forums for feedback and practicing the rules of constructive critique will undermine the Underminer.

Taking My Cookies and Going Home!

Leaving the group is the ultimate withdrawal. People may leave groups for many reasons, often good ones: not enough time, other interests, practical problems or the realization that their goals and values are different from the group's.

EXERCISE

Underminer Coaching Suggestions

Consider a project or plan that you take issue with. What would it be like to raise your objections directly, using the ground rules of constructive critique? Together create a script that shares your feelings, your chain of reasoning and tests assumptions. Role-play it, switching roles and notice what you feel both speaking the objections and hearing them.

What fears or resistance come up when you think about really saying it? Are there barriers in the group to open disagreement? If so, consider together how you might challenge them to create more safety for constructive conflict.

Other people leave the group for reasons that should concern the group: they felt unwelcome, disempowered, devalued or frustrated with the group's way of working. When we suspect such factors are at play, we do well to inquire why the person is leaving and whether there is anything we can do to remedy the situation.

But sometimes people leave a group as a power play, because they don't get their way in an argument or because the group challenges their behavior. When a disruptive or dysfunctional person leaves, don't mourn. When you are secretly feeling relieved that someone is gone, don't chase after them and beg them to come back.

When we do leave a group, for whatever reason, we can do so responsibly. We can clearly state our reasons for leaving and the chain of reasoning that led to our decision. Before we leave, we can train our successor so that our work can continue. We can pass on any needed information, contacts or resources and remain available for mentoring and consultation.

Strategies for Leaving

Interview the Person Leaving

Someone in the group may interview the person leaving and ask why. Are there conflicts or interpersonal issues that the group needs to address? Are there ways the group could relieve some of the real-life stresses of time and energy? Is there something the group needs to learn?

Hold a Clearing Session

Offer the person who is withdrawing a chance to participate in a group council to air problems and confront them safely, directly and with support.

Hold a Goodbye Ritual

Create a send-off for the person who is leaving, so she doesn't just fade away unnoticed. This can range from a ritual circle to a pizza party, whatever seems appropriate for the group.

Manipulate

When people are prevented from openly earning social power and respect, some will attempt to gain it by devious means. Sometimes those patterns become so ingrained that they continue to employ them even in situations where they are unnecessary and destructive.

E
X
E
R
C
I
S
E

Coaching Suggestions for Leaving the Group

When you contemplate leaving the group, have your coach ask you the following questions or consider them yourself and write the answers in your journal:

• Do I care whether the work of the group continues?

• If so, have I trained my successor?

• Have I passed on all relevant information and resources?

• Will I make myself available to advise and mentor my successor?

• Are there interpersonal issues or conflicts that I am ducking out of?

• If so, what would it be like to confront them directly?

If you are escaping unresolved conflicts, ask your coach to help you role-play out what it would be like to raise them, using all the communication tools we've given you.

Manipulation is hard to deal with because often it's not immediately apparent what is going on. Some difficult people express their distress by manipulating others — although they may not themselves be consciously aware that they are doing it. Manipulators use the Unilateral Control Model, often very subtly, trying to arrange the situation so their needs are met. Below are some common patterns of manipulation.

Rigid Framing

Every issue is framed as a life-or-death conflict between good and evil or between political righteousness and moral turpitude. You're either with us or against us, with no room for nuance.

Strategy — Challenge the Frame

Joe wants to charge RootBound members a monthly parking fee for using the cohousing lot. Donna wants to keep parking free of charge. "It's a climate change issue!" Joe declares. "Anyone who cares about the environment will understand why we should penalize gas-guzzling, carbon-spewing autos!"

If Donna proceeds to argue that she does, indeed, care about the environment, she's lost. Instead, she needs to set her own frame — and she can do so using the communication tools we've discussed in earlier chapters.

"Joe, there's another issue here. This is a question of how family-friendly we want to be as a community. When you frame the issue, as 'good environmentalist versus evil auto owners,' I feel frustrated, because I need room to express my own needs and advocate for values that I believe are also good values and are actually complementary. Would you be willing to listen to my point of view?"

Easing In

"Easing in can involve asking others questions or making statements that are designed to get others to figure out and state what you are privately thinking without your having to say it. It is an indirect approach designed to get others to see things your way for themselves."[7]

"OK, Donna," Joe says, "I do really respect you and want to hear your opinion. So, tell me — how do we get people to stop driving and pumping carbon into the atmosphere if we're afraid to penalize cars?"

Strategy — Don't Get Caught

My mother was a great easer-in and often peppered her admonishments with rhetorical questions. "What do you think of that!" she'd snap — and then wait for an answer, which I never knew how to give. My little brother, however, would simply reply, "Mom, I can't possibly answer that question!"

Sucking Up/Flattery/Splitting

Some people seek power, not by achievement but by association. They attempt to get close to powerful people, hoping some of that charisma will rub off and that they will gain respect by association. We all get a bit of a thrill from connecting to someone we admire or someone famous. I still remember with a happy glow the day I glimpsed George Harrison in the art department of Harrod's in London in 1971. But some people seek contact and favor from the powerful as a means to gaining power themselves.

Such behavior can be destructive to the group, because it decouples power from responsibility and creates channels of power that are not open or transparent.

Vicarious power-seekers are also dangerous to the people who hold power. Sucking up is also sucking out, and it can drain energy and attention. The more power you accrue, the more you must fend off people's projections and assumptions — and that gets exhausting. While you seem to be in the center of the spotlight of attention, you may actually feel very invisible as a real person.

Flattery is one method of manipulation people often use to gain favor. When we are the person being flattered, our first response may be to bask in the positive attention. But flattery is not the same as true praise or appreciation. Flattery is often global — "You are so wonderful!" If we succumb and surround ourselves with flatterers, we cut ourselves off from real sources of information and may make bad decisions. We are vulnerable, because the flatterer does not truly have our interests in mind, but their own.

Flattery often is only the opening salvo in splitting — the psychologists' term for seeing people as all good or all bad. Most of us learn, with maturity, that we are all a mix of marvelous and less-than-marvelous qualities, that we have our strengths and weaknesses, our moments of greatness and other moments when we may make terrible mistakes. But splitters see the world in black and white, all-good or all evil, leaving no room for nuance or principled disagreement.

Splitters begin by putting you up on a pedestal, but as soon as you disappoint them in some way (as inevitably you will do), they knock you down. Psychotherapists learn to be wary of the new client who begins by telling you all about how terrible their previous therapist was and how wonderful you are by contrast. For the wise, that's an alert that soon they may be telling someone else how terrible you are.

Strategies for Flattery

Clear and Fair Ways to Earn Power

When a group has clear and transparent ways to earn social power and a culture that values and practices constructive critique, sucking up and splitting will be discouraged but probably not eliminated.

Name and Challenge Aspects of the Syndrome

When we witness this syndrome, we can speak up, using our good communication tools, and say so. "Sally, I notice that whenever you speak in the group, you're looking at Pondweed and all your attention is directed to her. I feel hurt, as if you don't really see me or think that I'm important enough to pay attention to. Would you be willing to look across the circle when you speak?"

Alert the Target

When you are the target of flattery, it can be surprisingly hard to see. You may not realize that someone who is always nice to you is not behaving the same way to others. Sharing that information can be helpful — but be very careful to identify specific instances and use good communication skills so you don't slide into negative gossip.

When Someone Is Sucking up to You

Find an Ally/Informant

Find a friend who can offer another perspective on flatterers. Do they treat other people in the group as warmly as they treat you? Do they respond to your calls and e-mails and shut others out? Find ways to hold them accountable to the group.

Use Your Anchor to Your Core Self

Stay grounded, and practice bringing yourself back to your grounded, neutral place. Not all praise is flattery, and we deserve to enjoy and be fed by honest appreciation. So take a breath, take in what feeds you and release the rest.

Turn off the Torrent

Respond to a barrage of flattery by interrupting, gently, with a simple, "Thank you." Then change the subject.

Turn Flattery to Constructive Critique

Interrupt the flow with "thank you" and ask for specifics. "Thank you! Can you tell me specifically what you liked about the lecture? Were there any particular moments that stand out, or arguments you found persuasive? That will really help me to continue to improve my talks."

Set and Hold Boundaries

When you are pursued by a flatterer, you may need to set your own limits about how much time and attention to give — and what sort of attention. Someone who truly cares for you will respect your boundaries. Someone who is feeding off you energetically may become angry or flip into attack mode when you limit your attentions.

Flattery Coaching Suggestions

Mutual coaching can help us be aware when someone is sucking up and strategize on ways to shift the group dynamics. A coach can provide that other set of eyes to see the things that you don't.

A coach can also ask us the hard questions:

- What do you admire about X?
- What do you hope for from a relationship with X?

- How much time and energy are you asking of X?
- Can you see and accept X's flaws and vulnerabilities?
- If there is a quality in X that you admire, how can you develop that in yourself?
- If X has achieved things you admire or envy, how might you directly pursue similar achievements yourself?

Divide and Conquer

The Romans gained and held power by dividing their enemies and setting them against one another. Some people employ that strategy to gain power within groups. They may employ negative gossip, whispering campaigns, repeat or spread gossip and rumors or flatter some people while disparaging others. They may create their own center of power, case-building to gain supporters, gathering a clique together to band against someone else in the group. They may marshal their own band of Rebels to undermine group leadership.

Political groups often worry about infiltrators and informers. Divide and Conquer is one of the primary ploys used by infiltrators. Everyone who practices Divide and Conquer is not an agent — but a group that develops strategies to guard against this dynamic will also protect itself from some of the damage potentially caused by infiltrators.

Strategies for Divide and Conquer
Openness and Transparency Around Power

Clear ways to earn power and clear systems of accountability will provide an unfriendly habitat for the virus of division.

Constructive Critique and Open Conflict

Forums for feedback and a group culture that teaches and practices constructive critique will provide positive channels for the expression of disagreement and discontent.

Discourage Gossip and Encourage Direct Communication

Groups that develop a culture in which negative gossip is discouraged, in which people are expected to confront one another directly and given tools and support to engage in constructive conflict immunize themselves against viral disruption.

Clear agreements about conflict resolution and procedures to handle conflict create channels where discontent can be dealt with constructively.

Group Solidarity

Solidarity is the most powerful protection a group can have against divisiveness. Solidarity means that the group as a whole holds people to their agreements around conflict, supports one another in finding constructive ways to raise disagreements or give critical feedback and refuses to believe rumors or stories until they are checked out. Solidarity means standing behind the trust that members of the group have fairly earned, thinking well of one another's intentions or checking out our negative inferences before we repeat them as truth. Group solidarity might mean stopping a gossiper or saying, "Mugwort, how can I support you in raising that issue directly with Pondweed?"

Dissolving Factions

When Divide and Conquer has held sway and the group is polarized into cliques, efforts must be made to reestablish group unity. Those who are skilled at Divide and Conquer often identify real points of weakness or dissatisfaction in a group. Addressing this pattern can bring forth vital information that the group can use to strengthen itself and remedy its defects. When complaints and disagreements can be brought out into the open, they can be addressed.

> **EXERCISE**
>
> ### Divide/Conquer Coaching Suggestions
>
> Practice declining those gossip hooks:
>
> - "I really shouldn't say this, but ..."
> - "I'm so glad you recognize that you shouldn't say whatever it is. How can I support you in holding that boundary?'"
> - "This is supposed to be confidential, but ..."
> - "Great! Then let's keep it that way!"
>
> Create your own responses, and practice them!

Faction Coaching Suggestions

Discuss the costs and potential benefits of various approaches to dissolving factions in the group. Together come up with a plan to address the issue. If necessary, rehearse key conversations to practice good communication tools.

Strategies for Factions
One on One

Hold individual, one-on-one conversations with members of the dissenting faction, using active listening to hear their true concerns, turning attacks to constructive critique by asking for specifics and positive suggestions.

Bring the Problem to the Group

Name the problem aloud in the group, discussing the undiscussable and using good communication tools. Ask for group agreement to address the issue, by:

- Assigning members of different factions to work together, either on a project, a plan or on constructive critique for the group.
- Holding a group retreat or meeting, possibly with an outside facilitator, to bring dissatisfaction out into the open and address it constructively.

Snipers

Some people attack covertly, in ways that can be hard to immediately identify. Linguist Suzette Elgin says, "verbal violence all too often goes unrecognized, except at a level that you cannot even understand yourself. You know that you are suffering, and you vaguely know where the pain is coming from; but because the aggression is so well hidden, you are likely to blame yourself instead of the aggressor and to add to your own misery, like this: 'I can't understand why I always feel so stupid when I'm with her. She's always so considerate and she's such a nice person! There must be something wrong with me'."

She identifies several forms of subtle verbal attacks: "Even you ..." "Don't you even care ..." "If you really ..." "Everyone understands why ..."[8] "You could assemble that toy," is a statement of support and encouragement: it means, "The toy is easy to put together, and I believe you can do it." But add one word, even, and "Even you could assemble that toy," means: "The toy is really simple to put together, and you are mechanically inept and possibly not very bright."

Being a healer, counselor, therapist, teacher or a helper is a position of high social power. Being a patient or a student puts us below. Secure people accept that to learn or receive healing, we must sometimes temporarily stand below someone else, but insecure people may not be able to tolerate being in the down position and may snipe or covertly attack those they perceive as being above.

Just as a good parent knows that her ultimate success will come from her child's independence, a true healer aims to put herself out of a job. But an insecure person may cling to the role of healer or helper and the social power they confer, consciously or unconsciously perpetuating the need and the disease so they can remain in the up position..

Offers of healing and expressions of concern can be ways to assert dominance. "You look tired," may be a genuine statement of caring. But it can also mean, "You look like hell — old, weary and worn out." Or even, "I question your ability to continue functioning." It can be a negative suggestion — as soon as someone says you look tired, you begin to feel tired.

At one point, in the midst of a group meeting in a week-long intensive, someone remarked to the group that I looked tired. I snapped back, "Don't tell me I look tired — I hate that! If you want to support me, tell me I look fabulous!" For the rest of the week people did come up to me and tell me, "You look fabulous!" Each time someone did, I received a little burst of positive energy, and by the end of the intensive, I felt great!

Strategies for Dealing with Snipers

Make the Underlying Attack Visible

Instead of responding to the expressed concern, go directly to the underlying attack and bring it out, asking the questions that can reframe it into a constructive critique. Test your assumptions and share your chain of reasoning.

"I'm hearing something in your voice that sounds to me like doubt. I guess I'm inferring that you are not quite sure whether I'm capable of doing this job. Am I right about that? Let's talk about it. Are there specific things you feel I'm not dealing with competently?"

Name What You Feel

When our emotions or our own energy seem to be at odds with what we're hearing, we can say so, using our communication tools. "I appreciate your concern, but somehow I feel it comes laced with barbs. My sense is that you're angry about something, am I right?"

Sniper Coaching Suggestions

A coach can help us examine our own feelings and responses to covert attacks, identifying the attack hidden under sweet words and practicing our responses.

State What You Want

In non-violent communication, we state our feelings and needs and also make a request. When confronted with a sniper, we can also make a direct request for the behavior or the form of support we want. "Thanks for noticing that I look tired — would you be willing to take my turn at kitchen cleanup?"

Everyone Says

Another form of sniping masks the attacker's own complaints or critique as coming from others. "It's not me who is saying negative things about the organization, it's that other people bring me their concerns." Again, sometimes this may be true, and may point out real issues the group should address. But if the complaints are vague, chronic or undifferentiated, if they are about things that are impossible to address, suspect a covert power play.

> "Everyone says …"
> "Other people are saying …"
> "Lots of people in the group are saying …"

Everyone Says Strategies
Clear Channels for Feedback

A group culture that supports constructive critique and sets up clear forums for giving it is our best defense. When channels for feedback exist, we can respond by saying, "Oh, when you hear those complaints, it would be so wonderful if you'd direct them to the Feedback form on our web page. And now I have to go …."

Elicit the Underlying Attack and Turn It into Constructive Critique

"Let's talk about you. What are your feelings about the program?"
"Can you tell me specifically what's bothering you about the plan?"
"How did you see the incident, and what do you think should be done differently?"

Prescribe the Behavior

This is a technique I learned from Matt McKay and Peter Rogers, my supervisors in my internship at the Haight Ashbury Free Clinic as a graduate student in psychology.[9] Instead of resisting the negative behavior, prescribe it and amplify it to the point where it becomes an insupportable burden: "It's so wonderful that people feel free to come to you with their complaints. Would you be willing to write them up in detail and send them to our complaints committee each time you hear something bad about the group? Please include the context, the setting — and if you can reproduce the exact wording, that might be good, too. If the complainer is willing, get us their name, e-mail and full contact information. That will be so helpful in allowing us to respond and deal with these issues. And while you're at it, if you'd care to write up your recommendations, with supporting data for each, we can take that up in our next meeting ...."

The Divas — Narcissism

Some people need constant praise in order to feel good about themselves. They need to be the center of attention, and to be told again and again how wonderful they are — because deep inside, they feel insecure and empty.

I place the Diva under the section on manipulation because often they may use manipulative strategies in order to assure their supplies of attention and admiration. We all like praise, and we all like to be told we are fabulous, desirable and wonderful. But someone who is narcissistic needs that praise like a junky needs a fix. Cut it off, offer critique instead or fail to provide it, and you may provoke rage and eternal enmity.

Narcissism may be a cover for deeply wounded self-esteem. Bluster and bragging may substitute for a sense of true self-worth. I work with youth and young adults who come from deep poverty and are at-risk or already embroiled with the criminal justice system. The hard shell of bravado is the defense they erect against a world that continually tells them they are useless and worthless.

Setting limits or withdrawing attention from a narcissistic person may set off intense rage. Any hint of abandonment can shake their sense of self and evoke deep feelings of terror and anger. We do need to set limits, regardless of the impact, but be prepared for the backlash that might follow.

The key to working with narcissistic people is to recognize that we cannot fill the deep void in their self-esteem to make them feel happy or valued. We can, however, offer opportunities for real achievement and true praise and recognition where it is due. Many narcissistic people are, indeed, high achievers and may have enormous gifts to offer the group.

Diva Strategies

Don't Deepen the Wounds

Because the young people I work with in inner city community gardens have been scolded and denigrated all their lives, yelling, insulting and berating them has little or no effect on their behavior — it either rolls right off or simply hardens their resistance. In fact, they may get hooked on the negative attention — when that's the only sort of attention you've ever had, you may provoke it just to remind yourself that you exist.

So avoid shaming, blaming, attacking and name-calling. Instead, use good communication tools to share your own feelings, needs and perceptions.

Offer Grounded, Specific Praise

When a child is hooked on sugar, they may eat a lot and at the same time not be truly nourished. When a narcissistic person is hooked on flattery and empty praise, their inner hunger is not truly being satisfied. So, instead of offering insincere flattery, find those things you can truly praise and, following the guidelines for constructive critique, make your comments specific, timely and thoughtful.

Behavior Shaping

Rather than focusing on negative behaviors, offer praise and appreciation for any steps in the right direction. Don't wait until a person's behavior is perfect, but show appreciation for incremental changes that improve the situation.

Supportive Critique

Critique, no matter how constructive, can be hard to take regardless of how secure you are in your self-worth. Nonetheless, sometimes people make mistakes, and ignoring them does not further the work. But we can learn to hold one another accountable while supporting and feeding their basic sense of self-worth. In the garden, for example, the youth often make mistakes. Instead of shaming and blaming, I might say something like, "Lon, you are a sharp, intelligent guy. I know you are capable of observing and using your judgment. So — did you notice how strong that jet of water was when you watered the seedlings? Let's look at them — see, they are all knocked down now and some of them are killed. That makes me sad. What can we do to fix it?"

Opportunities for Real Achievement

Provide places for people to use their real talents, to shine and to receive praise and appreciation for real contributions.

Clear Boundaries

Clear expectations and boundaries are important, and neither narcissism nor low self-esteem are grounds for violating basic group agreements. If someone becomes so resentful at being held accountable that they throw a tantrum or leave the group, we may feel sad or disappointed, but the group may function more smoothly and effectively without them.

Personal Boundaries

Narcissistic people can be demanding and exhausting with their constant needs for attention. Set your own boundaries, give what you can, and when you can't, say so. Use your good communication skills, and express sincere regret and appreciation even as you set your limits: "Narcissa, I so wish I could go to your show tomorrow. It's always such a treat to hear you sing, and I am deeply disappointed to miss it. But I have another commitment I can't break."

PROBLEMS TOO BIG FOR THE GROUP

Some difficulties go far beyond the scope a group is equipped to handle. These would include serious mental illness, active drug or alcohol addiction and violent or threatening behavior. When these behaviors are present, few collaborative groups can function, unless their purpose or mission is to create support for these very problems.

Recognizing that a problem is beyond our capabilities is the first step in actually getting help and support. We may not be able to cope with an addict or a person having an intense breakdown ourselves, but we can be advocates and allies to help them find the help they need.

That support might be from the mainstream mental health system. We may at times be forced to call in police or social services. Groups may have widely differing views on the efficacy and ethics of medication or the effectiveness of 12-step programs or rehab. Nonetheless, all of these can sometimes make the difference between survival and catastrophe. We may not be able to find a perfect solution for a disturbed person, but we can be helpful in finding the best range of options that exist.

Mental illness can be a subjective category. One person's crazy may be another's inspired visionary. At times, we've been able to integrate people who are seriously disturbed into a group and allow both them and the group to have a positive experience. At other times, we've had to hospitalize people or remove them from the situation.

In making these difficult decisions, I keep in mind the difference between helping and enabling. *Enabling* means protecting people from facing the consequences of their choices and actions. Enabling an addiction or colluding with denial is not truly helpful or healing. While we may naturally want to cushion a friend's hard fall, sometimes an addict needs to hit bottom to break a negative cycle and spur true healing and change.

When deciding whether or not a deeply disturbed person can remain in the group, I ask four questions:

- Can we assure the basic physical safety of this person and others in the group?
- Can the group fulfill its function with this person present, without an enormous drain of time and energy?
- What contract has the group made? What is the work we set out to do together? Is providing support for this person's presence in the group part of that purpose?
- Can this person show up in the group in a state of consciousness that allows them to function, to be aware of others' needs and to benefit from the group's activities?

If the answer to any of these questions is no, I do not hesitate in asking the person to leave. However, I do try to arrange support and advocacy and to make sure the person in question has what they need to get to a safe situation.

HIDDEN AGENDAS

Most often in our collaborative groups, we are working with people who are acting in good faith. They may be infuriating or incompetent, but nonetheless we know they are honest and sincere. But at times, we encounter people who are not honest, who are working for their own ends or for other agendas.

Lies and Distortions

People lie for many different reasons. Some lie to gain advantage or cover up wrongdoing. Others lie to avoid conflict and dodge confrontation. Still others may tell stories to bolster their own importance. Many people distort their accounts of events because they experience them through the slightly warped lens of their own distress. Con artists may be adept at telling lies that hook our deepest needs and unspoken desires to further their own advantage.

The Internet opens up an enormous field for deceit. Some falsehoods might be relatively innocent — substituting a better-looking profile picture, exaggerating your achievements or contacts. But when online connections result in romantic or business relations based on untruths, fun turns to harm.

Truthful people may not recognize lies or distortions immediately. Calling someone a liar is a serious charge, and we may feel unwilling to confront someone without serious proof.

Protecting Our Groups from Deceit

Some simple practices can help a group protect itself against the untruthful.

Accountability

Clear systems of accountability, especially around money and finances, with more than one eye on the books will help protect against both con artists and honest mistakes.

Check out Stories and Rumors

Remember that every story has more than one side. A group culture that discourages rumor-mongering and gossip and establishes a regular practice of hearing all sides of a story before making a judgment can help protect against distortion.

"I'm Confused"

When we suspect a lie, rather than accusing, we can admit our vulnerability and confusion. "I'm confused," can be a powerful position to take. "I'm confused … you say that you deposited the check, and yet the bank balance doesn't show it. What do you think could have happened?"

A Path to Rebuild Trust

When trust has been broken, when a lie has been found out, the group must set clear boundaries and agreements about how trust can be reestablished. Spiritual and new-age groups often place a high value on forgiveness, but even God does not forgive us unless we first repent of the wrong we've done. Investing trust in some-one who has broken it without that person expressing remorse and making amends is not truly compassionate, but rather enables their continued bad behavior.

Infiltrators and Provocateurs

Groups that work for social change or mount political protests often fear that they will be monitored or infiltrated by the authorities, and many incidents have proven this fear to be a realistic one. Unfortunately, the police and political pow-ers regularly violate our civil rights by spying upon peace, environmental and social change groups.

Perhaps even more damaging than actual infiltration is the paranoia and sus-picion it engenders. When we suspect every newcomer of being a spy, how can we broaden our organization? If each time someone behaves badly, we accuse them of being a provocateur, how do we truly hold one another accountable?

One of the great strengths of non-violence as an organizing strategy is that it relieves our paranoia. We organize openly and honestly and stand behind what we do. Since part of our philosophy is our willingness to accept the consequences of our actions, we are not afraid of being found out.

But even the most open and non-violent of groups occasionally needs an ele-ment of surprise in their operations. How do we protect ourselves?

The suggestions in this book for clear and fair ways to earn power, for set-ting standards of behavior and holding people accountable, for offering honest and constructive feedback, for avoiding gossip and rumor-mongering and instead confronting people directly and constructively are all powerful protections against disrupters and those who would attempt to destroy the group.

If We Suspect Someone Is an Infiltrator

If we suspect someone of being an informer or infiltrator, there are several steps we can take. The first, and most important, is to reaffirm our group agreements about communication, constructive feedback, open and positive confrontation and accountability. We can also:

Check out Their Story

Get to know the person, in a friendly, not an interrogative way. Find out where they come from, how they got interested in the group or the issue, who they've worked with before, what they hope to accomplish in the group. Then, if warranted, check out the facts of their story.

Put Them to Work in Less Sensitive Ways

A police agent who is willing to scrub the floor or help chop the vegetables is giving us at least some good value for our tax dollars. Groups that have clear paths to earning power might start volunteers turning the compost piles before they are admitted to the strategy sessions.

Have Clear Avenues for Earning Trust and Power

An organization can be warm and welcoming and still say, "You know, we ask people to be around for at least six months so we can really get to know one another before we have you staffing the coms line during an action."

Hold Everyone Accountable for the Same Standards of Behavior

If charismatic leaders are allowed to be abusive to others, if some people can be rude while others cannot, we lay ourselves open for disruption.

PRESSING THE EJECT BUTTON

When someone's behavior is so consistently difficult that it undermines the group's effectiveness, when their problems are so deep that they are beyond the scope of the group's ability to cope or when they consistently violate group agreements, we may need to ask them to leave. Ejecting someone from the group is never an easy decision, and it is not something that should be done lightly or thoughtlessly. But at times, it may be the right decision.

My entire career as a writer would have been stillborn had I not kicked someone out of one of my very first classes on the Goddess many years ago. I was in my early 20s, newly teaching in San Francisco in the living room of my shared flat. We had a circle of about ten people, and one was a man who was so intrusive, rude and insulting that halfway through the session I offered him his money back (a big sacrifice for me at the time) and told him to leave, which he did. The class breathed a sigh of relief and carried on. In the room was Carol Christ, then working on her dissertation in religious studies at Yale, now one of the prime scholars in feminist religious studies, who later introduced me to the editor and publisher of my first book, *The Spiral Dance*. Also in the room were Naomi Goldenberg, who became another feminist scholar and writer on religion, and Mara Keller, who directed the program in Feminist Spirituality at California Institute of Integral Studies where I later taught. None of them would have returned, they told me, had I not gotten rid of our rather scary student.

Many times, a group is saved the trouble of ejecting someone by simply shifting its culture toward more health and clarity. Whenever we set clear standards and boundaries and demand that people function at a higher level of interpersonal relationships and integrity, some people will feel so uncomfortable that they leave.

If they don't, and the group asks them to go, it is important that they receive due process: a chance to answer charges directly and amend their behavior, a clear accounting of agreements that have been broken and procedures that have been followed and a clear accounting of what, if anything, they can do to regain trust. If someone is mentally ill or otherwise dysfunctional, the group may find someone to help them get treatment, counseling or practical help. Never kick someone out of a group in a way that endangers their health or safety: i.e., tossing them out into a snowstorm in the middle of the night. Give them a ride out to the bus stop in the morning, and make sure they have a warm coat and gloves.

MARTA FACILITATES ANDREW'S CHALLENGES

As RootBound gathered in the dining hall for their training date with Marta, Ella and Eli looked around nervously. Andrew had not come to the last two members' meetings, nor had he shown up for the day of Communication Training that Marta had led for a large percentage of RootBound's membership. But neither had he left the community.

As people took their seats, there was an air of anticipation in the room. The previous sessions had gone well, and a feeling of comradeship and connection now infused the community again, although there were still spats and bouts of gossip that erupted from time to time. But overall, Eli was beginning to feel confident again that RootBound would survive.

Just as the meeting was about to begin, Andrew entered. He loomed over the seated circle, surveyed them all with a baleful eye and finally chose a seat directly opposite Marta, folded his arms and stared at her.

The meeting began, and Marta swiftly led them into the discussion of how to define "verbal violence." Andrew sat and glowered.

Tension grew in Eli's stomach. He wanted to challenge Andrew, but he didn't want to disrupt the meeting or risk the good feelings that the group had developed. But as Andrew continued to radiate silent anger, Eli found himself feeling more and more agitated.

"Can someone give a specific example of something you consider verbal violence?" Marta asked.

"I can," burst from Eli's lips. "Andrew, when we were talking in the parking lot, and you said, 'I don't give a shit about what you feel' and stomped off, to me that was an example of verbal violence."

Immediately the room vibrated with suppressed tension.

Andrew shrugged. "I call it as I see it. To me, verbal violence is lies, secrecy and cover-ups."

Eli opened his mouth to speak, but it turned into more of a squawk as Ella stepped on his foot.

"Andrew, from what I'm hearing in your tone, and from some other things I've heard outside this meeting, I get the sense that you believe there has been some sort of cover-up here at RootBound, and you're angry about it. I'd like to check out that assumption — am I right?" Ella asked.

"Damn right!" Andrew agreed. "This is supposed to be some sort of shining light of collectivity, but I see us wallowing in the same muck of deceitfulness as everybody else. And frankly, it makes me sick."

"I hear how upset you are," Ella said. "But I'm confused. Can you tell me specifically what you feel is being covered up or lied about?"

"If you don't know, it's because you don't want to know," Andrew countered.

Don't buy into his frame, Ella reminded herself. Set my boundaries, and my own frame. She took a deep breath. "Andrew, I'd like to ask how you came to that conclusion? What makes you think I don't want to know, as opposed to, say, thinking that I'm just dumb as a box of hair?" She smiled, and the circle chuckled. "Would you be willing to share your chain of reasoning?"

"I think you don't want to know because Eli is at the bottom of it, and you're his bitch."

A shocked silence filled the room. Ella's eyes blazed. Eli jumped up, and Ella yanked him down.

Set my boundaries, Ella thought. "Andrew, it is not OK to use that kind of language about me or any other woman. That was a perfect example of verbal violence!. You owe me an apology, and every other woman here."

"Not just the women!" Acacia chimed in. "I may be a man, but I'm just as offended when I hear misogynist crap like that!"

Andrew looked around at the angry faces in the circle. "I'm sorry," he said. "I'm sorry you're offended by a word. I guess it's just a cultural thing — or maybe an age thing. Those of us in the hip-hop generation ..."

"Oh no you don't!" Amira Evans, a young, brilliant African American medical student jumped to her feet. "You got no claim to hip-hop, you blonde, blue-eyed poster child for an Aryan film fest!"

"Just go back to 'I'm sorry' and maybe stop there," Rick suggested. He felt he knew something about apologies.

"I'm sorry. I'm sorry I used that word. What I was trying to say is, Ella, you're Eli's partner. Of course you're not going to see where he's manipulating."

"I'm not his partner," Rick said, "And I'm equally confused."

"Oh, you! You are the prime beneficiary. How'd you get away with an act of violence without getting tossed out of here on your ass?"

"We had a mediation. ..." Rick said.

"You had some sort of a secret conclave with that woman!" Andrew pointed at Marta. "That women that Eli foisted on us! Then you waltz back in here and suddenly it's all pals and buddies, and the rest of us are supposed to strip down to loincloths and go dance in the woods!"

Marta knew it was time for her to take charge of the discussion once again. "Andrew, I am hearing that you were not happy about the way the issue of the swimming pool incident was resolved. Would you like to hear my chain of reasoning as to why I chose to take the two of them off for mediation?" Marta explained again why she chose to do the mediation in private, and asked the group if anyone else felt the subject should be revisited.

Edward was adamant that the subject, for him, was closed — and threatened to walk out if it were reopened. No one else raised a hand. Great moments in meeting facilitation, Marta thought to herself — when one side will walk out if you don't deal with something, and the other side will walk out if you do.

Ella knew she would shed no tears if Andrew left, but remembering what she'd read about trauma, fear and anger, she decided to make one last effort.

"Andrew, I'm hearing that lies and secrecy are really important to you — that you are sensitive to them, maybe more sensitive than the rest of us. I'm guessing here, and I don't want to put you on the spot, but I'm guessing that some bad stuff has happened to you in the past, involving secrets and cover-ups, and you carry the pain of that close to the surface. I can only imagine how that must hurt."

For just a moment, she saw softening in his eyes — then it was if a barrier snapped down again. He opened his mouth to speak, but Edward jumped in.

"I don't agree with you, man, but I see you really standing alone in this, and I feel for that aloneness. And I admire your courage in standing up for what you think, even if you don't have support. I'd actually like to suggest we take a bit of a break. Andrew, I'd like to invite you to come counsel with the guys in the men's circle, just for a bit. I promise you, no loincloths — but I think you might get some good support. Would you be willing to do that?"

Andrew nodded. For once, he was at a loss as to what to say.

"And I'd like to meet with the women!" Betty said firmly. "And anyone who is undecided, in between or in transition, come with us!"

The meeting adjourned for an hour. When it reconvened, Edward informed the group that Andrew was going to take some space and that Elm was going to stay with him. Some deep and painful personal issues were coming to the fore, and he needed time to integrate them.

Betty announced that the women's group had reached consensus that racial, gender, homophobic or other prejudicial slurs were part of how they defined verbal violence, and that they as women would not tolerate such things at RootBound.

"And now," Marta said, "are we ready to resume the topic of today's meeting. We certainly have much material to work with!"

❋ ❋ ❋ ❋

Yes, people can be difficult, disagreeable, frustrating and exasperating. But even the most difficult person may have great gems of wisdom and creativity to offer. We all have our difficult moments, and we all also have our moments when we shine like jewels. Attending to our group structure, lines of communication and boundaries will help create an environment that calls us to be our best selves.

CHAPTER 9

Groups that Work

ROOTBOUND ECOVILLAGE ONE YEAR LATER

On a Sunday close to the anniversary of the ill-fated picnic, a community brunch and pool party was in full swing at RootBound. Two barbecues were set up on opposite sides of the patio, one grilling tempeh and vegan soy dogs, the other serving free-range, organic, locally raised chicken and grass-fed beef burgers. Everything was served on RootBound's sturdy china, and Rick Ragle was head of the dishwashing crew.

Ella surveyed the scene with satisfaction. It had been a challenging year, but they'd come through. True, some people had left. Pyracantha had moved on, to join a vegan herb farm out in Sonoma County. After much mediation, Andrew, with the support of the men's group, had gotten counseling to help him face old memories of childhood abuse. The work was emotionally exhausting, and he'd decided what he needed most was solitude, not community, to let him integrate. So he'd moved into his own apartment, but he'd managed to leave on civil, even friendly terms.

Eli came over and put his arm around Ella. He too, was smiling. They'd done much hard work over the year. Marta had led RootBound through a series of what they called Community Development days: workshops in which they went through all the points on the Talisman of Healthy Groups. They revisited their vision, their mission, the values and goals. They restructured the community's governance, so that every function needed had its own circle of *responsables* that then sent representatives to the governing council. Members knew how to join circles, and that the path to respect and social power was through contributing to the community. RootBound ran very popular trainings in decision-making process and meeting facilitation, open to the larger community and required for new members. As a result, the day-to-day workings of the community were smooth. Of course, there were still disagreements and conflicts, but the community now had many tools available to approach them in constructive ways.

Eli still spent time on RootBound's issues, but when he was absent on his frequent trips, he had to admit that the community ran perfectly well without him. When he had one of his big ideas, he'd learned not to thrust it into the midst of another agenda, but to wait and present it during Big Idea Time — ten minutes allotted at the end of every meeting. His own speaking and consulting work continued to grow, and he was on the road more than ever. But he no longer paid TreePeople to do his shifts. The community had worked out a new policy for those members who were frequently away, allowing them to trade kitchen shifts for other sorts of work they could either do on the road or by helping to organize bigger work-weekends. The community had also chipped in to send three of the TreePeople to a gourmet vegan cooking class run by the chef from one of the city's premiere organic restaurants. As a result, the reviews of TreePeople's dinners had shifted from "avoid at all costs" to "don't miss it!" The community dining hall had become a lively, convivial place again.

Ella was thrilled with the changes. Adam, the Sterns' son, would be graduating high school in June and planned to travel for a year working on organic farms. Meredith, their daughter, had a full schedule of after-school rehearsals for the musical theater productions in which she performed. Ella herself was busier than ever, both with work and her own growing schedule of speaking engagements, and with political activities. Alarmed at mounting cutbacks which she saw as assaults on education, Ella had decided to run for the Oakland school board. RootBound provided her with many staunch supporters and with just as much community as she desired. If she wanted company in the evenings, she could always find a good meal at the dining hall. If she needed some time alone to regroup, she could heat up some take-out in her own kitchen and turn off the phone.

The men's group had met as a support group for three months and then decided that they needed a project. They'd created an annual wilderness camping trip for the teens, a rite of passage. The women's group, in the meantime, evolved into the

Women's Adventure Challenge. They'd gone white-water rafting, backpacking, bungie jumping, and a number of them staged a sit-in at the Chancellor's office to protest budget cuts at the university.

It had taken work and time to renew RootBound's spirit, Ella thought, but it was worth it. Now the community felt even stronger, because of what they'd been through.

Donna set out a large bowl of salad from the RootBound garden. In the big oak beside the dining hall, TreePeople were teaching a group of kids how to prusik up a tree. In the pool, the men's group were fighting to hold their ground against a determined assault by the women's group in a spirited game of water volleyball. Across the way, the teens were dancing on a mix of clay, sand and straw, making cob to build up the walls of what would someday become their new hangout space. Ella looked at her son, covered with mud, and her daughter, halfway up a tree. It was a good way to live, she thought, and she slid her arm around Eli's waist, tipped her head up and kissed him.

Her one sorrow was that Marta had not, after all, joined the community. Marta had been offered a two-year teaching contract at the University of Bolivia, charged with setting up a new sociology program that would integrate indigenous students. She'd accepted the call to adventure, with some regrets.

"But RootBound will still be here when I get back," she said. "I feel sure of that. And perhaps it is better this way. If I join at a later date, my role as mentor will have faded, and it will be easier for me to shift into the role of member."

A shrill whistle split the air. Heads turned as Edward climbed up on the retaining wall that edged the patio. "Gather round, people!" he cried. "Out of the pool, please! We have an announcement to make!"

RootBounders vaulted out of the pool, rappelled down from the trees or took plates in hand and gathered around him. Joan jumped up on the makeshift dais.

"We of the Community Building Committee want to honor the work we've all done this year. RootBound has had its share of conflicts — and I'm sure there's more to come. But we believe that we are stronger for it all. Am I right about that?"

A big cheer went up from the crowd.

"So we want to reward one person, the person we've decided has most contributed to RootBound's renewal. We thought about Eli, but then we went, 'Nah, his ego is big enough already!'" Eli himself led the laughter. "And then we thought about Ella, but we weren't sure what the impact would be on her political career if Fox News got ahold of it." More laughter.

"There was a big contingent that wanted to give it to Cuisine Sauvage, the folks who finally taught the TreePeople how to cook!" Edward went on to a burst of applause and cries of "Yes! Yes!"

"And there was Marta, of course, but she's not here," he continued. "So, we finally decided on one person, whose actions kicked off the whole shebang, who more than anyone else is responsible for propelling us into this phase of transformation. I give you … Rick Ragle! If he hadn't pushed me into the pool, we might still be eating dumpster pasta and grumbling behind people's backs!"

"And to celebrate you, Rick, we have a small ceremony," Joan said, grinning, and burst into a round of "For he's a jolly good fellow."

Joan and Edward jumped down from the wall. A swarm of the larger teens, clued in advance, joined them, sweeping Rick off his feet. They swung him back and forth, giving three loud cheers — and finally swung him out over the pool and let go. He went flying up, laughing, and landed with a huge splash. He jackknifed up, spied Justin doubled over with laughter on the pool's edge, and yanked him in. A wild water fight began, and soon half of RootBound was in the pool. Squirt guns and water balloons appeared as if by magic, and within a few moments everyone was sopping wet.

"Is this what Marta meant by 'creative conflict?'" Ella asked Eli as they surfaced in the middle of the deep end.

"That comes next, when we tackle RootBound's next controversy," Eli replied. "Which is?"

"Changing the community's name. We're not rootbound any more," he smiled, and then sputtered as Ella dunked him.

SUCCESSFUL COLLABORATIVE GROUPS

Today, the Internet and the spread of connectivity favor horizontal and decentralized groups in every area, from social networking to anti-capitalist agitating. What does it look like when a group organizes consciously and skillfully around principles of empowerment? Has it ever happened, successfully?

Yes, many times. From a group of friends deciding where to go out to dinner, to Indymedia and young Egyptians rising up and overthrowing a dictator, collaborative groups without command and control leadership have proved effective and powerful time and time again. And in spite of all pitfalls and frustrations, collaborative organization allows people to band together in ways that honor the core worth, the creativity and the potential in each of us.

RAINBOW GROCERY

Rainbow grocery is a worker-owned cooperative grocery that has served the community in San Francisco's Mission District since 1975. Rainbow carries high-quality, organic vegetarian food, including many products which are hard to find elsewhere, at reasonable prices. It supports local and organic growers and "strives to offer resources, education and a forum for informational exchange for many local communities and organizations."[1] It is a Certified Green Business which provides a living wage to its worker-owners and excellent benefits. Over the last 36 years, it has grown from a food-buying club to a tiny hole-in-the-wall shop to a full grocery store doing millions of dollars of business a year, with 200 worker-owners. There are many worker-owned collective businesses in San Francisco — including a worker-owned strip club, the Lusty Lady! — but Rainbow is one of the most successful and longest-running businesses of its kind.

Rainbow's history is both an inspiring and cautionary tale, for it is one of the few survivors of what was once envisioned as a network of small, community food stores, a "Peoples' Food System." Rainbow was started in the '70s by members of an ashram, a spiritual community who needed access to good-quality, healthy food. They saw their work in the store — which at that time was run completely by unpaid volunteers — as an act of service, part of their spiritual practice.

In the early 1970s, there were at least ten neighborhood cooperative food stores in the Bay Area, as well as two large consumer-owned cooperatives in Berkeley. The collectives banded together as a network, sharing a large warehouse. Unfortunately, the Common Operating Warehouse became embroiled in politics and the type of conflict that proved destructive to its mission and function. In 1981, a flood destroyed the warehouse stock, and it was unable to recover.

Rainbow, however, continued to thrive. It rapidly outgrew its tiny store on 16th Street, and with the help of $100,000 in loans from its own customers (as no bank was willing at the time to finance a collective) it moved into a larger space on Mission Street. The area, originally a kind of skid row, became the heart of San Francisco's counterculture. Soon after incorporating as a non-profit, Rainbow began to generate a surplus of funds, which it redistributed as higher pay for its workers and reinvestment in improvements in the store.

By the mid-1990s Rainbow was ready to expand again. It changed its legal structure to a cooperative — an organizational form which did not exist in the 1970s when Rainbow began. With its track record of many years of successful business, it was able to obtain loans backed by the city of San Francisco, and by moving into an area earmarked for redevelopment, it also received city funds to help stimulate the creation of jobs. With its move in 1996 to its present location, it more than doubled its number of worker-members.

Why did Rainbow survive when other collectives did not? Bill Crolius, one of Rainbow's founders, suggests a number of factors.

"Location is so critical, and we just lucked on a good location. The second thing is we came from a non-political place. We were a community centered around Maharaji, a teacher who teaches meditation. We had altruistic motivations. The ashram was run very collectively; it was co-ed, people worked and gave their money. We were doing communal living, everything shared, brotherly love. We had an enthusiasm to be giving."[2]

Ryan Sarnataro, who joined the collective in the early years from outside the ashram, also stressed the importance of service. "Rainbow, more than some of the other stores, was very customer responsive. There was an attitude in the store — food for people not for profit.

"You had people like me and so many others who were all smart people who could run their own businesses and here we were, working for $1.50 an hour. But because there wasn't a management structure to get in the way, we could really create the real wealth. For me as a 20-something, it was a really great experience, to be working, not for yourself, but for the common good."

Rainbow also encouraged individuals to take risks and exercise leadership. According to Ryan, "one thing that served Rainbow really well was to give people the latitude to go out and do things. Buyers could buy stuff. For example, Rainbow used to be open six days a week. I thought it would be good to be open on Sunday. So the collective said, if you can find the people to do it, go ahead and do it. That is really important — to be able to allow parts of the collective to be able to move forward. You can't be too stuck on everybody being equal because people aren't equal. You've got to be able to let leaders emerge."[3]

"People need a good hook in their mouth to pull them up and evolve," Bill

Crolius said. "I was so insecure as a teenager — ashram life helped me so much. There was overt love for me. And then when I went to Rainbow — we had three or four ashram people, then a lot more who weren't interested in the ashram but they were really interested in love. You could see people getting off on the common good, finding a path that made them feel good.

"We kind of recognized that as we got bigger, we were going to go past this threshold for making decisions, so we wrote into the bylaws a kind of federal system so that people could maintain that small, family feeling, not get lost in meetings of 100 people. For stuff that affects the whole, we elect people who can be responsible. You identify people who are coming from that common good and you authorize them to make decisions for you."[4]

Laura Kemp has worked at Rainbow since May of 1996, when it moved to its current location. When Laura was hired at Rainbow, "It afforded me and my family an income, enabled us to have healthcare for the family for the very first time, and we could eat really well, eat healthy food at an affordable price because I enjoy a discount as a member. What appealed to me was being part of a group that works together without having a boss, in cooperation with others, being on an equal par."[5]

Rainbow's structure is an example of the complexity that comes with collaboration. Rainbow has 15 departments, and each runs with much autonomy. Each has its own hiring committee and coordinating committee. When workers are hired, they are given a three-month trial before they are invited in as a member of their departmental collective.

Rainbow does not run by consensus, but votes on all its issues. "If we tried to reach consensus on every aspect of running a business, we wouldn't get very far at all," Laura explained. "But anyone can effect change, and knowing that, whether you choose to or not, is empowering."

Once you become a collective member, you are eligible to become a corporate member after you put in 1,000 hours of work or 9 months. Prospective corporate members must also go through a number of training workshops in co-op history, customer service, collective history, safety orientation and financial skills. These trainings were instituted when members realized that most new workers had no experience of working collectively. Prospective corporate members must also pass a test, and then they are eligible to buy one share in the cooperative, for ten dollars. At that point, they become worker-owners and can vote in membership meetings and nominate themselves for any of the corporate committees.

Day-to-day business is primarily run by the departments, but Rainbow also has a Storewide Steering Committee which deals with operational questions that cannot be handled by individual departments. A Board of Directors, elected each year, handles legal and financial issues. A Public Relations committee takes care of advertising and PR, and together with a Donations Committee, decides on grants which Rainbow makes to many local non-profits and social change organizations. As well, Rainbow gives back-door food donations to soup kitchens and groups such as Food Not Bombs that provide free food for protests and community events.

Rainbow also has an Ecology Committee that looks for ways the store can continue to reduce its carbon footprint and serve as a model green business. They do in-store recycling, composting, battery recycling, cork recycling, bicycle parking and more. The Space Committee, a subcommittee of the Storewide Steering Committee, looks after renovations and building maintenance.

The Effective Meetings Committee is responsible for the monthly membership meetings which all 240 worker-owners are invited to attend. Anyone can bring proposals to those meetings, and if people are new to the process, they can get help from the Effective Meetings Committee in drafting their proposals, making sure they cover all necessary aspects: community impact, environmental and financial impact, pros and cons.

Rainbow offers all its workers excellent benefits and generous healthcare, although like all businesses they are struggling with the increasing costs of healthcare. Workers start at a base wage, and the Board of Directors considers the Cost of Living Adjustment (COLA) pay raises annually. Workers who join committees get paid for the extra hours of committee work. But there are no differentials of pay between managers and line workers as everyone is both. Pay increases come with seniority and increased hours.

Rainbow also invests time, energy and money in training. It offers its workers training in meeting facilitation and runs regular anti-oppression workshops. A Conflict Resolution Team consists of people trained in mediation. If a worker has a problem, they can go to the team, openly or anonymously, and request help. A department might also call the team in to help resolve disputes and disagreements. A Civil Rights Advocacy Committee intervenes in cases when discrimination or harassment is alleged.

Rainbow is a powerful example of a social business: not a charity, but a thriving enterprise with a larger social purpose than profit for profit's sake. It offers its workers not just a living wage, but a sense of empowerment and efficacy, a true workplace democracy. And it successfully competes with huge, profitable chains such as Whole Foods and major grocery stores in the highly competitive Bay Area.

Orientation to service, attention to business and respect for the skills and accountability of sound business practices all helped Rainbow survive. Somehow, Rainbow succeeded in finding a viable balance between the idealogical and the practical and continues to thrive.

THE 1999 SEATTLE BLOCKADE THAT SHUT DOWN THE WORLD TRADE ORGANIZATION

Throughout the 1990s, corporate globalization seemed to be an irresistible force marching across the world, leaving the corpses of local businesses, small farmers and the poor in its wake. The conventional wisdom said that removing barriers to trade and undoing safety and environmental regulations would create greater economic prosperity for everyone. Privatizing services that had once been the responsibility of governments would create new markets for companies to make profits on everything from mail to education to prisons. Increased wealth for the well-off would trickle down to the poor in the form of jobs and opportunities that would be more effective than social programs.

Reality did not support the claims of the globalizers, and in fact the gap in wealth increased as the rich got richer and the poor lost what little they had. In the US, the wealth gap increased over 50% between the 1960s and the turn of the century.[6] Neo-liberal globalization allowed corporations to roam the planet in search of cheaper labor, lax environmental laws and ever-greater profits — at the expense of communities that lost their economic base. The IMF and World Bank forced poorer countries in the global South to privatize their public resources and cut social programs in order to service onerous debts to wealthier countries. Unions and workers who had fought for generations to receive a fair share of the profits they produced lost ground. Safety and environmental protections were abandoned. By 1994, 385 billionaires controlled as much wealth as the world's poorest 2.7 billion people.[7]

The World Trade Organization had built its power as an overarching arbiter of global trade. By joining the WTO, nations essentially gave up some of their sovereignty, their right to regulate their own business and commerce. The WTO could pass rulings that would override environmental, labor or safety laws, and those rulings were made in closed-door meetings by an anonymous group of three bureaucrats whose names were not known and who were not elected nor accountable. So, for example, a US law prohibiting the importing of tuna caught in nets that killed endangered sea turtles was ruled an "unfair restraint of trade." Environmental laws, safety standards and child labor prohibitions were all under attack.

Civil society around the world challenged these assumptions. Successful campaigns had been waged by an international coalition against the Multilateral Agreement on Investments, which would have opened up even more avenues for destructive global financial schemes. The 1994 Zapatista rebellion in Mexico was sparked by the devastation that the North American Free Trade Agreement brought upon indigenous communities and poor farmers. Youthful activists in Britain had mounted a powerful and creative direct action in June of 1999, growing out of the Reclaim the Streets Movement, in coordination with a new global network called People's Global Action. All of these networks grew in power as a result of the Internet which connected organizers and activists worldwide.

The World Trade Organization planned its annual meeting in Seattle, for November 30, 1999, and many groups began organizing a year ahead. Some of those groups were organized conventionally. Unions planned a huge protest march. A coalition of NGOs and non-profits planned a counter-convention with an impressive list of speakers. A Peoples' March was organized to highlight issues of jobs and poverty. The Ruckus Society ran a week-long training camp, educating young activists in both the political and economic issues involved and in techniques of non-violent direct action.

The Direct Action Network planned a non-violent blockade of the conference itself, and they organized using the decentralized model common in antinuclear actions of the late 1970s and 1980s and anti-intervention groups of the 1980s such as the Pledge of Resistance. These groups were organized into affinity groups and spokescouncils that supported coordinated autonomous actions. The WTO mobilization was also influenced by the road blockades, tree sits and other tactics used by Earth First and forest defenders to stop clearcut logging. Indeed, it seemed that all of the progressive movements in the US converged in Seattle: one of the slogans was "Teamsters and Turtles United At Last!," referencing the solidarity between unions and environmentalists.

The Direct Action Network had interlocking circles of organization. A core group of organizers up and down the West Coast did much of the preliminary planning. Seattle area groups took on the logistics and hands-on organizing. They worked collaboratively, and within their group made decisions by consensus. Working groups were formed who took on specific aspects of the planning such as scenario, communications, training and maintaining the convergence space. They also made decisions by consensus. They reported back to regular coordinating meetings.

As the action plan developed, people who wished to participate were encouraged to form affinity groups — small groups which would take action together and would also provide for their own basic supplies, transportation and support. The affinity groups made decisions by consensus and sent representatives to spokescouncils, where overall decisions and final planning were done.

The organizers created a framework for the blockade; a gathering time and a rough plan to begin with a simultaneous shutdown all around the convention center, followed by two converging marches that could help re-enforce blockades. They drew pie slices onto a map of the downtown area and divided it into sections. Affinity groups chose areas to blockade and chose their own methods within the non-violent guidelines. Some would simply stand and sing, others would lock down, chaining themselves to lumps of concrete or fixtures on the streets. Others erected tripods and suspended themselves above the street, refusing to move voluntarily and forcing police to risk doing them physical harm if they attempted to remove the obstruction. No central command knew exactly when blockades would begin or where exactly in their sectors they would happen, making them very difficult to stop.

The convergence began several days before the official meeting was scheduled. Thousands of people were trained in everything from non-violent direct action, to media skills to jail solidarity and magical activism. Spokescouncils were held that coordinated the plans of over a thousand affinity groups. Overall, between the union march and the planned blockade, there were over 60,000 people on the streets on the first day of action.

I was not part of the original planning, but I came up a few days early to help do trainings. The mobilization attracted a large number of my personal friends and connections from up and down the West Coast, some of whom were old buddies that I originally met when we had blockaded at Diablo Canyon almost 20 years before. We formed a cluster of affinity groups and chose our section.

Here's an excerpt from an account I wrote: "Now I mostly remember snatches of images from the day: setting off in the morning with one of the marches, banners flying, giant puppets hovering above the crowd, drums thundering and feeling a sense of joy and liberation that never deserted me even in the worst times of the next few days. Our Pagan cluster dancing by the Union sound stage most of the day in one corner that stayed fairly quiet and peaceful. Rounding the corner to find smashed windows, burning dumpsters, casualties weeping on the curb from the tear gas — a new kind of war zone. Hearing that we had indeed shut the meeting down! Trying to facilitate a meeting that night with a thousand people at once pumped, traumatized, triumphant and fearful, with someone running in at intervals to yell, 'The cops — they're coming this way! They're tear gassing everyone, and they're five blocks away!' 'The cops — they're coming this way! They're tear gassing everyone, and they're three blocks away!' 'The cops — they're coming this way! They're tear gassing everyone, and they're right outside the door!'

"The next morning, after the Mayor declared downtown Seattle a closed, protest-free zone, most of us headed down there to defy the order we considered unconstitutional and a violation of our rights. We sat down in the road, got arrested, and went to jail for the next five days. During that time, the talks we had set out to protest fell apart, as delegates from the global South, emboldened by our presence on the streets, walked out.

"The blockade in Seattle was probably the single most successful political action I've been involved in over more than four decades of activism. It had a catalytic affect on the movement for global justice and it galvanized me into doing more street actions and mobilizations than any sensible middle-aged gardener really ought to do."[8]

The Seattle blockade inspired a decade of actions around the world organized in similar ways. Decentralized networks have enormous resilience — there is no head to cut off, no leader to take out. They can inspire a great sense of personal agency and empowerment, because everyone taking part is there voluntarily, and each person's voice is heard in making decisions.

David Solnit, one of the core organizers, wrote, "We won because we were strategic, well organized, and part of strong local, regional, national, and international networks. Decentralized networks are more flexible and stronger than top-down hierarchies like police agencies and city authorities, and this played to our advantage. Many individuals and allied groups who had minimal contact with the Direct Action Network understood and supported the strategy, and participated in the action without ever attending a meeting or bothering to identify with a specific group."[9]

The experience of Seattle shows some of the strengths of the empowerment model, but it also points up some of its challenges. Networks with no central command and control structure offer greater freedom, but they may face challenges in setting boundaries and holding people accountable to agreements.

The Direct Action Network agreed to a set of organizing principles such as affinity group-based action, spokes coordination and encouraging jail solidarity. They also had the following set of guidelines for the action:

Action Guidelines

All participants in this action are asked to agree to these action guidelines. Having this basic agreement will allow people from many backgrounds, movements and beliefs to work together for this action. They are not philosophical or political requirements placed upon you or judgments about the validity of some tactics over others. These guidelines are basic agreements that create a basis for trust, so we can work together for this action and know what to expect from each other.

1) We will use no violence, physical or verbal towards any person.
2) We will carry no weapons.
3) We will not bring or use any alcohol or illegal drugs.
4) We will not destroy property.[10]

A loose coalition of affinity groups informally called the black bloc never agreed to the Direct Action Network's prohibition against property damage. Many people in both the Direct Action Network and the black bloc identified with forms of anarchism: an idealistic political culture and philosophy that rejects coercive power and envisions a world organized on free associations, voluntary agreements, self-responsibility and direct democracy. But the black bloc looked much more like the popular conception of anarchists. Masked, dressed in black, drawing their political models from *autonome* groups that emerged out of the anti-fascist movement in Germany, they believed that contesting corporate and state power justified attacking property and the symbols of corporate domination such as

McDonald's or Starbucks. They broke windows throughout the downtown area and, though they were few in number, garnered a large share of media attention.

Whether their actions helped or hindered the larger movement is something that will probably continue to be debated for decades to come. For those of us arriving from out of town who had not been part of the ongoing meetings — and especially for us older activists who were accustomed to a model of non-violence that did not include property damage — their actions were an unwelcome surprise. Of the dozens of people who were part of our cluster, few would have come to a mobilization where we knew people would be tossing bricks through windows — if for no other reason than that we're older and slower than your average rock-thrower, and far more likely to be the ones the police catch up with, whether or not we're the ones who have done the damage.

In later mobilizations, we did find ways to organize successfully in concert with various black bloc activists and even, at times, to collaborate on rituals, marches and media. Lisa Fithian, one of the organizers from Seattle, convened a process in Washington DC in September of 2001, prior to the IMF-World Bank meeting, where labor union reps, religious leaders and black bloc youth met to discuss how to be in the streets together. They crafted a set of agreements that enabled diverse groups to act in solidarity together. They included standards for personal behavior, such as "Challenge and critique other groups and individuals in constructive ways and in a spirit of respect." As well, they suggested codes of conduct on the street — "Don't put people at risk who have not chosen it" — and approaches to media — "Do not condemn other demonstrators."[11] These agreements were used successfully in many mobilizations over the years.

Decentralization allows for great autonomy, but it can be difficult to achieve unity. When we do away with coercion, we must find other ways to assure cohesion. "Diversity of tactics" may at times allow groups with widely varying political philosophies to work together, but it can also be an easy out that lets us avoid wrestling with hard questions, arguing out the pros and cons of various tactics and hammering out compromises we can all support.

Decentralized networks are often also ephemeral as institutions. The Direct Action Network continued to exist for a year or two after Seattle, but eventually dissolved, partly from unresolved conflicts, partly because organizing bodies tend to spring up as needed for actions. While the Direct Action Network did not survive as an institution, many of the friendships and relationships formed in Seattle endure and form an ongoing network of allies who continue to work together effectively.

RECLAIMING

Reclaiming, my own extended network of Goddess worshippers, spiritual teachers and Pagan communities, is an example of a decentralized group that has lasted for three decades or more, growing, changing and evolving along the way. Reclaiming's story may illuminate some of the challenges of balancing the flexibility and spontaneity of empowered decentralization with the longevity and stability of institutions.

Reclaiming had its origins in the loose networks of groups exploring feminist spirituality in the late 1970s. Weaving together our feminist critique of patriarchal power with the spiritual explorations of the 1960s, we forged our own new rituals and traditions, drawing on remnants of the ancient Goddess religions that, we were discovering, lay at the root of European culture as well as many other cultures around the world. It was a tremendously creative time, when we felt inspired and empowered to find our own ways of connection to spirit that also honored our agency as women and as men who were allies of empowered women. Ritual brought together art, poetry, mask-making, music, drumming, as well as many of the techniques of meditation and consciousness-shifting that were part of the new-age movements arising at the same time.

On the Winter Solstice of 1980, a group of us celebrated with an all-night vigil. Ronald Reagan had just been elected as US president, and we lamented the sense of political despair that we felt. By that dawn, we decided to create a political despair ritual, timed for the next major Pagan holiday — Brigid's Day, February 1 — shortly after Inauguration Day.

> "The heart of the ritual took place in small groups, which gathered around a bowl of salt water. We passed the bowl counterclockwise, and each person answered the question, Where in your life do you feel powerless? She or he breathed into the salt water, letting go of despair, and then washed with the water.
>
> "When the circle was complete, we chanted and raised power to transform the sadness and despair in the water into energy we could use for change.

"Then we passed the bowl clockwise. Each person answered the questions, Where in your life do you feel power? After each person spoke, the circle said, 'We bless your power,' and the person took back some of the water and washed again.

The answers became a litany: 'I feel power when I go ahead and say what I'm afraid to say,' 'I feel power when I weave.' 'I felt power when I gave birth to my child.' 'I feel power when I write.'

"Then we poured all our water into a big bowl on the altar, and lit a large cauldron. Each person had brought a candle, and individuals lit candles from the cauldron, and stated some commitment to an act of power. The room gradually filled with light, and we sang and danced with candles until the power peaked."[12]

The ritual inspired us to look for ways to take action, and soon we learned that many people were organizing a blockade against the nuclear power plant due to open atop an earthquake fault at Diablo Canyon in central California. We formed an affinity group to take part in the action, and many of us went down to the blockade and remained for the three weeks that the action endured. At Diablo, we learned the empowerment model of organizing and developed skills at consensus decision-making. When we returned home at the end of the blockade and rejoined our friends, we had become a collective.

We needed a name. Because we offered so many courses called things like Reclaiming our Power, Reclaiming the Goddess or Reclaiming our Magic, we decided to call ourselves Reclaiming.

At first, we organized on the model we'd learned in the action. Our collective, though small, was entirely open and anyone who was interested could come to meetings and take part in decisions. After a few unfortunate experiences (culminating in a bipolar individual nobody knew well literally attempting to climb the walls during a meeting), we decided this was not a viable model for an ongoing organization. We closed the collective. People could still join, but they had to be invited in.

Our activities continued to grow, and our meetings grew longer and longer. We organized a retreat in the early 1980s and carried out the first of many restructurings of the collective. Instead of all of us making decisions on every aspect of the work, we created *cells* that took on specific functions, like putting out the newsletter, teaching classes or planning public rituals.

We continued to grow, sometimes at a pace that left us overwhelmed and exhausted. At one retreat, we decided to halt our expansion for a while to focus on our own process, to take an "in breath" rather than always breathing out.

By the mid 1980s, we felt pretty pleased with ourselves. We were growing, teaching, creating ritual and modeling shared power. I was also beginning to do more travelling and teaching, and people from far away often asked how they could train in our model. We decided to host an intensive, where people from out of town could come and receive the benefits of our community. The first one was held in 1985, and a group of people came to San Francisco, were housed in our homes and met together each day for a week. We began by collectively setting an agenda and then taught what people were interested in. Co-creating the agenda was, we thought, a perfect way to teach our collectivist model in practice — but some of the students found the process frustrating and wanted more of a structured program.

We also received feedback that people wanted more intensity — a residential setting somewhere out of town. So in the summer of 1986 we hosted two week-long retreats, back to back, on the Mendocino Coast. Someone who heard about that retreat asked us to come to Vancouver and teach a Witch Camp, so in 1987 five of us went north to teach, returning home to California to teach another camp our own collective organized near Santa Cruz. But our organizing group ran into conflicts, and at the end of that rather exhausting month, we decided that it was easier to let other people organize for us and to focus on teaching.

After our first Witch Camp in Vancouver, the community wanted another, and two students organized one in the Midwest. Our goal was not to continue forever travelling to various camps, but to train local people both to create rituals and classes in their own areas and to eventually take over teaching the camp. The next year, we recruited student teachers.

For a number of years, we continued to do two camps each summer — then, in the mid-1990s, the number suddenly jumped. We had continued to train teachers, who were now giving courses and planning rituals in their own communities. Suddenly we had camps in the Midwest, in Texas, in West Virginia and even back in California, as well as Canada, England and Germany.

For a few years, I taught at every camp. Because I was the writer whose books people knew and one of the founders of the tradition, the camps felt they needed me to draw people in. Although we had many other excellent and inspiring teachers, mine was the name that people knew. Because many people had read my books, they had a sense of how we approached spirituality and what our values and ethics might be.

Being in the center of intense spiritual work for seven or eight weeks out of the year, working intensely with teams creating series of rituals that night after night would transport a hundred people to the otherworld and back and mediating the powerful emotions that would inevitably arise was exhilarating. I felt stretched to my limits — which is right where I like to be — and could have happily stayed in that position forever.

But one day, walking back to my cabin in one of our camps, I heard an inner voice say clearly, "Get out of the center!" I knew that I had to begin a long process of pulling back, that as long as I had to be in the middle of everything, I would become a bottleneck that would strangle the growth of our tradition. I began slowly withdrawing from attending each camp. Over time, our teachers' group from San Francisco had also been slowly turning over more control to the local teachers we had trained.

At the same time as we were starting to pull back, we began to realize that we had no decision-making structure for the camps. In the beginning, when the teachers all came from the Bay Area, it made sense for our local teachers' cell to decide how many camps to teach, who would go to each and what some of our basic policies should be. But as we began to develop skilled teachers in other communities, they began to clamor for some power in making these decisions.

We had also been talking about how exciting it would be some day to get teachers and organizers from all over the country to come together. A group in Portland, Oregon, put together a gathering, and at my and some others' instigation, we included time to meet and form some new governance structure.

At the meeting, we formed a new Witch Camp Council, on a spokescouncil model with representatives from different camps and geographic areas. From the beginning, there were tensions that the structure could not resolve. Many teachers felt that their "home community" was not geographic, but more a network of close friends that they had developed over time, teaching together in many locations. Others lived where they were the lone teacher in an isolated area and had no geographic group to go back to. The structure did not adequately allow for their representation.

The other problem that became apparent over time was that the spokescouncil was not empowered. Spokes could discuss issues and formulate proposals, but had no power to make decisions. Proposals had to be brought back to home communities and decided at a later meeting. Meetings were expensive — bringing representatives together from far-flung communities meant lots of air travel. So face-to-face meetings took place only once a year, with an online meeting in between. The length of time between meetings made decision-making slow and cumbersome.

And "bringing it back to the home community" was more of an ideal than a reality, for most home communities didn't really exist as such. In the Bay Area, we had groups, public rituals and a teachers' cell to whom representatives could report, but in other areas, camps met once a year, for camp, but not in between.

Nonetheless, the Council did function, and was a clear step forward in truly democratic organizing from the days when a few of us in California made all the decisions. Generally, the meetings were marked by respectful and thoughtful attention and good facilitation. The Council also provided a couple of slots at each meeting for elders who would not represent a community but would hold the memory and history of the organization.

At the same time, our home community in the Bay Area was undergoing structural challenges. We knew that we in the original collective needed to let go of power. To do so, we felt, we needed to formalize our values in some way. We all shared values that we understood, intuitively, but in the 17 or 18 years of the collective's existence, we had never written down a statement of our principles — in part, because one of our values was intellectual freedom, and we distrusted dogma of all kinds.

So we began a process of looking at both our guiding principles and our structure. We began with a weekend retreat, in which we brainstormed what our values were and had many deep discussions. That was followed by an evening meeting to start prioritizing and winnowing down the lists — a meeting that turned out to be horrible in spite of a good outside facilitator. People arrived late, stated that they had to leave early, and at the very end, one of our beloved elders announced that she had cancer. We left without setting another meeting date, and for some weeks it seemed likely that the collective would simply die by default, never meeting again.

During that time, I and another collective member took a permaculture design course. In that course, we learned about how designers get community input through a process called a design charette — from the French word for cart.

Small groups take on a problem, each comes up with their solution, and then the solutions can be compared and contrasted. The group as a whole can take various features from each. We thought that this might be an effective way to tackle our restructuring and our principles.

When we got home, we called together a new collective meeting. We inspired people to come by announcing that we were going to consider adding new members — a topic which we knew would arouse indignation and passion, as we had previously agreed not to do so until we finished restructuring. Most of the collective showed up to tell us off — and we were able to put forth the idea of working in charettes over the summer and coming together again for a weekend retreat in the fall. We formed the charettes by bringing people together who lived in proximity and could easily meet. More importantly, we put people together in the charettes who generally were in opposing factions of the collective.

Not every charette met and completed its work, but by the autumn retreat, enough groups had come up with proposals that we were able to complete our task. In that weekend, we wrote up the Principles of Unity, created a new structure for our local Bay Area Reclaiming group and formally dissolved the old collective. In its place, we now had a spokescouncil, formed of representatives from the groups that actually did the work of the organization.

The following weekend, near Austin, Texas, we held the first meeting of the Witch Camp Council. We created structures for decision-making, for coordination and for having giving some centralized coordinated input into the choices of teachers that individual camps might make.

We did not, however, create any sort of governance structure for Reclaiming as a whole. We had agreed that groups around the world could identify as Reclaiming if they agreed to the Principles of Unity, but we had no structure for overall decision-making or coordination. At the time, I felt we had exhausted our capacity for creating new organizational structure and that we needed to give the new structures time to work. If more organization was needed, it would become apparent over time. And if it emerged organically, it would be more fitted to the real needs and workings of the group than if we tried to create it by fiat.

The new structures held well enough that, over time, I was able to drop back from teaching all the Witch Camps to teaching one every few years, from being at every spokescouncil meeting to not needing to attend at all, from being the instigator of major structural changes to being a supportive witness of other people's insights and efforts. By stepping back, I opened up more room for others to step forward and take on roles of leadership. Our community has continued to grow — not always as rapidly as during that period of expansion in the 1990s, but slowly and steadily. And I have had time and energy to explore and develop other areas of interest.

About seven years after we created our new structure, a group within Reclaiming were inspired to again create an all-Reclaiming gathering which they called Dandelion. It took place in Texas, near Austin, and we had three wonderful days of connection, ritual and discussions. Some new creative endeavors were born, including a Free Activist Witch Camp run on a new model — costs kept low by camping in National Forests, teachers, organizers and cooks working for free, people paying what they could afford.

By the second Dandelion, the Witch Camp spokescouncil had begun to find itself in a challenging position. As the camps and their communities developed, there was less need for the centralized organization to decide on camp matters. But at the same time, other issues arose from time to time that people insisted on bringing to the Council because there was no other body to decide them. But the Witch Camp Spokescouncil felt that these issues were outside its mandate. So they proposed the creation of a new body they called BIRCH: Broader Intra-Reclaiming Councils Hub.

A second Dandelion meeting was held in Massachusetts in 2006. At that meeting, BIRCH was officially formed. By now, we had learned a few lessons about group process, and the way we went about forming BIRCH was a more positive lesson. First, we discussed the matter informally, online and in our groups and meetings, for about a year before the official meeting. During that time, we had opportunities to hear people's ideas and concerns without the pressure of immediately making a big decision.

At the Dandelion gathering, we spent the first two days in workshops, doing rituals and generally having fun. We reserved only one day for official meetings. We scheduled long mealtimes, and at lunches and dinners, we proposed topics for discussion — the larger issues that had bearing on forming our new level of organization. Over a meal, we could talk about the deep issues we never have time to discuss in meetings — questions like, "What are our core values?" "How do we think climate change will affect the way we do things?" "What do we most love about Reclaiming? What drives us nuts?" We could harvest some of the thoughts and insights from those discussions formally by writing them up on sheets of paper or reporting back to a gathering. But even more importantly, over the course of those meals, a rough sense of the group, as the Quakers put it, began to develop.

When the meeting came, we were able to come up with a structure and founding documents with relative ease. When one issue of wording became an impasse, we were able to set it aside and empowered a small group of those who were most deeply attached to either side to work out a compromise.

At our most recent gathering, in the autumn of 2010, we were able to address some important issues with respect and grace. We could contemplate a change in the wording of the Principles of Unity to make them more inclusive and welcoming to transgender folks, and use the process we had set up earlier for doing so: the issue was brought up in online discussion for a few weeks before the gathering, so that people who were interested in it had incentive to come. We had some lively and emotional discussion during the gathering and came up with a few suggested changes in wording to bring back home. We left with the understanding that this would simply begin a process of discussion that would continue throughout the time leading up to the next Dandelion — probably two years or so. We encouraged people during that time to hold gatherings to talk about gender, to speak about their own experiences and to consider possible wording changes. We also agreed to post something about the process on our website next to the Principles of Unity, so that the general public would know that this discussion was under way.

Looking back on our growth, I would call Reclaiming an accidental institution. We didn't set out to create an institution, and many of us were extremely wary of organizations accruing centralized power. We set out to do work that we felt passionate about, to create the minimal structure necessary to support the work and to organize in the most open, egalitarian way. What we discovered, to our surprise, is that each time we grew, our open, egalitarian structure needed to change. Like the chitin of an insect's exoskeleton, what had once served us became constricting each time we outgrew it. What at one time furthered egalitarianism and connection became exclusive and elitist. As an emergent organization, each stage of growth put us through a phase shift that required a new structure. We were less like a tree — growing taller and broader in the same form — and more like a butterfly, needing to completely rebuild our body with each new phase of growth.

As those of us who founded Reclaiming grow older, our new challenge is to pass on our learning and our traditions to a new generation. In the last few years, more of our camps have opened to families with children, and more of our communities have begun holding programs for children and teens. New people have taken up the work of ensuring that, whatever happens eventually to our organization, our values will continue to seed new life in times to come. For many of us, Reclaiming has been for three decades now a core part of our spirituality, our connection to community and our lives.

Reclaiming endures, but the measure of a group's success is not just how long it exists, although those of us in spiritual traditions naturally want to think they will live on after us. But many teachers, writers, artists, musicians, dancers, poets and activists have participated in Reclaiming's activities and been inspired, challenged and encouraged in their endeavors. Some Reclaiming teachers have left the organization but gone on to do their own important work or found groups of their own. Many others in Reclaiming have written books, songs, articles, academic papers, made films, photographs, paintings, sculptures and other creative works. Still others pursue vocations in healing, teaching, organizing and many other forms of service. With all of our conflicts and growing pains, Reclaiming has provided nurturing for the creative spirit, comradeship for those on the front lines of activism, comfort for wounded bodies and souls and a vision of a better world for more than three decades, and all of that is part of the measure of its success.

LESSONS FROM SUCCESS

What can we learn from these examples? Although *The Empowerment Manual* focuses mostly on the workings of small groups, *collaboration can work on a larger scale*. Interlocking circles can link up in many ways to guide larger organizations from the bottom up, rather than the top down.

Ideals and values are important; they are the guiding force that drives people to organize together and work together. But groups that survive find ways to balance the ideal with the pragmatic needs of the moment. They are flexible, rather than rigid, and accepting rather than judgmental. They value diversity rather than orthodoxy, problem-solving over toeing a party line.

Successful groups balance unity with autonomy. They have a bias toward freedom and impose the minimal structure necessary. But they do have structure and often hold a unifying vision and set of core values.

Collaborative groups that last over time reinvent themselves periodically. They may need to change their structure, organization and ways of working as they grow and develop. They are not static, but dynamic, not artifacts, but living organisms.

Collaborative groups come in all shapes and sizes, small, large, simple and complex. They might be a group of kids deciding what game to play, a mobilization of activists that challenges entrenched power, an intentional community of idealists exploring new ways to live together, a successful cooperative business, a family or a group of friends. When they function well, they can be places of learning, joy and empowerment, that allow our creativity to flourish. They can provide the support and structure we need to change the world.

But to function well, collaborative groups must negotiate many challenges. First, *they must find a common vision* that reflects shared values and set a clear intention that can be realized by achieving common goals. *They must understand the many different forms of power and find ways to let people fairly earn social power* within the group. Earned authority must be balanced by responsibility. Members may not play equal roles in the group, but they must have equal opportunity to earn more rank and rewards. The group's structure must be clear and transparent.

Effective groups develop and practice good communication skills that can build connection and trust. They learn to give constructive feedback and to embrace conflicts and disagreements about ideas and plans without descending into personal attack. They establish systems of accountability, and they also engage in many sorts of activities that can build trust and connection.

Empowering groups are not leaderless but leaderful, providing training, support for many people to step into a variety of leadership roles and to find many different ways of offering their skills and passions. *They embrace conflict rather than avoid it* and learn to passionately argue for ideas and positions without attacking persons. They create an environment that favors positive behaviors and interactions and discourages the problematic behaviors that cause group ruptures.

Finally, *they provide appropriate support and training* so that members can learn the necessary skills to help the group function. *They draw from positive examples and believe in the possibility of success.*

As the world grows more and more connected, as the larger command and control structures fail to provide the means of a dignified life to so many people or to address the enormous challenges of climate change, environmental destruction, war and violence, more and more the hope of the world comes to rest on the efforts of voluntary groups fired with vision and passion. When we shift away from the oppressive power of domination and cultivate spirit, compassion and empowerment, we unleash enormous forces of creativity and human energy. When we can harness those forces effectively, we truly become the change we want to see and embody the future of freedom and interconnection that we hope to create. It is my hope that *The Empowerment Manual* will be helpful to those who wish to connect and conspire to build that new world on a foundation of justice, harmony with nature and love for one another. Resting on those piers, our structures will withstand the storms and offer shelter and nurturing for the endeavors that renew the world.

Endnotes

Chapter 1: A New Era of Empowerment

1. Diana Leafe Christian. *Creating a Life Together: Practical Tools to Grow Ecovillages and Intentional Communities.* New Society, 2003, p. 5.
2. Ori Brafman and Rod A. Beckstrom. *The Starfish and the Spider: The Unstoppable Power of Leaderless Organizations.* Penguin, 2008, p. 50.
3. See especially Starhawk. T*ruth or Dare: Encounters with Power, Authority and Mystery.* Harper, 1987 and Starhawk and Hilary Valentine. *The Twelve Wild Swans: A Journey to the Realm of Magic, Healing, and Action.* Harper, 2000. A recorded version of the grounding and anchor to core self exercises, along with many guided meditations, can be found on my audio CD *Earth Magic.*
4. *The Twelve Wild Swans,* pp. 41-43.

Chapter 3: The Circle of Vision

1. George Lakoff. *Don't Think of an Elephant: Know Your Values and Frame the Debate — The Essential Guide for Progressives.* Chelsea Green, 2004.
2. Alan Savory. *Holistic Management: A New Framework for Decision Making.* Covelo, 1999, pp. 81-82.

Chapter 4: The Axis of Action

1. Margo Adair and William Aal. Tools for Change website. [online]. [cited May 11, 2011]. toolsforchange.org/resources/org-handouts/AI%20interview%20%20hand %20out%20power.pdf. Their website also includes many valuable resources, books and meditation CDs by the late Margo Adair.

2. Delfina Vanucci and Richard Singer. *Come Hell or High Water: A Handbook on Collective Process Gone Awry.* AK Press, 2010, p. 39.

3. Laurence Mishel. "CEO-to-worker Pay Imbalance Grows." Economic Policy Institute website, June 21, 2006. [online]. [cited May 12, 2011]. epi.org/economic_snapshots/entry/webfeatures_snapshots_20060621/.

4. Jeanne Sahadi. "CEO Pay: 364 times more than workers." CNN Money, August 29, 2007. [online]. [cited May 12, 2011]. money.cnn.com/2007/08/28/news/economy/ceo_pay_workers/index.htm.

5. F. John Reh. "Pareto's Principle: The 80/20 Rule." About.com Management. [online]. [cited May 13, 2011]. management.about.com/cs/generalmanagement/a/Pareto081202.htm.

Chapter 5: The Axis of Learning

1. Jo Freeman. "The Tyranny of Structurelessness." 1970. [online]. [cited May 13, 2011]. jofreeman.com/joreen/tyranny.htm. See also Cathy Levine. "The Tyranny of Tyranny." [online]. [cited May 13, 2011]. libcom.org/library/tyranny-of-tyranny-cathy-levine.

2. George Lakey. *Facilitating Group Learning: Strategies for Success with Adult Learners.* Jossey-Bass, 2010, pp. 46-47. See also Berit Lakey et al. *Grassroots and Nonprofit Leadership.* Training for Change website. [online]. [cited May 13, 2011]. trainingforchange.org/grassroots_and_nonprofit_leadership.

3. Arthur Ransome. *We Didn't Mean to Go to Sea.* Puffin, 1972, p. 263.

4. Roger Schwarz. *The Skilled Facilitator: A Comprehensive Resource for Consultants, Facilitators, Managers, Trainers, and Coaches.* Jossey-Bass, 2002, pp. 70-73.

5. Beatrice Briggs. "Gossip as a Group Dynamic" in Kosha Anja Joubert and Robin Alfred, eds. *Beyond You and Me: Inspirations and Wisdom for Building Community.* Permanent Publications, 2007, pp.126-127.

6. Luisah Teish. *Jambalaya: The Natural Woman's Book of Personal Charms and Practical Rituals.* Harper, 1985, p. 21.

7. Lisa Fithian. "FBI Informant Brandon Darby: Sexism, Ego and Lies." The Rag Blog. [online]. [cited May 13, 2011]. theragblog.blogspot.com/2010/03/lisa-fithian-fbi-informant-brandon.html.

8. Marshall B. Rosenberg. *Nonviolent Communication: A Language of Compassion.* PuddleDancer, 2002, pp. 83-85.

9. George Lakoff. *The Political Mind: Why You Can't Understand 21st-Century American Politics with an 18th-Century Brain.* Viking, 2008, p. 22.

10. A good summary of Peter Senge's work on the learning organization can be found at: Peter M. Senge. "The Fifth Discipline: The Art and Practice of the Learning Organization." Audubon Area Community Services website. [online]. [cited May 17, 2011]. audubon-area.org/NewFiles/sengesum.pdf. See also: Peter M. Senge. *The Fifth Discipline: The Art and Practice of the Learning Organization,* rev. ed. Crown, 2006.

11. *The Twelve Wild Swans,* pp. 256-258.

12. Marshall Goldsmith and Mark Reiter. *What Got You Here Won't Get You There: How Successful People Become More Successful.* Hyperion, 2007, pp. 170-171.

13. There are several different ways of naming and elaborating the rungs on the ladder. My own formulation draws on Rick Ross. "The Ladder of Influence" in Peter M. Senge et al. *The Fifth Discipline Field Book: Strategies and Tools for Building a Learning Organization.* Crown, 1994, pp. 242-246 and *The Skilled Facilitator,* pp. 99-104.

14. Ross in *The Fifth Discipline Field Book*, p. 244.

15. *Nonviolent Communication,* pp. 6-7. An excellent short summary of Rosenberg's work can be found at: Marshall B. Rosenberg. "Chapter One: Giving from the Heart, the Heart of Nonviolent Communication." Center for Nonviolent Communication. [online]. [cited May 17, 2011]. cnvc.org/Training/nvc-chapter-1.

16. *The Skilled Facilitator,* p. 97.

17. This issue is discussed in more depth in The Five-Fold Path of Productive Meetings.

18. Thanks to Jen Aramath of Akashic Transformations for suggesting these questions. Personal communication.

19. "Mehrabian's Communication Research" Businessballs.com. [online]. [cited May 19, 2011]. businessballs.com/mehrabiancommunications.htm. A. Mehrabian. *Silent Messages: Implicit Communication of Emotions and Attitudes,* 2d ed. Wadsworth, 1981. Currently distributed by Albert Mehrabian (e-mail: am@kaaj.com).

20. Diana Leafe Christian. "Starting a New Ecovillage: Structural Conflict and Nine Ways to Resolve It." in *Beyond You and Me,* p. 53.

21. Patrick Lencioni. *The Three Signs of a Miserable Job : A Fable for Managers (And Their Employees).* Jossey-Bass, 2007, pp. 235-236.

22. Ryan Sarnataro. Personal communication.

23. *Three Signs of a Miserable Job,* p. 221.

24. I especially recommend Starhawk. *The Earth Path: Grounding Your Spirit in the Rhythms of Nature.* Harper, 2005; pp. 166-188 in *The Twelve Wild Swans* and chapter 11 in *Truth or Dare.* While not every group is open to expressions of

spirituality, there are many ways to allow people deeper connection without using sectarian language, subscribing to dogma or holding hands and singing "Kumbaya." My previous books contain many ideas for rituals and ceremonies.

Chapter 6: Leadership Roles for Leaderless Groups

1. *The Starfish and the Spider,* p. 20.
2. Ibid.
3. *Truth or Dare,* p. 277.
4. Thistle. Personal communication.
5. Daniel Goleman, Richard Boyatzis and Annie McKee. *Primal Leadership: Learning to Lead with Emotional Intelligence.* Harvard Business, 2002, pp. 53-88.
6. *What Got You Here Won't Get You There,* pp. 35-111.

Chapter 7: Group Conflict

1. Bruce Tuckman. "Developmental Sequence in Small Groups." *Psychological Bulletin,* Vol. 63, No. 6 (1965), pp. 384-399 at p. 396. [online]. [cited June 2, 2011]. aneesha.ceit.uq.edu.au/drupal/sites/default/files/Tuckman%201965.pdf.
2. *Truth or Dare,* pp. 265-268.
3. Starhawk. *Dreaming the Dark: Magic, Sex and Politics.* Beacon, 1982, p. 129.
4. *Nonviolent Communication,* pp. 71-90.
5. *The Fifth Discipline Fieldbook,* pp. 245-246.
6. Tools for Change Mediation courtesy of Bill Aal and Margo Adair, toolsforchange.org/.
7. *Come Hell or High Water,* p. 83.
8. Restorative Justice Online Blog. [online]. [cited May 23, 2011]. restorativejustice.org/.
9. Retorative Justice Online Blog. "What Is Restorative Justice?" [online]. [cited May 23, 2011]. restorativejustice.org/university-classroom/01introduction.

Chapter 8: Dealing with Difficult People

1. Bill Wiersma. *The Big AHA! Breakthroughs in Resolving and Preventing Workplace Conflict.* Ravel Media, 2007, pp. 13 and 14.
2. Marshall Goldsmith. Daily Questions article: "Questions That Make a Difference Every Day." [online]. [cited May 24, 2011]. marshallgoldsmithlibrary.com/html/marshall/resources.html.
3. Judith Herman, quoted in Steven Wineman. *Power-Under: Trauma and Non-Violent Social Change,* 2003, p. 51. [online]. [cited May 24, 2011]. peacemakerinstitute.org/Readings/Power_Under.pdf.

4. Ibid., p. 48.
5. Ibid., pp. 50 and 56-57.
6. *Truth or Dare,* Chapter 3.
7. *The Skilled Facilitator,* p. 74.
8. Suzette Haden Elgin. *The Gentle Art of Verbal Self-Defense.* Dorset Press, 1980. p. 2.
9. Peter Rogers and Matthew McKay have co-authored a number of books, including: Matthew McKay and Peter Rogers. *The Anger Control Workbook.* New Harbinger, 2000; Matthew McKay, Peter Rogers and Judith McKay. *When Anger Hurts: Quieting the Storm Within,* 2d ed. New Harbinger, 2003.

Chapter 9: Groups that Work

1. Rainbow Grocery website. [online]. [cited May 26, 2011]. rainbow.coop/mission/.
2. Bill Crolius, personal communication, March 24, 2011.
3. Ryan Sarnataro, personal communication, March 24, 2011.
4. Bill Crolius.
5. Laura Kemp, personal communication, March 23, 2011.
6. Jeanne Sahadi. "Wealth Gap Widens." CNN Money, August 29, 2006. [online]. [cited May 26, 2011]. money.cnn.com/2006/08/29/news/economy/wealth_gap/.
7. David Korten. *When Corporations Rule the World,* 2d ed. Berret-Koehler, 2001, p. 90.
8. Starhawk. "November 30: Ten Years Since Seattle Climate Change Action." The Real Battle in Seattle website. [online]. [cited May 26, 2011]. realbattleinseattle.org/node/188.
9. David Solnit. "The Battle for Reality." *YES! Magazine,* July 30, 2008. [online]. [cited May 25, 2011]. yesmagazine.org/issues/purple-america/the-battle-for-reality.
10. Thanks to David Solnit for providing these guidelines.
11. Thanks to Lisa Fithian for providing these guidelines.
12. *Truth or Dare,* pp. 304-305.

Bibliography and References

Adair, Margo. *Meditations on Everything Under the Sun.* Gabriola Island, BC: New Society, 2001.

Adair, Margo. *Working Inside Out: Tools for Change.* Naperville, Illinois: Sourcebooks/ Media Fusion, 1984, 2003

Adair, Margo. *Working Inside Out: Tools for Change.* Wingbow, 1985.

Adair, Margo and William Aal. *Tools for Change website.* [online]. [cited May 11, 2011]. toolsforchange.org/resources/org-handouts/AI%20interview%20%20hand% 20out%20power.pdf.

Beck, Don Edward and Christopher C. Cowan. *Spiral Dynamics: Mastering Values, Leadership and Change.* Blackwell, 1996.

Beck, John and Sharon Villines. *We the People: Consenting to a Deeper Democracy.* Sociocracy.Info, 2007.

Beer, Jennifer E. and Eileen Stief. *The Mediator's Handbook,* 3rd ed. New Society, 1998.

Brafman, Ori and Rod A. Beckstrom. *The Starfish and the Spider: The Unstoppable Power of Leaderless Organizations.* Penguin, 2008.

Briggs, Beatrice. "Gossip as a Group Dynamic" in Kosha Anja Joubert and Robin Alfred, eds. *Beyond You and Me: Inspirations and Wisdom for Building Community.* Permanent Publications, 2007.

Briggs, Beatrice. *Introduction to Consensus.* 2000. Self-published, distributed by IIFAC (International Institute for Facilitation and Change). [online]. [cited June 6, 2011]. iifac.org/php/pp_buypage.php?lang=en&product=manual.

Brown, Michael Jacoby. *Building Powerful Community Organizations: A Personal Guide to Creating Groups that Can Solve Problems and Change the World.* Long Haul, 2006.

Butler, C.T. and Amy Rothstein Butler, *On Conflict and Consensus: A Handbook on Formal Consensus Decision Making.* Food Not Bombs, 1991.

Christian, Diana Leafe. *Creating a Life Together: Practical Tools to Grow Ecovillages and Intentional Communities.* New Society, 2003.

Christian, Diana Leafe. *Finding Community:How to Join an Ecovillage or Intentional Community.* New Society, 2007.

Christian, Diana Leafe. "Starting a New Ecovillage: Structural Conflict and Nine Ways to Resolve It" in Joubert, Kosha Anja and Robin Alfred, eds. *Beyond You and Me: Inspirations and Wisdom for Building Community.* Permanent Publications, 2007.

Curtis, Joan C. *Managing Sticky Situations at Work: Communication Secrets for Success in the Workplace.* Praeger, 2009.

Elgin, Suzette Haden. *The Gentle Art of Verbal Self-Defense.* Dorset Press, 1980.

Finzel, Hans. *The Top Ten Mistakes Leaders Make.* David C. Cooke, 2007.

Fithian, Lisa. "FBI Informant Brandon Darby: Sexism, Ego and Lies." The Rag Blog. [online]. [cited May 13, 2011]. theragblog.blogspot.com/2010/03/lisa-fithian-fbi-informant-brandon.html.

Freeman, Jo. "The Tyranny of Structurelessness." 1970. [online]. [cited May 13, 2011].jofreeman.com/joreen/tyranny.htm.

Goldsmith, Marshall. Daily Questions article: "Questions That Make a Difference Every Day." [online]. [cited May 24, 2011]. marshallgoldsmithlibrary.com/html/marshall/resources.html.

Goldsmith, Marshall. *Succession: Are You Ready?* Harvard Business, 2009.

Goldsmith, Marshall and Mark Reiter. *What Got You Here Won't Get You There: How Successful People Become More Successful.* Hyperion, 2007.

Goleman, Daniel, Richard Boyatzis and Annie McKee. *Primal Leadership: Learning to Lead with Emotional Intelligence.* Harvard Business, 2002.

Grinder, John and Richard Bandler, *Trance-Formations: Neuro-Linguistic Programming and the Structure of Hypnosis.* Real People, 1981.

Harvard Business School Press. *Leading Teams: Expert Solutions to Everyday Challenges.* Harvard Business, 2006.

Hawken, Paul. *Blessed Unrest: How the Largest Social Movement in the World Came into Being and Why No One Saw It Coming.* Viking, 2007.

Indymedia website. [online]. [cited June 6, 2011]. indymedia.org/en/index.shtml.

Joubert, Kosha Anja and Robin Alfred, eds. *Beyond You and Me: Inspirations and Wisdom for Building Community.* Permanent Publications, 2007.

Kaner, Sam, Lenny Lind, Catherine Toldi, Sarah Fisk and Duane Berger. *Facilitator's Guide to Participatory Decision-Making,* 2d. ed. Jossey-Bass, 2007.

Kohn, Stephen E. and Vincent D. O'Connell. *The 6 Habits of Highly Effective Teams.* Career, 2007.

Korten, David C. *The Post-Corporate World: Life After Capitalism.* Kumarian, 1999.

Korten, David C. *When Corporations Rule the World,* 2d ed. Berret-Koehler, 2001.

Lakey, Berit et al. *Grassroots and Nonprofit Leadership.* Training for Change website. [online]. [cited May 13, 2011]. trainingforchange.org/grassroots_and_nonprofit_leadership.

Lakey, Berit, George Lakey, Rod Napier and Janice Robinson. *Grassroots and Nonprofit Leadership: A Guide for Organizations in Changing Times.* New Society, 1998.

Lakey, George. *Facilitating Group Learning: Strategies for Success with Adult Learners.* Jossey-Bass, 2010.

Lakoff. George. *Don't Think of An Elephant: Know Your Values and Frame the Debate — The Essential Guide for Progressives.* Chelsea Green, 2004.

Lakoff, George. *Moral Politics: How Liberals and Conservatives Think,* 2d ed. University of Chicago, 2002.

Lakoff, George. *The Political Mind: Why You Can't Understand 21st-Century American Politics with an 18th-Century Brain.* Viking, 2008.

Lencioni, Patrick. *Death By Meeting: A Leadership Fable ... About Solving the Most Painful Problem in Business.* Jossey-Bass, 2004.

Lencioni, Patrick. *The Five Dysfunctions of a Team: A Leadership Fable.* Jossey-Bass, 2002.

Lencioni, Patrick. *The Three Signs of a Miserable Job: A Fable for Managers (And Their Employees).* Jossey-Bass, 2007.

Levine, Cathy. "The Tyranny of Tyranny." [online]. [cited May 13, 2011]. libcom.org/library/tyranny-of-tyranny-cathy-levine.

Mason, Paul A., M.S. and Randi Kreger. *Stop Walking on Eggshells: Taking your Life Back When Someone You Care About Has Borderline Personality Disorder,* 2nd ed. Oakland, CA: New Harbinger Publications, 2010.

Maxwell, John C. *The 21 Irrefutable Laws of Leadership: Follow Them and People Will Follow You,* 10th ed. Thomas Nelson, 2007.

McKay, Matthew and Peter Rogers. *The Anger Control Workbook.* New Harbinger, 2000.

McKay, Matthew, Peter Rogers and Judith McKay. *When Anger Hurts: Quieting the Storm Within,* 2nd ed. New Harbinger, 2003.

Mehrabian, A. *Silent Messages: Implicit Communication of Emotions and Attitudes,* 2nd ed. Wadsworth, 1981.

"Mehrabian's Communication Research." Businessballs.com. [online]. [cited May 19, 2011]. businessballs.com/mehrabiancommunications.htm.

Mertes, Tom, ed. *A Movement of Movements: Is Another World Really Possible?* Verso, 2004.

Mindell, Arnold. *Sitting in the Fire: Large Group Transformation through Diversity and Conflict.* Lao Tse, 1995.

Mishel, Laurence. "CEO-to-worker Pay Imbalance Grows." Economic Policy Institute website, June 21, 2006. [online]. [cited May 12, 2011]. epi.org/economic_snapshots/entry/webfeatures_snapshots_20060621/.

Moyer, Bill, JoAnn McAllister, Mary Lou Finley and Steven Soifer, *Doing Democracy: The MAP Model for Organizing Social Movements.* New Society, 2001.

Occidental Arts and Ecology Center website. [online]. [cited June 6, 2011]. oaec.org/.

Ojai Foundation website. [online]. cited June 6,2011]. ojaifoundation.org/Council.

Open Space World website. [online] [cited June 6, 2011]. openspaceworld.org/cgi/wiki.cgi?AboutOpenSpace.

Patterson, Kerry, Joseph Grenny, Ron McMillan and Al Switzler. *Crucial Conversations: Tools for Talking When Stakes Are High.* McGraw-Hill, 2002.

Pearson, Christine and Christine Porath. *The Cost of Bad Behavior: How Incivility Is Damaging Your Business and What To Do About It.* Penguin, 2009.

Rainbow Grocery website. [online]. [cited May 26, 2011]. rainbow.coop/mission/.

Ransome, Arthur. *We Didn't Mean to Go to Sea.* Puffin, 1972.

Reh, F. John. "Pareto's Principle: The 80/20 Rule." About.com Management. [online]. [cited May 13, 2011]. management.about.com/cs/generalmanagement/a/Pareto081202.htm.

Restorative Justice Online Blog. [online]. [cited May 23, 2011]. restorativejustice.org/.

Rosenberg, Marshall B. "Chapter One: Giving from the Heart, the Heart of Nonviolent Communication." Center for Nonviolent Communication. [online]. [cited May 17, 2011]. cnvc.org/Training/nvc-chapter-1.

Rosenberg, Marshall B. *Nonviolent Communication; A Language of Compassion.* PuddleDancer, 2002.

Ross, Rick. "The Ladder of Inference" in Peter M. Senge et al. *The Fifth Discipline Field Book: Strategies and Tools for Building a Learning Organization.* Crown, 1994.

Ross, Rick and Art Kleine. "The Left-Hand Column" in Senge, PeterM., Art Keliner, Charlotte Roberts, Richard Ross, George Roth and Bryan Smith. *The Dance of Change: The Challenges to Sustaining Momentum in Learning Organizations.* New York: Doubleday, 1999.

Sahadi, Jeanne. "CEO Pay: 364 times more than workers." CNN Money, August 29, 2007. [online]. [cited May 12, 2011]. money.cnn.com/2007/08/28/news/economy/ceo_pay_workers/index.htm.

Sahadi, Jeanne. "Wealth Gap Widens." CNN Money, August 29, 2006. [online]. [cited May 26, 2011]. money.cnn.com/2006/08/29/news/economy/wealth_gap/.

Sartor, Linda. "Collaboration and How to Facilitate It: A Cooperative Inquiry." Ph.D. diss., California Institute of Integral Studies, 2007.

Savory, Alan. *Holistic Management: A New Framework for Decision Making.* Covelo, 1999.

Schwarz, Roger. *The Skilled Facilitator: A Comprehensive Resource for Consultants, Facilitators, Managers, Trainers, and Coaches.* Jossey-Bass, 2002.

Senge, Peter M. *The Fifth Discipline: The Art and Practice of the Learning Organization* rev ed. Crown, 2006.

Senge, Peter M. "The Fifth Discipline: The Art and Practice of the Learning Organization." Audubon Area Community Services website. [online]. [cited May 17, 2011]. audubon-area.org/NewFiles/sengesum.pdf.

Senge, Peter M., Art Kleiner, Charlotte Roberts, George Roth, Rick Ross and Bryan Smith. *The Dance of Change: The Challenges to Sustaining Momentum in Learning Organizations.* Crown, 1999.

Senge, Peter M., Art Kleiner, Charlotte Roberts and Rick Ross. *The Fifth Discipline Field Book: Strategies and Tools for Building a Learning Organization.* Crown, 1994.

Shore, Zachary. *Blunder: Why Smart People Make Bad Decisions.* Bloomsbury, 2008.

Solnit, David, ed. *Globalize Liberation: How to Uproot the System and Build a Better World.* City Lights, 2003.

Solnit, David. "The Battle for Reality." *YES! Magazine,* July 30, 2008. [online]. [cited May 25, 2011]. yesmagazine.org/issues/purple-america/the-battle-for-reality.

Stanfield, R. Brian, ed. *The Art of Focused Conversation: 100 Ways to Access Group Wisdom in the Workplace.* New Society, 2000.

Starhawk. *Dreaming the Dark: Magic, Sex and Politics.* Beacon, 1982.

Starhawk. *Earth Magic: Sacred Rituals for Connecting to Nature's Power.* Sounds True Audio CD 978-1-59179-415-8, 2005.

Starhawk. *The Earth Path: Grounding Your Spirit in the Rhythms of Nature.* Harper, 2005.

Starhawk. "November 30: Ten Years Since Seattle Climate Change Action." The Real Battle in Seattle website. [online]. [cited May 26, 2011]. realbattleinseattle.org/node/188.

Starhawk. *Truth or Dare: Encounters With Power, Authority and Mystery.* Harper, 1987.

Starhawk. *Webs of Power: Notes from the Global Uprising.* New Society, 2002.

Starhawk and Hilary Valentine. *The Twelve Wild Swans: A Journey to the Realm of Magic, Healing, and Action.* Harper, 2000.

Stout, Linda. *Collective Visioning: How Groups Can Work Together for a Just and Sustainable Future.* Berrett-Koehler, 2011.

Teish, Luisah. *Jambalaya: The Natural Woman's Book of Personal Charms and Practical Rituals.* Harper, 1985.

Tuckman, Bruce. "Developmental Sequence in Small Groups." *Psychological Bulletin,* Vol. 63, No. 6 (1965), pp. 384-399. [online]. [cited June 2, 2011]. aneesha.ceit.uq.edu.au/drupal/sites/default/files/Tuckman%201965.pdf.

Vanucci, Delfina and Richard Singer. *Come Hell or High Water: A Handbook on Collective Process Gone Awry.* AK Press, 2010.

Wiersma, Bill. *The Big AHA! Breakthroughs in Resolving and Preventing Workplace Conflict.* Ravel Media, 2007.

Wineman, Steven. *Power-Under: Trauma and Non-Violent Social Change,* 2003, p. 51. [online]. [cited May 24, 2011]. peacemakerinstitute.org/Readings/Power_Under.pdf.

World Café website. [online]. [cited June 6, 2011]. theworldcafe.com/.

Zimbardo, Philip. T*he Lucifer Effect: Understanding How Good People Turn Evil.* Random House, 2007.

Zimmerman, Jack and Virginia Coyle. *The Way of Council,* 2nd ed. Bramble, 2009.

Index

It's not over yet …

Download a bonus chapter: "The Five-Fold Path of Productive Meetings" at

www.starhawk.org/Five-Fold_Path.html

Continue the discussion at

www.starhawk.org

About the Author

STARHAWK is the author or coauthor of 11 previous books including *The Spiral Dance,* the now-classic ecotopian novel, *The Fifth Sacred Thing, The Earth Path* and the Nautilus Award-winning picture book for children, *The Last Wild Witch.*

She is a founder, director and core teacher for Earth Activist Trainings (earthactivisttraining.org), with permaculture design courses with a focus on organizing and a grounding in spirit.

Starhawk and director Donna Read collaborated on a trilogy of documentaries for the National Film Board of Canada. Together as Belili Productions (Belili.org) they released *Signs Out of Time,* a documentary on the life and work of archaeologist Marija Gimbutas in 2004 and *Permaculture: The Growing Edge* in 2010.

Starhawk is currently working with Yerba Buena Productions to bring her novel *The Fifth Sacred Thing* to the screen. See FifthSacredThingMovie.com

Starhawk travels globally lecturing and is a committed activist for peace, global justice and the environment.

Starhawk's website: www.starhawk.org

Starhawk's blog: www.starhawksblog.org

If you have enjoyed *The Empowerment Manual,* you might also enjoy other

BOOKS TO BUILD A NEW SOCIETY

Our books provide positive solutions for people who want to
make a difference. We specialize in:

**Sustainable Living • Green Building • Peak Oil • Renewable Energy·
Environment & Economy • Natural Building & Appropriate Technology
Progressive Leadership • Resistance and Community
Educational & Parenting Resources**

New Society Publishers

ENVIRONMENTAL BENEFITS STATEMENT

New Society Publishers has chosen to produce this book on recycled paper made with
100% post consumer waste, processed chlorine free, and old growth free.

For every 5,000 books printed, New Society saves the following resources:[1]

41	Trees
3,696	Pounds of Solid Waste
4,066	Gallons of Water
5,304	Kilowatt Hours of Electricity
6,718	Pounds of Greenhouse Gases
29	Pounds of HAPs, VOCs, and AOX Combined
10	Cubic Yards of Landfill Space

[1]Environmental benefits are calculated based on research done by the Environmental Defense Fund and
other members of the Paper Task Force who study the environmental impacts of the paper industry.

For a full list of NSP's titles, please call 1-800-567-6772 *or check out our website* at:

www.newsociety.com

NEW SOCIETY PUBLISHERS
Deep Green for over 30 years